God's Call to

Planet Earth

David Wilson

Table of Contents

Introduction

Welcome, dear reader, to this book, *God's Call to Planet Earth*. Some might raise their eyebrows and say, "What exactly is God's call?" God's message from the fall of man in Eden to the time when the door of mercy forever shuts has been "look unto Me, and be ye saved, all the ends of the earth: for I am God, and there is none else" (Isaiah 45:22). However, as in the days of Noah before the flood, God has in the last days a message to Planet Earth before His coming. I believe that the last chapters in the book of Revelation, particularly chapter 14 and onward, is God's call to Planet Earth.

As you open the book of Revelation, from chapter 1 to chapter 22, you will see a timeline developing from John's day to the coming of the Lord, and to the earth made new, when sin and sinners are no more. In Revelation 13 we find the description of the beast, and we read how another two-horned beast, that appears as a lamb but speaks as a dragon, creates an image or likeness of the first beast. This will be the time when the mark of the beast will be implemented worldwide. This mark, regardless of the final form it takes and the manner of its implementation, will show our allegiance to the commandments of men. It will further demonstrate, willingly or not, our mistaken recognition of the authority of the religion of men over true faith and the authority of God's Word, the Bible.

In Revelation 14, beginning in the first five verses, you will find the description of the 144,000. These are the people of God who overcome the beast, his mark, and the number of his name. In Revelation 14:6 we find an angel depicted as flying in the midst of heaven. Jesus addressed His messages for the seven churches, beginning in Revelation chapter 2, to the angel of those churches, meaning "a messenger, envoy, one who is sent, an angel, a messenger from God."[1] Angels in the book of Revelation are messengers. They can be angels from heaven or human messengers who are ordained and chosen of God to bear His message.

Jesus said, "As My Father has sent Me, even so send I you" (John 20:21). God has always used men to reach other men with His warnings and His offer of salvation from sin. Thus it is in Revelation 14. Here are found three angels, representing three messages to be given to the world. Beginning in verse 14 we find a figurative description of a harvest, and the "harvest is the end of the world" (Matthew 13:39). This represents the harvest of the righteous and the harvest of the wicked. The outcome of the two groups depicted in the harvest is based upon the message of the three angels and the response to that message. The development of character, in relationship to accepting that message or rejecting it, will determine where we are in the harvest, whether we are found sealed, righteous, and saved, or marked by the beast, unrighteous, and lost.

This is not an unusual concept, for in the Bible we learn that the acceptance or rejection of God's message determines one's destiny. Noah was "a preacher of righteousness" (2 Peter 2:5), and by his preaching "he condemned the world, and became heir of the righteousness which is by faith" (Hebrews 11:7). Further, Jesus said, "As the days of Noah were, so shall also the coming of the Son of man be" (Matthew 24:37).

When the world did not receive the warning of God through Noah, they sealed their destiny. The message of God through Noah and its acceptance or rejection determined the fate of all who were living at that time. Jesus said there are many lessons to learn from the days of Noah for the last days. Therefore, the messages of God, whether accepted, neglected, or rejected and set aside, will determine one's eternal destiny.

"Now the word of the Lord came unto Jonah the son of Amittai, saying, Arise, go to Nineveh, that great city, and cry against it; for their wickedness is come up before Me" (Jonah 1:1–2). We read here that God gave Jonah a message to speak to the city of Nineveh.

He went and preached, and the Ninevites repented, and God withdrew His judgments. (See Jonah 2:1–10.) The acceptance or rejection of God's message through His prophet would determine the fate of every living thing in the city of Nineveh.

Jesus said, "He that rejecteth Me, and receiveth not My words, hath one that judgeth him: the word that I have spoken, the same shall judge him in the last day" (John 12:48). God has always used men to give messages to determine "who is on the Lord's side" (Exodus 32:26). God through His servants gives messages to draw people to decisions. "And Elijah came unto all the people, and said, How long halt ye between two opinions? if the Lord be God, follow him: but if Baal, then follow him" (1 Kings 18:21).

Thus we find, in Revelation 14, the message that is to be given before and during the implementation of the mark of the beast. As we follow the message of Revelation 14 to the end of the chapter, we see that it deals with last-day events. The angels represent God's servants who bear a testing message. Two classes will be developed. Those who will be marked by the beast and those who will be sealed by God.

My friend, your daily life and decisions for or against the truth of God will determine where you will be in the great harvest at the end of the world. I urge you, therefore, to read *God's Call to Planet Earth*.

Endnotes

1. Greek lexicon based on *Thayer's Lexicon* and *Smith's Bible Dictionary* plus others; keyed to the large Kittel and the *Theological Dictionary of the New Testament*. Online Bible CD 2.5.3, Macintosh Version, 1996.

Section One
God's Invitation

Chapter One

The Everlasting Gospel

A nd I saw another angel fly in the midst of heaven, having the everlasting gospel to preach unto them that dwell on the earth, and to every nation, and kindred, and tongue, and people. (Revelation 14:6)

Throughout the book of Revelation previous to this verse there have been angels bearing messages from God. Now John sees another angel messenger coming to this world. My friend, this is not going to be a literal angel flying above the earth that mankind will see. God has always used angels to assist men and to protect men, but He uses men to reach other men and to warn other men. We see this principle with Noah, with Jonah, with the prophets throughout the Old Testament, and even with Jesus.

Jesus came as a man and lived among us, though He was also "God manifest in the flesh" (1 Timothy 3:16). We learn further, "The Word was made flesh, and dwelt among us, (and we beheld His glory, the glory as of the only begotten of the Father,) full of grace and truth" (John 1:14). Jesus came as a man to reveal heaven's principles and to reveal God's righteousness. Jesus did not come as God only; He came as a man to show us what the Father was like. Consistently throughout Scripture we find that God uses men to reach other men.

A messenger is seen flying in the midst of heaven, having the everlasting gospel to preach to every man, woman, and child. This is a worldwide message. The message is the gospel in the setting of the last hours of earth's history.

There is no new gospel. The gospel of salvation, which will save men from their sins, has been the same since the fall of Adam and Eve and will be the same to the end of time. "For by grace are ye saved through faith; and that not of yourselves: it is the gift of God: not of works, lest any man should boast" (Ephesians 2:8–9).

Salvation has always been by grace through faith and has always been the gift of God. In the Old Testament, sacrifice and works never saved anyone. It was by faith in the shed blood and sacrifice of animals representing the coming Messiah, which for that time was the gospel in symbols.

"What shall we say then that Abraham our father, as pertaining to the flesh, hath found? For if Abraham were justified by works, he hath whereof to glory; but not before God. For what saith the scripture? Abraham believed God, and it was counted unto him for righteousness" (Romans 4:1–3). Abraham was counted righteous not by anything he did, but by believing in God, trusting in God, and by giving his heart, mind, and strength to God.

It is a failure by men at the end of time to accept the gospel because of neglect, rejection, or substitution that will lead them to accept the mark and be eternally lost. Most of mankind will become spiritually confused, for "all nations drink of the wine of the wrath of her [Babylon's] fornication [spiritual adultery]" (Revelation 14:8).

Let us now begin to look at the everlasting gospel, which is centered in Christ, "the Lamb of God, which taketh away the sin of the world" (John 1:29).

> "And many other signs truly did Jesus in the presence of His disciples, which are not written in this book; but these are written, that ye might believe that Jesus is the Christ, the son of God; and that believing ye might have life through His name." (John 20:30–31)

We are to have faith; we are to believe in order to be saved. But what is it that we must have faith in? What is it that we are to believe? The life, death, and resurrection of Christ is the focus of our faith. "And this is life eternal, that they might know Thee the only true God, and Jesus Christ, whom Thou hast sent" (John 17:3). There is nothing we can do to recommend ourselves to God. We are utterly dependent on Him. Even our faith gains no merit with God, for it is He who sends the Holy Spirit to draw us to the great demonstration of love and the salvation purchased for us on Calvary. It is God's Holy Spirit that draws a man to perceive His grace and unmerited favor and places a desire in our hearts to entrust our lives, our eternal well–being, to Jesus Christ in complete confidence in what He has done to gain our salvation. This is the essence of the gospel. And it is this that the religion of Babylon counterfeits, or substitutes with religious ritual, works, and the doctrines of men, thus leading men away from God and the good news of the gospel to falsehood, mistakenly believing that they are following Him.

The Good News in the Life of Christ

> The Spirit of the Lord is upon me, because he hath anointed me to preach the gospel to the poor; he hath sent me to heal the brokenhearted, to preach deliverance to the captives, and recovering of sight to the blind, to set at liberty them that are bruised, to preach the acceptable year of the Lord. And he closed the book, and he gave it again to the minister, and sat down. And the eyes of all them that were in the synagogue were fastened on him. And he began to say unto them, This day is this scripture fulfilled in your ears. (Luke 4:18–21)

In the synagogue of Nazareth, Jesus read from Isaiah a prophecy telling of His own work and ministry as the Messiah. (See Isaiah 61:1–2.)

Jesus came to preach the gospel to "the poor," those who recognize their need. And how is it that we recognize our need? It is only by God's Spirit, which draws us to Him. We cannot accept the gospel or give heed to the three angels' messages unless God draws our hearts.

God is no respecter of persons but desires to save "every nation, and kindred, and tongue, and people" (Revelation 14:6). However, we must be aware that the devil, through the falsehood of unclean spirits and the three-fold religion of Babylon, desires to lead us away from the gospel into a counterfeit system of religion that in the end will separate us from God and eternal life. (See Revelation 16:13–14.)

Jesus went on to say, "He hath sent Me to heal the broken-hearted." Jesus' ministry is to heal the broken emotions and tarnished hopes caused by the bitterness of sin, to heal us emotionally, mentally, and spiritually. The gospel is not simply a theory; it is a power that affects the very life and being of a man.

Jesus, that day long ago in Nazareth, described His work further, stating that He came "to preach deliverance to the captives." He did not mean those who are held in the prisons of the nations of this world. Rather, this deliverance is from the captivity brought about by the destructive and delusive habits of sin. When we truly believe from the heart and surrender in faith to Jesus, accepting the good news of the everlasting gospel of God's love and mercy, God will deliver us. The gospel brings deliverance from sin and guilt and condemnation, and "the wages of sin [which] is death" (Romans 6:23), eternal separation from God.

He empowers us, though we are full of sin, for we are delivered and set free as our will is sanctified and renewed and enabled to choose the right, and reject the wrong through the indwelling of Christ within. The deliverance brought to us through the gospel of Christ develops in us strength of character as we yield to Him day by day.

The gospel of Christ is to bring "recovery of sight to the blind," to those whose spiritual understanding has been desensitized and blinded by the delusions of sin and falsehood. When we accept the gospel, there is a transformation of our worldview as we begin to see things with new eyes according to God's Word.

The gospel of Christ is "to set at liberty them that are bruised." Sin brings to each one broken dreams, bitter disappointments, and often shattered lives. Mankind, in a vain attempt to heal the bruises caused by sin, often seeks healing in false ideas of God and spirituality, in drugs and alcohol, and in a variety of sensual indulgences and stimulation. All these things and many more only worsen our spiritual and emotional sickness.

The prophet Isaiah describes mankind's spiritual condition. "The whole head is sick, and the whole heart faint. From the sole of the foot even unto the head there is no soundness in it; but wounds, and bruises, and putrifying sores: they have not been closed, neither bound up, neither mollified with ointment" (Isaiah 1:5–6).

Despite our condition, God's longsuffering love cries out through the everlasting gospel given by the angel messengers in these last days. He says to us, "Though your sins be as scarlet, they shall be as white as snow; though they be red like crimson, they shall be as wool" (Isaiah 1:18).

Despite God's timeless message of love in the everlasting gospel, the book of Revelation reveals that most of mankind will accept the beautiful side of evil, a religion that is cloaked in apparent good and beauty but leads us away from God. This religion is represented by a woman, "Mystery Babylon," representing all the counterfeit religions of the world in the last days. All who reject, neglect, or substitute something for the gospel of Christ will drink of the falsehood coming from the beautiful golden cup of Babylon's deception. (See Revelation 17:1–5.)

> For it became him, for whom are all things, and by whom are all things, in bringing many sons unto glory, to make the captain of their salvation perfect through sufferings. For both he that sanctifieth and they who are sanctified are all of one: for which cause he is not ashamed to call them brethren. (Hebrews 2:10–11)

> Though he were a Son, yet learned he obedience by the things which he suffered; and being made perfect, he became the author of eternal salvation unto all them that obey him. (Hebrews 5:8–9)

Represented as angels, God's last message through His people is a call to the world to believe and accept the gospel. We are to believe in Jesus, His life, His death, and His resurrection. In Christ's life and teachings we learn what God requires of us, and what heaven's principles are in contrast to the false paths and religions of men. Jesus, by His life, showed us what God is like, that we might want to serve Him.

Jesus, "in the beginning was the Word, and the Word was with God, and the Word was God" (John 1:1). Yet Jesus became a man that He might be our example. Further, He learned obedience in the sense that, day by day in His humanity He, as we do, had to yield to God rather than to the very real temptations and calls to compromise all around Him. Jesus was tempted in all points like as we are. (See Hebrews 4:15.) He suffered the trials and tribulations of man, yet without sin. His life is our great example. In contrast, the religion of Babylon would have us look to men, his institutions, his creeds, his pomp and ceremony, his saints and mediators. However, the everlasting gospel is centered upon Jesus, who is "the way, the truth, and the life" (John 14:6). Jesus alone is the true way to life and salvation that cannot be found in the clever religious counterfeits and the many lords and gods of this world.

Jesus lived a perfect life that He could be a perfect sacrifice, and His righteous life is accredited to us who believe and have faith. This is why God can save us though we are sinners. God must uphold His law and the eternal, unchanging standard of heaven. Yet He justifies and pardons all who accept the perfect sacrifice and obedient life of His Son in their place.

The Good News Is that the Life of Christ Is to Be Ours

Forasmuch then as Christ hath suffered for us in the flesh, arm yourselves likewise with the same mind: for he that hath suffered in the flesh hath ceased from sin; That he no longer should live the rest of his time in the flesh to the lusts of men, but to the will of God. (1 Peter 4:1–2)

For even hereunto were ye called: because Christ also suffered for us, leaving us an example, that ye should follow his steps: who did no sin, neither was guile found in his mouth: who, when he was reviled, reviled not again; when he suffered, he threatened not; but committed himself to him that judgeth righteously: who his own self bare our sins in his own body on the tree, that we, being dead to sins, should live unto righteousness: by whose stripes ye were healed. For ye were as sheep going astray; but are now returned unto the Shepherd and Bishop of your souls. (1 Peter 2:21–25)

As we by faith accept the life, death, and resurrection of Christ, the life of Jesus is accredited to us, and the death of Jesus pays the debt for our sins. Further, the life of Jesus is worked out in us by faith as His mind becomes our mind, "by the washing of regeneration, and renewing of the Holy Ghost" (Titus 3:5). Through the revelation of God's love as seen in Christ, we are drawn to His life and experience His death as we give Him our heart, mind, and strength. This leads us to desire to follow Christ rather than the lusts and sins of men. Yet the counterfeit religion revealed in the book of Revelation offers mankind a means of being saved by his own works, or saved in his sins. These are the fatal attractions of all the false religions that mankind so readily seeks.

The Good News in the Death of Christ

For when we were yet without strength, in due time Christ died for the ungodly. For scarcely for a righteous man will one die: yet peradventure for a good man some would even dare to die. But God commendeth his love toward us, in that, while we were yet sinners, Christ died for us. Much more then, being now justified by his blood, we shall be saved from wrath through him. For if, when we were enemies, we were reconciled to God by the death of his Son, much more, being reconciled, we shall be saved by his life. (Romans 5:6–10)

The coming of Christ to this world came at the right time and was according to the prophecy of Daniel 9. This prophecy refers to the seventy-week time period when a day equals a year.

(See Numbers 14:34.) God marked off 490 years of prophetic time from the commandment to restore and rebuild Jerusalem after the Babylonian captivity until Jesus Christ was anointed of the Holy Spirit, when He was baptized by John, marking the start of His three-and-a-half-year ministry. In the midst of that week of seven prophetic years, the Messiah was to be cut off for the sins of mankind.

This "due time" is prophetic time. It was the time that God had ordained and spoken through the prophet hundreds of years before. The prophecies are given that we might know that God is true, and that we would trust Him and trust His Word.

Listen, my friend, God demonstrated "His love toward us in that while we were yet sinners, Christ died for us." Jesus died our death. Whatever your religion or culture, no matter what your race, Jesus died for you. For every individual is subject to the condemnation and death penalty of sin. The Bible reveals the wages of sin is death and all men have sinned. All of us have come short of the glory of God. (See Romans 6:23; Romans 3:23.) We have come short of God's perfect standard, of His law. We are in rebellion; thus, we need the gospel to transform us. We need the gospel to save us from the just condemnation and wrath of God.

The everlasting gospel, through the angel's loud voice, indicates the intensity and great importance of the message that is calling the people of this planet to look upon Jesus, to know, understand, and receive Him as Savior, and to accept His death and sacrifice. However, what does much of the world do? We try to save ourselves by works, by following man-made religion to gain acceptance with God.

Many people have a false concept that says, "All I have to do is make a profession of God; it does not have to affect my life." The world is being conditioned to accept the false religion of Mystery Babylon. The crisis of the last days is over worship. "Shall I obey God or shall I obey man?" What we do with Christ, with the gospel, determines our destiny.

Those who accept the falsehood of salvation in sin or salvation by works will end up receiving the mark of the beast. They will reject the gospel or put something else in its place, rejecting God even as they claim to be serving Him.

For he hath made him to be sin for us, who knew no sin; that we might be made the righteousness of God in him. (2 Corinthians 5:21)

God sent Jesus as a sacrifice and substitute for us. He was actually made sin when, upon the cross, He felt the wrath of God due for mankind's sin: your sins and mine. He experienced the guilt and condemnation of every man. Jesus died for all, this includes you and I. The good news of the death of Christ is that He can free mankind from the guilt, condemnation, and eternal damnation that are the result of sin.

My friend, there is no other means of salvation other than Jesus. Every other attempt to gain acceptance with God and gain eternal life and the happiness all mankind desires, as sincere as it may be, is a false path. If our religion and spirituality ignores, sets aside, or substitutes the death of Jesus for any another means of acceptance with God, it can only lead to eternal loss, for we are yet in our sins, subject to the justice of God and the wages for our sins, which is death. Mankind cannot merit God's favor by anything he does, and God cannot save man in sin. The only remedy is grace, God's unmerited favor and kindness accepted by faith.

Forasmuch as ye know that ye were not redeemed with corruptible things, as silver and gold, from your vain conversation received by tradition from your fathers; But with the precious blood of Christ, as of a lamb without blemish and without spot. (1 Peter 1:18–19)

The word *redeem* means "to buy back." We were on our way to destruction, but Jesus came, lived a perfect life, and died upon the cross of Calvary, taking upon Himself our guilt and our sins, that He might buy us back from the sentence of death and deliver us so that we might have life. We can believe it or disbelieve it, yet it is true.

Mankind may try to gain acceptance with God, but his efforts are all doomed to failure. Nothing we can do will redeem our souls, no amount of good works, no pilgrimages, no religious zeal, sincerity, or profession, no amount of humanitarian charity. There is no intercessor, in heaven or on earth, that can substitute for the gospel of Jesus Christ. No human devising will replace the salvation that is in Jesus alone. This is why those who neglect, reject, or substitute something else in the place of the gospel end up as Revelation 14 describes, becoming part of the system of Babylon, a global system of false religion.

We can be fervent in praying five times a day, we can be ardent in adoring the Host for hours at a time, and we can be zealous in giving service to our religious practices. We can piously and dutifully go on pilgrimages and be obedient to the doctrines and creeds of churches. Yet it is all in vain. There is no other gospel; there is no means of salvation other than in Christ. Christ's death is accredited to us if we believe that He took our place in dying our death. Jesus was our substitute in experiencing our condemnation. We can pass from death unto life if we accept the gospel, the good news of the life, death, and resurrection of Christ for us.

Christ's Death Is to be Ours

> Giving thanks unto the Father, which hath made us meet to be partakers of the inheritance of the saints in light: who hath delivered us from the power of darkness, and hath translated us into the kingdom of his dear Son: in whom we have redemption through his blood, even the forgiveness of sins. (Colossians 1:12–14)

We are redeemed from sin through Jesus' shed blood and His death. Further, we are delivered from the power of darkness. This is a real experience, my friend. We are delivered from the darkness of sin and Satan's kingdom. We are translated into "the kingdom of His dear Son." If there is a kingdom, there must be a king. The acceptance of the gospel leads us to make Jesus our King, Lord, and Master.

Jesus, in His life as a man, "made Himself of no reputation, and took upon Him the form of a servant" (Philippians 2:7). His life is to be ours, for we are told, "Let this mind be in you, which was also in Christ Jesus" (2:5). Jesus went further, for "as a man, He humbled Himself, and became obedient unto death, even the death of the cross" (2:8). Therefore, if we accept Christ as Redeemer we must accept Him as King. Then not only is His death credited to our account, but "the love of Christ constraineth us; because we thus judge, that if one died for all, then were all dead" (2 Corinthians 5:14). What does that mean? "They which live should not henceforth live unto themselves, but unto him which died for them, and rose again" (verse 15).

To be saved by the death of Christ and from the guilt and condemnation of sin means that "our old man is crucified with Him, that the body of sin might be destroyed, that henceforth we should not serve sin" (Romans 6:6). This is the power of Christ's death; it not only frees us from the guilt of sin, but also enables us to overcome sin as we surrender heart, mind, and strength to Him, making Him Savior and King.

Many at the end of time will acknowledge various lords and gods. Others will declare Jesus as Lord, though they have not accepted His death in their own lives, leading them to "fear God, and give glory to Him" (Revelation 14:7). Therefore, they fall under the delusions and falsehood of Babylon.

> But Christ being come an high priest of good things to come, by a greater and more perfect tabernacle, not made with hands, that is to say, not of this building; neither by the blood of goats and calves, but by his own blood he entered in once into the holy place, having obtained eternal redemption for us. For if the blood of bulls and of goats, and the ashes of an heifer sprinkling the unclean, sanctifieth to the purifying of the flesh: how much more shall the blood of Christ, who through the eternal Spirit offered himself without spot to God, purge your conscience from dead works to serve the living God? (Hebrews 9:11–14)

Jesus' death is credited to us, so let us praise God for that. If we truly have faith in the death of Jesus, He begins to work out in us a transformation of character. The death of Christ, when it's accepted and believed, becomes our death, leading to the cleansing of our conscience. This is the work of God upon the heart of a man as he yields his will in self-surrender; a death, as it were. Then day by day we "put on the new man, which after God is created in righteousness and true holiness" (Ephesians 4:24).

The forgiveness of sin is not the only result of the death of Jesus. He made the sacrifice for our sins, not only so that the guilt and condemnation of sins might be removed, but also that He might restore us to Himself. The human heart, moved by the love of Christ and the power of the gospel, makes a willing surrender, which is death. By death we become "obedient children, not fashioning [ourselves] according to the former lusts in [our] ignorance: but as He which hath called you is holy," so we are called and enabled to be "holy in all manner of conversation" (1 Peter 1:14–15).

The Good News in the Resurrection of Christ

> … [Jesus] was delivered for our offences, and was raised again for our justification. Therefore being justified by faith, we have peace with God through our Lord Jesus Christ. (Romans 4:25; 5:1)

> [Jesus] was betrayed and put to death because of our misdeeds and was raised to secure our justification (our acquittal). (Romans 4:25 AMP)

Many of the religions of the world recognize that Jesus was a good man but do not accept Him as the Son of God, as the sacrifice and Savior for all mankind.

Just believing in Jesus' life is nothing unless you believe He was the revelation of God, and that His righteous life is credited to those who believe in Him. Just believing that Jesus existed and was a good man or a prophet has no saving virtue.

Many people believe that Jesus lived and died, but not that He was resurrected. Yes, He was a good man, they say, perhaps even a messenger of God, but He did not rise from the grave. If Jesus is still in the grave, my friend, regardless of what religious belief or philosophy you subscribe to, "your faith is vain; ye are yet in your sins" (1 Corinthians 15:17).

The reality is that salvation is only in the Lord Jesus Christ. Jesus was God manifest in the flesh. He showed us how to live, and He showed us what God was like. This man, the God man, who took upon Himself the guilt and woe and condemnation for the sins of the whole world, was raised from the grave for our acquittal. This is the gospel, the good news of salvation:

> That if thou shalt confess with thy mouth the Lord Jesus, and shalt believe in thine heart that God hath raised him from the dead, thou shalt be saved. (Romans 10:9)

> Blessed be the God and Father of our Lord Jesus Christ, which according to his abundant mercy hath begotten us again unto a lively hope by the resurrection of Jesus Christ from the dead, to an inheritance incorruptible, and undefiled, and that fadeth not away, reserved in heaven for you, who are kept by the power of God through faith unto salvation ready to be revealed in the last time. Wherein ye greatly rejoice, though now for a season, if need be, ye are in heaviness through manifold temptations. (1 Peter 1:3–6)

Jesus is not a dead or dying Savior, He is a risen Savior. Further, Jesus wants to give us His life. If we believe in Him, Jesus will credit to us His death so that we do not have to die eternally. In addition, Jesus, who was raised again, wants to give us resurrection life now, a new empowered life to live for God and to give Him glory.

The Good News Is that the Resurrection Life of Christ Is to Be Ours

> Buried with him in baptism, wherein also ye are risen with him through the faith of the operation of God, who hath raised him from the dead. And you, being dead in your

sins and the uncircumcision of your flesh, hath he quickened together with him, having forgiven you all trespasses. (Colossians 2:12–13)

But God, who is rich in mercy, for his great love wherewith he loved us, Even when we were dead in sins, hath quickened us together with Christ, (by grace ye are saved;) And hath raised us up together, and made us sit together in heavenly places in Christ Jesus. (Ephesians 2:4–6)

Knowing that Christ being raised from the dead dieth no more; death hath no more dominion over him. For in that he died, he died unto sin once: but in that he liveth, he liveth unto God. Likewise, reckon ye also yourselves to be dead indeed unto sin, but alive unto God through Jesus Christ our Lord. Let not sin therefore reign in your mortal body, that ye should obey it in the lusts thereof. (Romans 6:9–12)

The resurrection power that brought Christ from the grave is the same power that delivers us who are "dead in trespasses and sins" (Ephesians 2:1). Christ is "the resurrection, and the life" (John 11:25), and the power of His resurrection sets us "free from the law of sin and death" (Romans 8:2). Through Christ, the dominion of evil in our hearts may be broken, and through faith the soul can be kept from sin. We are to be "crucified with Christ"; this means we share His death. Further, we are to share in His resurrection. "I live; yet not I, but Christ liveth in me: and the life which I now live in the flesh I live by the faith of the Son of God, who loved me, and gave Himself for me" (Galatians 2:20).

It is by virtue of this union with Christ, by faith now in this life, that we are to come forth from the grave—not simply as a demonstration of the power of Christ, but because, through faith, His resurrection life has become ours.

Revelation 14 shows us the outcomes of those who reject the gospel and those who accept it. This gospel of the kingdom, which is to go to the whole world with a loud voice, is God's last message. The rejection of the gospel through neglect or substitution will eventually lead to the mark of the beast and eternal loss. "And this is the record, that God hath given to us eternal life, and this life is in His Son" (1 John 5:11).

Eternal life is not in human works; it's not in pilgrimages; it is not in the intercession of Mary; it is not in anything that man can do. No church affiliation, religious zeal, or time spent in purgatory or a hundred reincarnations will gain for anyone eternal life. Without Jesus' perfect life being credited to us, without Jesus taking our place and paying for our sins by His death, and without Jesus' resurrection life becoming ours by faith, we are lost. Truly, Jesus is the gospel and the message that is to go to every nation, kindred, tongue, and people.

Chapter Two

Restoration—
The Everlasting Gospel

And I saw another angel fly in the midst of heaven, having the everlasting gospel to preach unto them that dwell on the earth, and to every nation, and kindred, and tongue, and people. (Revelation 14:6)

The angel messenger is seen flying in the midst of heaven, to draw the attention of the world to the everlasting gospel. This messenger is to preach unto them who dwell on the earth, showing this is a worldwide message.

The cross is the very center of the whole plan of salvation; it is the gospel. The cross is the great demonstration of the grace and love of God for humanity, for you and for me. Not only has Christ paid the penalty for sin, but the power of the gospel is the power of restoration.

Let us begin to explore from the Scriptures God's great plan for the restoration of man from sin.

Where was thou when I laid the foundations of the earth, declare if thou hast understanding. When the morning stars sang together, and all the sons of God shouted for joy? (Job 38:4, 7)

Here is depicted a time of rejoicing and blessing, when heaven saw this new planet, the whole solar system, being created by the spoken word of God. However, it was not simply making a new planet or making the wonderful variety of animals that was the cause of rejoicing. As wonderful as the solar system and the intricacies and beauty of the earth are, the most important feature of

God's creation was man. This was what brought the rejoicing. All the sons of God were gathered to view His creative majesty and power, and man was the crowning act of that creation.

All of heaven, as depicted here in Job, took a deep and joyful interest in the creation of this world and especially of man, for human beings were a new and distinct order. The book of Genesis says, "Let us make man after our own image" (Genesis 1:26). God had a special purpose in making man.

God spoke into existence the sun, the moon, the stars, the animals, and earth's life support system. However, when it came to man, the Bible reveals that "the Lord God formed man of the dust of the ground, and breathed into his nostrils the breath of life; and man became a living soul" (Genesis 2:7). God did not simply speak man into existence by the might of His power; He formed man from the dust of the ground. This special manner of creation shows the intimacy that God, at the very beginning, desired to have with mankind.

As Adam came from the Creator's hand, his physical, mental, and spiritual nature had a likeness to his Maker, for man's purpose was to reflect the glory of his Creator. The longer man should live, the more fully he would reveal God's image and reflect the glory of his Creator.

In the days of the prophet Isaiah, though the world and man had been terribly marred by sin, God's purpose for Israel (and indeed for all mankind) repeats creation's purpose, for we read: "Even every one that is called by My name: for I have created him for My glory, I have formed him; yea, I have made him" (Isaiah 43:7).

God created us for His glory. This is not a selfish glory as we think of in this world, where we want to take glory to ourselves. God is not like us. When He created man for His glory it was also to bless man and fulfill man's fondest hopes of happiness and fulfillment, which could only be in God. This was to be to God's glory as the Creator.

In the beginning, God spoke with man face to face. Heart-to-heart communion with his Maker was his privilege. If Adam had remained faithful, this would have been the succeeding generations' privilege forever. Throughout eternal ages, man would have continued to gain new revelations of knowledge and discover more sources of happiness in knowing and serving God. Man would have gained deeper insights into the wisdom and power and love of God. Man would have fulfilled the purpose of his creation, which was to reflect the image of Him who "formed man of the dust of the ground" (Genesis 2:7). God designed that man, the crowning work of His creation, would express His thought and reveal His glory. This was man's purpose and destiny.

We are all too familiar with the sin of Adam and Eve and of the continual fall of mankind ever since, as well as our own sins and shortcomings and failures. As we look upon this world cursed with sin and sorrow, we are made acutely aware of the tragic result of sin. Many in this world love sin, but we need to understand that sin is a curse, and that is why this world is in such chaos. It is not because there is a lack of resources and money. It is not because there is so much disease or that science has not yet found answers to our problems. Rather, the real reason this planet is in turmoil is sin, as "evil men and seducers ... wax worse and worse, deceiving, and being deceived" (2 Timothy 3:13) while the "imagination of the thoughts of his [mankind's] heart ... [is] only evil continually" (Genesis 6:5).

The result of man's sin is that his physical powers were weakened, his mental capacity was lessened, his spiritual vision was dimmed, and he became subject to death. Yet Adam and succeeding generations were not left without hope, for God in love and mercy devised a plan of salvation and a second chance was granted. As soon as there was sin, there was a Savior: Jesus, "the Lamb slain from the foundation of the world" (Revelation 13:8).

Sin did not come as a surprise to God; He already had a plan to restore man, to bring us back to the purpose for which we were created. This is the work of redemption and this is the great object of the gospel. The gospel of Jesus Christ not only redeems man by paying the penalty for sin, it also brings the renewing work of grace and love in restoring man to his Maker.

This restoration does not add anything to God's work of salvation. It is simply the outgrowth, the fruit of being born again; it is the power of the gospel to change sinners to saints.

Enmity Natural and Supernatural

> And I will put enmity between thee and the woman, and between thy seed and her seed; it shall bruise thy head, and thou shalt bruise his heel. (Genesis 3:15)

This is the first promise in the Scripture of the gospel, of the power of God to enable man to resist the devil, and of the promised Messiah. Jesus would be bruised because of our sin, for we read, "He was wounded for our transgressions, He was bruised for our iniquities" (Isaiah 53:5). However, through that bruising Christ would bring deliverance, salvation, and an end to Satan's reign.

It is the grace of Christ, which the Spirit implants in the soul, that creates in man enmity against Satan. Without this converting and enabling grace and renewing power, man would continue to be the captive of Satan, a servant to sin. As we were once at ease with sin and strangers to righteousness, now as we experience Christ's redeeming love and our lives are enabled by His grace, there is a conflict where previously there had been peace. There is a divine transaction that begins as God places in our hearts enmity toward Satan and his principles. As our hearts are drawn from Satan there is a corresponding love that grows, deepens, and develops toward God and for His principles of truth and righteousness.

Whoever is seen to hate sin instead of loving it, whoever resists sin and conquers the passions of evil that have held control over heart and life, reveals the working of a principle wholly from above. This is the work of the gospel, for it creates enmity in our hearts toward Satan and his rule of evil that we once enjoyed.

All who are not committed to God and are not true followers of Christ are willingly or unwillingly servants of Satan. You see, in the unregenerate heart there is love of sin and an attitude to cherish and excuse it, which is proof of Satan's dominion over us. In the renewed heart there is hatred of sin and determined resistance against it by the enabling grace of Christ.

Revelation 13 reveals that the worshipers of the beast are actually worshipers of the dragon or Satan. (See Revelation 13:4.) In addition, Revelation 14 reveals the entire world will be taken in the snare of Babylonian religion, receiving the mark of the beast if they do not know and experience the power of the gospel that is evidenced by a love for God and obedience to His word and law.

> Because the carnal mind is enmity against God: for it is not subject [obedient] to the law of God, neither indeed can be. (Romans 8:7)

The above verse reveals to us the nature of the carnal, unregenerate mind, the mind that has not been touched by the Spirit of God and the gospel. The carnal mind has enmity against God; there is hostility. How is this hostility manifested? Our world today is very religious, as most of mankind follows some kind of religion or spiritual philosophy. Very few in this world would say, "God, I hate You." Rather, most people simply ignore and neglect God, even though they profess religion. In addition, their hatred for God is shown by the fact that they are not subject (in other words, obedient) to the law of God. In fact, apart from the transforming work of Christ through the gospel, man cannot obey God's law. This is why most of the world will follow the religion of Babylon which is man-centered religion, contrary to the law and word of God. It is the religion of the carnal, unregenerate nature.

Romans 8:7 reveals to us the natural enmity all of us have toward God when left to follow our own sinful and selfish ways. However, by the work of grace and redeeming love, God wants to work out a change in our lives.

> And you that were sometimes alienated and enemies in your minds by wicked works, yet now hath he [Christ] reconciled. In the body of his flesh through death, to present you holy and unblameable and unreproveable in his sight. (Colossians 1:21–22)

To be alienated means to be an enemy of God, manifested by wicked works, the root of which is in our minds. However, becoming one with Christ makes man free.

The work of the gospel is the work of reconciliation. A mind that once ignored, rejected, or despised God is to be reconciled and brought again into harmony with Him. The gospel is not to work a change in God but in man. God has always loved us; however, He must work on our hearts without violating our will or our conscience. This change of heart leads us to accept the sacrifice of Christ in our place, and leads us to love and serve Him. This is the result of our reconciliation with God. In addition, this reconciliation is manifested by an ever-growing and deepening love and obedience to Him; it is the healing and restoration of our wicked minds, the source of all our sinful works.

> Ye adulterers and adulteresses, know ye not that the friendship of the world is enmity with God? Whosoever therefore will be a friend of the world is an enemy of God. (James 4:4)

> Love not the world, neither the things that are in the world. If any man love the world, the love of the Father is not in him. For all that is in the world, the lust of the flesh, and the lust of the eyes, and the pride of life, is not of the Father, but is of the world. (1 John 2:16)

To be a friend with the world is to follow the world's principles, its way of thinking, which is contrary to God's Word, and to follow its wickedness and sin. If we are friends with the world, we have enmity toward God. Therefore, our profession of religion, regardless of what religion it may be, is vain and useless. It does not come from God at all.

In contrast, "the gospel of Christ: ... is the power of God unto salvation to every one that believeth" (Romans 1:16). The purpose of the gospel is not simply to provide for the forgiveness of sins, but to restore the harmony and relationship with God that sin has taken away.

> And they that are Christ's have crucified the flesh with the affections and lusts. (Galatians 5:24)

For the grace of God that bringeth salvation hath appeared to all men. Teaching us that, denying ungodliness and worldly lusts, we should live soberly, righteously, and godly, in this present world. (Titus 2:11–12)

God's grace, working upon the heart of men, falls freely upon all mankind, irrespective of religion, race, or nationality. God is no respecter of persons, for He loves all men. What is the effect of grace if it is received and responded to? It leads us to accept Jesus' death for the forgiveness of sins, which in turn changes our hearts, leading us to put to death and crucify our natural heart. This is not something worked up by religious fervor; it is the work of the gospel to change the heart of man.

We learn further that grace works in us, teaching us and enabling us to deny ungodliness and worldly lust, that we might have a sound mind, living temperately, righteously, and godly in this present world.

If the power of redeeming love transforming our hearts is not experienced, we will come under the influence of the religion of Babylon. This encompasses all the religions of man, based as they are on the various ideas of salvation by works or salvation in sin.

Restoration of the Mind

Sin brought a break in the relationship between man and God, and sin demanded death. Jesus' death on the cross paid that penalty. However, paying the penalty for sin is not the only result of Christ's death. Any newborn baby, and indeed any newborn animal, if it is healthy, will start growing and developing. Moreover, the mother and the father do not love that child any more because it is growing and developing into eventual adulthood. That growth and development is the outcome of birth. So is the new birth and subsequent restoration brought about by the gospel. Both forgiveness and restoration are the result of the sacrifice of Jesus Christ, accepted by faith.

The love and mercy of God that reaches into our hearts and moves us to accept Christ as our Savior is the same grace, love, and power that begins a process of restoring us to the image of our Maker. Many people believe that Jesus died for their sins, but they are not overcoming the world. They still have in their hearts, to some degree, an animosity and enmity toward God. They will seldom admit it, they do not even recognize it in most cases, but it is manifested by disobedience to the law and principles of God. Loving the things of the world, the lust of the flesh and the lust of the eyes, and the pride of life demonstrate the enmity that is still within the heart.

Oh, friends, as true as it is that Jesus died for our sins, it is just as true that God wants to restore us. This work of restoration, and this growth of character development, is the proof of having received the gospel. Sadly, most of the world will reject the gospel. Yet, desiring salvation, they will turn to the delusions of false religion.

To open their eyes, and to turn them from darkness to light, and from the power of Satan unto God, that they may receive forgiveness of sins, and inheritance among them which are sanctified by faith that is in me. (Acts 26:18)

The above verse describes Christ's commission to the apostle Paul: the ministry of the gospel. Now listen to what Paul's message was and what effect it was to have upon those who received it: "to open their eyes." This is not simply the gift of healing; rather, it is speaking of "the eyes of your understanding being enlightened" (Ephesians 1:18). This is referring to the mind, the faculty of knowing or understanding.

The grace of God moving upon the heart of a man begins to work out in us a new mind. Thus, our spiritually darkened understanding begins to see the light of God's love. The delusions of sin and Satan, which are accompanied by the darkness of error and falsehood, begin to be replaced by the light of the gospel. This light of understanding, with the subsequent diminishing and eventual banishing of the darkness, is to grow and brighten like the ever-increasing splendor of the sun. Therefore, "the path of the just [justified] is as the shining light, that shineth more and more unto the perfect day" (Proverbs 4:18).

> "The light [of the gospel, shining] out of darkness, hath shined in our hearts, to give the light of the knowledge of the glory of God in the face of Jesus Christ." (2 Corinthians 4:6)

Previous to the light of the gospel shining in our minds, "the god of this world ...blinded the minds of them which believe not [you and I, all of mankind], lest the light of the glorious gospel of Christ, who is the image of God, should shine unto them" (2 Corinthians 4:4).

Turning from darkness to light is moving from the life of sin and rebellion and estrangement from God to a life of wanting to love and serve God, being freed from the power of Satan.

The power of forgiveness is the power of the gospel, for the sin-hardened heart of man to be drawn to God and desire His forgiveness is the work of the Spirit upon our hearts. A work that draws, leading to pardon; a work that fixes our hope and confidence upon Him who is "the way, the truth, and the life" (John 14:6). Not all who make a profession of religion have an inheritance of eternal life, though this is the hope of billions of people. For in rejecting, neglecting, or placing something in the place of the gospel, man is actually deluded by the false religious ideas of Babylon. Thus they are still estranged from God and need salvation. The inheritance is only for those "which are sanctified by faith that is in Me." We cannot separate forgiveness and justification from sanctification. They are each the work of grace. The gospel that brings salvation, delivering us from the darkness and power of Satan, is to justify, forgive, and restore, and its end is eternal life.

Called to God's Glory

> Whereunto he called you by our gospel, to the obtaining of the glory of our Lord Jesus Christ. (2 Thessalonians 2:14)

The gospel is calling us to the glory of the character of Christ. The rebellious human heart, which often couldn't care less about God, ignores Him, rejects Him, or just does not have much interest in Him. Mysteriously, however, through divine love and mercy, the Holy Spirit begins to enlighten the minds of all who will not resist. Sometimes we become open to the Holy Spirit because of sorrows, trials, and perplexities in our lives.

Sin separates us from God; therefore, the gospel is not simply a way to pay for our sins and then leave us alone. No, the gospel is God's wonderful, loving means of being just; His laws and principles are upheld even though sin demands death. God is just but He is also the justifier of those who believe in Jesus, because Jesus took our penalty. The penalty had to be paid, whether we accept it or not, and Christ, in paying that penalty, has given man a second chance. The purpose of the gospel is restoration, bringing us back into harmony with God, that once again we might fulfill the purpose for our creation: to reflect the glory of God. This is to begin here and now and last throughout eternity, "to the praise of the glory of His grace, wherein He hath made us accepted in the beloved" (Ephesians 1:6).

One of the messages of Revelation 14 deals with the mark of the beast, a mark of rebellion, a sign of worship that acknowledges the beast above God. The beast will appear in the name of God and in the place of God, claiming that he is God's representative on earth. The world will think this is the great power of God. However, those who experience the everlasting gospel will recognize this beast as the counterfeit that it is. Those who do not experience the gospel will worship the beast. "All that dwell upon the earth shall worship him, whose names are not written in the book of life of the Lamb slain from the foundation of the world" (Revelation 13:8).

There are going to be many who accept the beast, who worship the beast, who think that in doing so they are following and serving God. They have never had their eyes opened. They have not turned from the darkness of sin and falsehood to the light of the glorious truth of the gospel. They were not freed from the power of Satan to come under the lordship of Christ. They worship the beast, Satan's vicar, because they have not experienced the gospel. This is serious, my friend. God has called us by the "gospel, to the obtaining of the glory of our Lord Jesus Christ" (2 Thessalonians 2:14). Apart from experiencing the everlasting gospel, we will become spiritually drunk on the delusive falsehoods of Babylon. (See Revelation 18:3.)

Becoming the Sons of God

> But as many as received him, to them gave he power to become the sons of God, even to them that believe on his name. (John 1:12)

Receiving Christ is not a mere verbal acknowledgement; it is not simply an intellectual assent. To receive Jesus means to believe, entrusting yourself and giving your heart, mind, and strength to Him who died for us.

The book of James says even "the devils also believe, and tremble" (James 2:19). Yet this belief has no saving virtue. Many people in the world say they believe in Jesus. However, what Jesus is it? For "as the serpent beguiled Eve through his subtilty, so … [many] minds … [will] be corrupted from the simplicity that is in Christ" (2 Corinthians 11:3). Many in the world are corrupted because they accept "another Jesus … another spirit … another gospel" (2 Corinthians 11:4). Further, we have been warned by Christ, "Take heed that no man deceive you. For many shall come in My name, saying, I am Christ; and shall deceive many" (Matthew 24:4–5).

Simply believing in Jesus as a historical figure, or intellectually as the Savior, is of no value unless you believe to the point of entrusting your life to Him as Redeemer and King. Further, to receive the real Christ rather than an antichrist is to receive the power of forgiveness, which is the power of God unto salvation, a power that begins to restore us. This is the power to become the sons of God, and if we are the sons of God, we are going to live like it, following God's laws and His principles and His Word. This the adherents of the religion of Babylon do not do.

> But now being made free from sin, and become servants to God, ye have your fruit unto holiness, and the end everlasting life. (Romans 6:22)

Freedom comes when we accept what Jesus has done for us intellectually, of course, but also from the heart made soft and subdued by the Holy Spirit working in us. We are made free from guilt and condemnation, the "wages of sin [which] is death" (Romans 6:23). As soon as we are freed from the guilt and condemnation of sin, as we surrender and yield our hearts and minds to God, we become God's servants. Becoming a servant of God develops in us a life of holiness; it is the work of restoring in us the character of God, and the end or outcome of such a life lived for God is everlasting life.

The Gospel Creates a New Man

> That ye put off concerning the former conversation the old man, which is corrupt according to the deceitful lusts. And be renewed in the spirit of your mind. And that ye put on the new man, which after God is created in righteousness and true holiness. (Ephesians 4:22–24)

The old man is the man of the flesh: the man who was estranged from God, who loved sin, who ignored, despised, or rejected God. The new man is the one who has accepted the death of Jesus Christ, who has made Jesus his Lord. The new man is the one who, by the power of Christ, begins a warfare to resist the promptings of sin and the pulls of the flesh. For this body will not change until Jesus changes it at the resurrection, when this mortal shall put on immortality. (See 1 Corinthians 15:51–54.) However, when we accept Him and as we surrender our hearts day by day, He renews our minds that we might willingly choose to serve and follow Him. The Christian life is all about warfare. Paul says:

Thou therefore endure hardness, as a good soldier of Jesus Christ. No man that warreth entangleth himself with the affairs of this life; that he may please him who hath chosen him to be a soldier. And if a man also strive for masteries, yet is he not crowned, except he strive lawfully. (2 Timothy 2:3–5)

Sin has made such inroads into our lives and into the human experience that even with God's help, and God's justifying and sanctifying enabling grace, we still need to choose the way of the Lord. This at times involves the discipline and hardship that is seen in the life of a soldier. However, we do not work alone. For "God has brought you into union with Christ Jesus, and God has made Christ to be our wisdom. By Him we are put right with God; we become God's holy people and are set free" (1 Corinthians 1:30 TEV).

God's purpose through the everlasting gospel is to renew the mind, to begin to bring us back into harmony with Himself, the oneness mankind lost at the beginning through Adam's fall.

To put on the new man is not something we can obtain alone through meditation techniques or by going to the right church or by special counseling. Absolutely not! The true renewal of the mind and life is the work of creation upon the human heart. It is the creative power of God that gives us the desire and willingness to serve and follow Him. God could just magically change our character, but He will not violate our will. God requires the surrender of the will, the cooperation of man to save him and to restore him, because He wants our surrender to come from our hearts, because God's kingdom is based upon love.

We are to put away the old man, which is the old behavior, the partnership with evil and evil associates. This is possible only if we are renewed, "created in righteousness and true holiness." The word *renewed* means "to renovate; i.e., to reform."[1]

Pursuing this definition further, we find that *renovate* means "to renew; to restore to the first state, or to a good state, after decay, destruction or deprivation."[2] Sin has brought decay and deprivation upon this planet, into your life and mine; sin has destroyed and is destroying nations, families, and individuals. But praise

God, He wants to change all of that, and it begins in the heart of man. The gospel calls every man, the Spirit woos and draws every man, the death of Jesus upon the cross was sufficient to pay the debt of sin for every man, but man must yield and surrender, allowing himself to be drawn. If we surrender, God begins the work of renewing our hearts, our minds, and our lives. This is the power of the gospel, the work of redemption.

The Gospel Is the Power of God

> For the preaching of the cross is to them that perish foolishness; but unto us which are saved it is the power of God. (1 Corinthians 1:18)

It is not enough to hear the story of the cross. The cross must become our story, as the Holy Spirit moves upon our hearts, as we recognize and accept that it was our sin that crucified the Lord of glory; it was for me that He died. When we accept that, when it becomes a reality in our lives, we can know and experience the power of God unto salvation, the power of the gospel. For Christ upon the cross, dying for your sins and mine, is the gospel. "Christ crucified" is unto us "which are called, … the power of God, and the wisdom of God" (1 Corinthians 1:23–24).

The gospel is the power of God. What power is that? It is nothing less than the new birth. And how is this manifested in the life? When we speak of the new heart brought about by the acceptance of the gospel, we are speaking of the mind, the life, the whole being. To experience a changed heart leads to the withdrawal of affections from the world, which is then fastened upon Christ. To have a new heart is to have a new mind, new purposes, and new motives. What then is the sign of a new heart, the power of the gospel? It is a changed life that lives to please and serve God. Being born again leads us to a daily, hourly dying to selfishness and pride. True conversion will make us honest in our dealings with our fellow men, and it makes us faithful in our everyday work. And why this change? Because we have a "faith which worketh by love" (Galatians 5:6), as "the love of God is shed abroad in our hearts by the Holy Ghost which is given unto us" (Romans 5:5).

> But now ye also put off all these; anger, wrath, malice, blasphemy, filthy communication out of your mouth. Lie not one to another, seeing that ye have put off the old man with his deeds; And have put on the new man, which is renewed in knowledge after the image of him that created him. (Colossians 3:8–10)

Knowledge does not save us, though it is true that to a certain degree social influences and other external factors and education may modify the life. However, only the knowledge of God, His principles, and His love, mercy, and kindness has the power and ability to renew us in the spirit of the mind. This knowledge is intellectual, but it is also experiential. As we receive God's Word into our hearts, it has creative power.

The mind gradually adapts to the subjects and environments upon which it is allowed to dwell. It becomes assimilated to that which it is accustomed to behold. We are told in Colossians 3 that the power of the gospel is to set us free from anger, wrath, malice, blasphemy, and lying. We are to put off the old man with his deeds. We are to put on the new man, which is renewed in knowledge after the image of Him who created him. Where are we spending our time? Where are we focusing our attention? Whatever we focus our attention on is what we will become.

It is the law of the intellectual and spiritual nature of man that by beholding we become changed. That is why the world is changing the church today. Because the church is beholding the world. It is not beholding Christ; it is not beholding His Word. The mind, and consequently the life and religious beliefs and practices, gradually adapts itself to that which it dwells upon. Therefore, the church is becoming like the world because it is dwelling on the principles and things of the world. The church has not known the power of the gospel, the church at large is not even preaching the gospel. Therefore, we have comfortable sinners attending churches, being made at ease by an easy message. Sadly, many are fallen from God, departing "from the faith, giving heed to seducing spirits, and doctrines of devils" (1 Timothy 4:1).

> Not every one that saith unto me, Lord, Lord, shall enter into the kingdom of heaven; but he that doeth the will of my Father which is in heaven. Many will say to me in that day, Lord, Lord, have we not prophesied in thy name? and in thy name have cast out devils? and in thy name done many wonderful works? And then will I profess unto them, I never knew you: depart from me, ye that work iniquity. (Matthew 7:21–23)

Do the people described above believe in the death of Jesus Christ? Yes, they believe in Jesus, but they never surrendered, they never yielded, they never experienced the power of the gospel. Thus, they will be worshipers of the beast, believing that they are serving God. This is the tragic result that will come to everyone who neglects, rejects, or substitutes the gospel for the religion of men.

The Gospel Brings a New Life

> Therefore if any man be in Christ, he is a new creature: old things are passed away; behold, all things are become new. (2 Corinthians 5:17)

> Therefore if any person is [in grafted] in Christ (the Messiah) he is a new creation (a new creature altogether); the old [previous moral and spiritual condition] has passed away. Behold, the fresh and new has come! (2 Corinthians 5:17 AMP)

The power of the gospel is centered in the cross, but the cross must become ours. Not in the sense that we can do anything to pay for our sins—that is not possible. The cross must become ours as "the love of Christ constraineth us; because we

42

thus judge, that if one died for all, then were all dead: and that He died for all, that they which live should not henceforth live unto themselves, but unto Him which died for them, and rose again" (2 Corinthians 5:14–15)

As the Holy Spirit draws us, we are enabled to surrender our hearts and minds. This surrender, to a God of love whom we do not see, is like being crucified. This is why anyone who is "in Christ" (meaning surrendered to Christ, making Him Lord and Savior) is a new creature. A new life has begun. The new life seeks to please God and live for Him, thereby beginning to live the life that was the original purpose for man's creation.

We may not be able to explain or understand the change He has made and is making in our hearts, and we may be saddened about our past and current shortcomings. Even if that is the case, "this one thing I do, forgetting those things which are behind, and reaching forth unto those things which are before, I press toward the mark for the prize of the high calling of God in Christ Jesus" (Philippians 3:13–14).

> For the grace of God that bringeth salvation hath appeared to all men, Teaching us that, denying ungodliness and worldly lusts, we should live soberly, righteously, and godly, in this present world; Looking for that blessed hope, and the glorious appearing of the great God and our Saviour Jesus Christ. Who gave himself for us, that he might redeem us from all iniquity, and purify unto himself a peculiar people, zealous of good works. (Titus 2:11–14)

Jesus is the light that "lighteth every man that cometh into the world" (John 1:9). Further, it is by His Spirit that He seeks to spiritually enlighten, to give understanding and a saving knowledge of God to all men. This is accomplished by grace, an influence of love and mercy that is brought to the heart of every man, though very few men respond to it. Yet even if men neglect the gospel, reject it, or put something else in its place, and even "if we believe not, yet He abideth faithful: He cannot deny Himself" (2 Timothy 2:13). Why does God remain faithful in the midst of most of mankind's unbelief and lack of faith? "Herein is love, not that we loved God, but that He loved us, and sent His Son to be the propitiation for our sins" (1 John 4:10).

The spirit of grace teaches and transforms those who open their hearts to the love of God and respond to the everlasting gospel. Under the spirit of grace, instead of living an ungodly life, which is a disregard of God and His commands, a life of sin, we now have an ever-increasing desire for godliness. It is the grace of God received into the life that enables us to "flee these things; and follow after righteousness, godliness, faith, love, patience, meekness" (1 Timothy 6:11).

Not only does the grace of God draw and renew, giving us a desire to deny ungodliness and worldly lusts, it transforms and restores, leading its recipients to live soberly, with a sound mind and self-control. The transforming and restoring work of grace leads us to live righteously and godly here and now in this present world. And what does it mean to live a godly life? It is "living in obedience to God's commands, from a principle of love to him and reverence of his character and precepts." It is to be "pious; conformed to God's law."[3]

This is why Revelation 14 reveals that the gospel will develop a people "that keep the commandments of God, and the faith of Jesus" (Revelation 14:12). The vast majority of earth's teeming multitudes, many of whom are professors of religion, do not really love God and have never been transformed by grace; therefore, they will worship the beast, often sincerely, yet rejecting God for the religion and commandments of men.

Jesus die not die to save man in sin; rather, He paid the penalty for our sins and has given us His Spirit, "that He might redeem us from all iniquity, and purify unto Himself a peculiar people, zealous of good works" (Titus 2:14).

God's glory is shown in His mercy to the children of men, and His glory will be restored day by day in the hearts of those who partake of His mercy. "That ye may be blameless and harmless, the sons of God, without rebuke, in the midst of a crooked and perverse nation, among whom ye shine as lights in the world" (Philippians 2:15).

Those who neglect this glorious offer of love will go into further darkness and sin, often pursuing religion in one form or another. False religion develops in men the mind of Satan, leading mankind to accept the beautiful side of evil. However, that is the way of death.

I pray, my friend, that you will open your heart to the Lord, that you might let His love fill your soul and transform your mind so that this day you might truly be a child of God.

I pray that you might know the love of God and experience the gospel, "the power of God unto salvation to every one that believeth" (Romans 1:16). Amen.

Endnotes

1. James Strong LL.D., S.T.D., *Strong's Exhaustive Concordance* (Grand Rapids, Michigan: Baker Book House, 1987).
2. Noah Webster, *American Dictionary of the English Language* (San Francisco, California: Foundation for American Christian Education, 1967).
3. Ibid.

Chapter Three

Saying with a Loud Voice, "Fear God"

S aying with a loud voice, Fear God, and give glory to him; for the hour of his judgment is come: and worship him that made heaven, and earth, and the sea, and the fountains of waters. (Revelation 14:7)

When God gives a message with a loud voice, calling the world to fear Him, is He thundering from heaven, commanding us to be afraid of Him as a vengeful God? No! God gives warnings, to be sure, for He is just and will punish sin. However, the Bible also says, "For I know the plans I have for you, says the Lord. They are plans for good and not for evil, to give you a future and a hope" (Jeremiah 29:11 TLB). This has always been the attitude of God toward humanity.

To fear God is simply to give Him reverence. This comes about not through the religion of men but through the experience of the gospel. It is by the message of the gospel that we know the love of God through Christ. By faith we have seen the risen Savior, and our great High Priest, who has been touched with the feeling of our infirmities.

This call to fear God is a call to enter into a relationship with the Creator. However, if we ignore, despise, or neglect such a privilege as to know and fear God it will lead us to be a part of spiritual Babylon. To all who are under the influence of the philosophy and religion of Babylon, and willingly remain so, there "remaineth no more sacrifice for sins, but a certain fearful looking for of judgment and fiery indignation, which shall devour the adversaries" (Hebrews 10:26–27).

Therefore, the call to fear God is also a message to separate ourselves from sin and from following man and his religions, doctrines, and delusions. "The fear of man bringeth a snare: but whoso putteth his trust in the Lord shall be safe" (Proverbs 29:25).

Satan's lie, the final delusion that he will bring upon the whole world, is the mark of the beast, which sets the stage for his appearance as Antichrist, the one in place of Christ. Then his proud boast, as recorded by the prophet Isaiah, will come to pass: "I will ascend into heaven, I will exalt my throne above the stars of God: I will sit also upon the mount of the congregation, in the sides of the north: I will ascend above the heights of the clouds; I will be like the most High" (Isaiah 14:13–14).

The fear of man, which brings the snare and ends in death, is vain worship, "teaching for doctrines the commandments of men" (Matthew 15:9). Fearing man means being spoiled "by his so-called philosophy and intellectualism and vain deceit (idle fancies and plain nonsense), following human tradition (men's ideas of the material rather than the spiritual world), just crude notions following the rudimentary and elemental teachings of the universe and disregarding [the teachings of] Christ (the Messiah)" (Colossians 2:8 AMP).

In contrast to the fear of man, we will learn in this chapter what it really means to fear God, which is our only safety for this life and hope for eternity.

> In good men, the fear of God is a holy awe or reverence
> of God and his laws, which springs from a just view and
> real love of the divine character, leading the subjects of it
> to hate and shun everything that can offend such a holy
> being, and inclining them to aim at perfect obedience.[1]

To truly fear God is not the experience of the natural man; it is the result of being born again, of experiencing the everlasting gospel.

In the book of Revelation there are two classes of people in the last days: the worshipers of the beast and the worshipers of God. The worshipers of the beast are spoken of as having a mark on their right hand or their forehead, which is a mark of man-made religion. It is the authority of men recognized, followed, and worshiped above God and His word and law. The worshipers of God are sealed, having the Father's name on their foreheads. This means they have been transformed by grace; God's will, word, and law are supreme in their life by faith and love.

We fear God; we obey Him, not because we are afraid of hell-fire or because we have a desire for the reward of eternal life and heaven. We can only love someone as we come to know them. Therefore, God invites us, in the message of the everlasting gospel, to know Him and thereby love, obey, and fear Him. If our allegiance to God is based on a superficial hope of reward or fear of punishment, in the end we do not obey because that is not adequate motivation, for only true heart service that leads us to fear God is acceptable worship. God in love will use stern warnings, which we see throughout Scripture. Further, He allows or brings judgments and trials upon men and nations if that is what it takes to get our attention. However, He wants us to grow beyond that and to know and love Him.

> And the Lord said unto Satan, Hast thou considered my servant Job, that there is none like him in the earth, a perfect and an upright man, one that feareth God, and escheweth evil? and still he holdeth fast his integrity, although thou movedst me against him, to destroy him without cause. (Job 2:3)

Job was bitterly tested, but he was sustained in that bitter testing, and he came out, tried in the fire, having a greater understanding and love for God than he ever had.

Job was God's servant, His representative. God wants to have servants today who will stand against Satan and his accusations, who will rightly represent Him. The description of Job's character shows us what it means to fear God. Job is described as being a perfect and upright man, meaning one who is straight, not deviating from correct moral principles. The messengers of Revelation 14 cry with a loud voice at this hour because we live in a perverse world with a compromised Christianity. Believers who are straight and upright, who are not deviating from correct moral principles, are a minority in this world. God is calling the world to experience the gospel and to come back to uprightness and moral correctness, to fear Him.

We read further of Job that he "eschweth evil." *Eschew* means "to turn aside," "to depart," to "avoid."[2] God is calling the world to fear Him and to shun evil. God's standard, and the result of truly following Him, is that we will "abstain from all appearance of evil" (1 Thessalonians 5:22). If we are not fleeing from evil, we are in a conditioning process as our minds are being marked. The mark of the beast is not a sudden event someday in the future; we are determining our destiny today. Those who shall receive the mark are the ones who neglect, ignore, reject, pervert, and distort the everlasting gospel. The first angel's message determines our destiny, whether we will be found in Babylon and end up receiving the mark of the beast, or whether we will be sealed on the forehead with the name of God.

> By mercy and truth iniquity is purged: and by the fear of the Lord men depart from evil. (Proverbs 16:6)

God uses warnings and judgments to awaken man from the delusions of sin. We see this throughout the Bible, especially in the book of Revelation. Though at times effective to draw the attention of men and nations, warnings and judgments cannot really change the heart; only God's love known and experienced can accomplish a real change. The real issue of the message of Revelation 14 is, who has your heart?

In knowing God's mercy and understanding His truth, rebellion and sin are purged from the life. This is the work of the everlasting gospel, and Christ is the greatest demonstration of God's mercy. "God commendeth His love toward us, in that, while we were yet sinners, Christ died for us" (Romans 5:8). Therefore, it is to the extent that Christ is made known to us intellectually and from the heart that the love and mercy of God changes us, cleansing us from sin and leading us to fear Him and depart from evil.

Not until we have experienced for ourselves God's mercy, love, and truth can we begin to fear Him. Indeed, it is the only true reason we fear, love, and honor Him.

The work of God through His Spirit is to humble man so that he may recognize his lost condition and his utter inability to save himself. This the worshipers of the beast will not accept. For man wants some means of saving himself or to be saved in his sin and compromise. The religion of Babylon appeals to both classes.

It was sin that crucified Jesus, the very One so many of us claim to worship and serve. Then how is it that we can be left to continue in our sins? Jesus did not come simply to remove the guilt and condemnation. He came to save us from our sins. Therefore, His message to the world is to fear Him, to put away sin, to put away rebellion, to have a true and abiding relationship with Him that makes us love to obey because obedience is pleasing to God.

> Having therefore these promises, dearly beloved, let us cleanse ourselves from all filthiness of the flesh and spirit, perfecting holiness in the fear of God. (2 Corinthians 7:1)

Sin defiles both mind and body; however, as we take hold of the promises of God, the promise of His love and mercy works in our hearts to cleanse us from the defiling results of sin. The power of God works to change the inner man, the mind and thoughts and outward actions, the flesh. This cannot be done through religion and ritual; it comes only as we appropriate by faith the promises of God's Word.

While many of the world's religious adherents recognize the depravity of man and seek to overcome and please God, this effort is in vain, for it relies on what man can do rather than God's promises. Holiness, which is the result of fearing and loving God, is the work of God in the heart of man and our daily surrender. It is not the result of what man can accomplish by philosophy, religion, or ceremony.

The result of accepting the everlasting gospel is that we will love and honor God, which results in holiness of life, a wholehearted service "with all thy heart, and with all thy soul, and with all thy strength, and with all thy mind" (Luke 10:27). The religion and philosophies of Babylon will take your entire mind, strength, and will. Therefore, God's call to fear Him is really the issue of who will have your heart and allegiance: Christ or Satan. There is no middle ground.

> And he said, Lay not thine hand upon the lad, neither do thou any thing unto him: for now I know that thou fearest God, seeing thou hast not withheld thy son, thine only son from me. (Genesis 22:12)

The story of Abraham and God's command to him to sacrifice his son provides an example of what it means to fear God.

Abraham walked with the Lord, had heard His voice, and knew God personally. Abraham's love for God was demonstrated by the fact that he was willing to do whatever God said, even, in this instance, sacrificing the son of promise. Do you love God enough to go against your own will, your own understanding?

To fear God means to trust and obey. It begins when, by faith, we accept the grace of God and receive the salvation that is in Christ. Abraham believed God and obeyed the call to leave his home and follow Him. No doubt the family he left behind in Ur of the Chaldees sought his allegiance, as the world will demand ours. The command of God and the commandments of men pull in different directions. The everlasting gospel of salvation by grace through faith in Christ, and the many voices and pathways of man's religion, also pull in different directions. Therefore, to every human heart, the Spirit speaks, seeking to "reprove ... of sin, and of righteousness, and of judgment" (John 16:8). To hear the voice of God's reproof leads to the acceptance of the gospel, resulting in obedience, faith, and love. This is what it means to fear God.

Many, if not most, people claim to love God or follow some deity and religious philosophy. But that is not enough. We must hear God's voice through His Word and, like Abraham, follow it. Only then can we truly come to know, trust, and fear God and give glory to Him rather than man-made religion, for the fear of man only leads to death.

Be not wise in thine own eyes: fear the Lord, and depart
from evil. (Proverbs 3:7)

In every generation and in every endeavor of human life, from
religion to science, from morality to politics, man largely follows
what is right in his own mind rather than the true and unchanging moral standard of God as found in the Bible. This will be a
marked characteristic of all who will follow the beast willingly or
who choose to "go along to get along."

When a person accepts the everlasting gospel, this delusion
of following the wisdom of man is broken. For the mystery of
redeeming love and the power of grace bring to our hearts and
minds new thoughts, new motives. The wisdom from above that
begins to fill our souls leads us to love and reverence God, to fear
Him. The result of this transformation of heart and mind is that
we will depart from evil.

The fear of the Lord is to hate evil: pride, and arrogancy,
and the evil way, and the froward mouth, do I hate.
(Proverbs 8:13)

True love and reverence for God will lead us to have an increasing hatred of evil, which is in contrast to the acceptance of evil
by most of mankind. As man increasingly sets aside the wisdom
of God for human wisdom, even our sense of right and wrong is
blurred. One man's evil is another man's entertainment and fun. Yet
God's Word is clear, for it teaches that those who know the true God
will hate evil, which includes the prideful, arrogant ways of man.

In our world we reward people for pride in business, politics,
sports, entertainment, and other endeavors. Yet we are often religious in our pride and arrogance. That is why the call to fear God
is not only an invitation to know and love God, it is also a warning
to put aside evil and man-centered philosophy and religion. The
prophet has warned such religion is vain; it is the fear of man. "This
people draw near Me with their mouth, and with their lips do honour Me, but have removed their heart far from Me, and their fear
toward Me is taught by the precept of men" (Isaiah 29:13).

God is calling us to fear Him, to put away evil in all its forms. This would include a growing distaste for "perverted and twisted speech" (Proverbs 8:13 AMP), and "evil ways and false words" (8:13 TEV). This is not only language that is course or vile, but includes all speech and sentiments that are contrary to heaven's principles and sound doctrine. "In all things shewing thyself a pattern of good works: in doctrine shewing uncorruptness, gravity, sincerity, sound speech, that cannot be condemned; that he that is of the contrary part may be ashamed, having no evil thing to say of you" (Titus 2:7–8). Some might say God requires too much. Friend, that is the attitude of the unconverted, unregenerate heart, and it shows that we are yet in our sins and do not know and fear God.

> The fear of the Lord is the instruction of wisdom; and before honour is humility. (Proverbs 15:33)

Eternal wisdom has as its source a relationship with God, leading us to fear Him. Further, the knowledge of God is the way of humility, for humility is the direct result of experiencing the everlasting gospel. For the sinful and prideful heart of man must see his nothingness in God's sight, and this requires the intervention of God in our lives and the humility of heart to accept His grace. "Let there be tears for the wrong things you have done. Let there be sorrow and sincere grief. Let there be sadness instead of laughter, and gloom instead of joy. Then when you realize your worthlessness before the Lord, He will lift you up, encourage and help you" (James 4:9–10 TLB).

The fear of the Lord leads us to the true source of wisdom. "For the wisdom of this world is foolishness with God. For it is written, He taketh the wise in their own craftiness. And again, The Lord knoweth the thoughts of the wise, that they are vain" (1 Corinthians 3:19–20).

God cannot instruct us until we know humility, which is the result of the wisdom of God known and experienced. For "the wisdom that is from above is first pure, then peaceable, gentle, and easy to be intreated, full of mercy and good fruits, without partiality, and without hypocrisy" (James 3:17).

There is another wisdom seeking our attention that leads us away from God, for it despises humility and the honor of God, that it might glory in sin and the prideful ways of man. The Bible describes it this way: "But if ye have bitter envying and strife in your hearts, glory not, and lie not against the truth. This wisdom descendeth not from above, but is earthly, sensual, devilish. For where envying and strife is, there is confusion and every evil work" (James 3:14–16).

> Teach me Your way, O Lord, that I may walk and live in Your truth; direct and unite my heart [solely, reverently] to fear and honor Your name. (Psalm 86:11 AMP)

Are you willing to say to God, "Teach me Your way"? God is not going to force you; God does not work like that. He wants us to give service and worship to Him from a willing heart.

God's question to us is, "Are you willing to allow Me to teach you My wisdom? To teach you to fear and love Me?" Are you willing to be taught of the Lord, that your heart might be united with God? This does not come naturally to man, and it cannot be found in the religion and philosophy of Babylon. It is the direct result of experiencing the everlasting gospel.

If we allow God to teach us, we are going to live by the truth of His Word. If we are not living by His Word, somebody else is teaching us. The question is, Who? If we are not living by the Word, if we are not being taught by the Word of God, the holy Bible, if we are not living in obedience to God's commandments guided by the Spirit, then another spirit is uniting our hearts to itself.

Who is teaching you? Each of us is being influenced and taught by the spirit of light and truth or the spirit of darkness and error.

> The fear of the Lord is the beginning of wisdom: a good understanding have all they that do his commandments: his praise endureth forever. (Psalm 111:10)

All the wisdom of this world that is true begins and ends with the recognition of God as the Creator. The fear of the Lord, leading us to obedience, is the beginning of wisdom; all other wisdom is superficial. Though there are many brilliant minds in the world whose research and discoveries seem beyond the scope of human abilities, most of these people are disobedient to God's commandments and do not know or love God. Such "knowledge puffeth up [is prideful]. ... And if any man think that he knoweth any thing, he knoweth nothing yet as he ought to know" (1 Corinthians 8:1–2). The wisdom of the world is foolishness if it leads man away from God; even much of the religious wisdom that mankind follows leads away from the true God. Thus, the heaven-sent message of the last days is the call to fear God, to separate from the prideful ways of man wherever they are found.

> And now, Israel, what doth the Lord thy God require of thee, but to fear the Lord thy God, to walk in all his ways, and to love him, and to serve the Lord thy God with all thy heart and with all thy soul, to keep the commandments of the Lord, and his statutes, which I command thee this day for thy good? Behold, the heaven and the heaven of heavens is the Lord's thy God, the earth also, with all that therein is. (Deuteronomy 10:12–14)

Mankind cannot command love, and neither will God. Love awakens love. "We love Him, because He first loved us" (1 John 4:19). God is not going to command us to love Him and then, when we are unable to give this love, cast us aside and destroy us. God loves us first. That is how we can love Him, and that is why the messages of Revelation 14 are centered on the greatest demonstration of love for all time: the cross of Calvary. Jesus was the gospel when hanging on the cross. For "the gospel of Christ ... is the power of God unto salvation to every one that believeth" (Romans 1:16). This is the only means by which mankind can render to God the fear and love He deserves. God demonstrated His love for us while we were yet sinners, by sending His son to die for us. (See Romans 5:8.)

To ancient Israel, and now in these last days to the world, God is saying, "It is required of man to fear and to reverence Me, to live by My laws and My principles, and to render to Me loving service, giving all thy heart and soul." This will be the response if we have experienced the gospel. To walk in His ways and to serve Him will be the very desire of our hearts. However, the system of Babylon deceives, flatters, and corrupts. In the end, force, threats, and eventual death will come to all who do not receive the mark.

God is calling us to serve Him "with all thy heart and with all thy soul, to keep the commandments of the Lord, and His statutes, which I command thee this day for thy good. Behold, the heaven and the heaven of heavens is the Lord's thy God, the earth also, with all that therein is."

The pledge of God's desire and ability to give us the above experience is the fact that the earth is His and all that dwell therein; He is the Creator! He will create in you a new heart, a new life, if you will let Him.

Counterfeit Fear

> And the Lord said, Forasmuch as this people draw near Me with their mouth and honor Me with their lips but remove their hearts and minds far from Me, and their fear and reverence for Me are a commandment of men that is learned by repetition [without any thought as to the meaning] ... (Isaiah 29:13 AMP)

This counterfeit fear of God, taught by the precepts and doctrines of men, is the reason Revelation 14 has as part of the last message the call to fear God. If we do not fear God, leading us to reverence and obey Him, then all our worship is in vain. If we do not truly fear God, then we fear men. This is shown by following the dictates of our own hearts or the doctrines, philosophies, and religions of men. The end result of this is that we will be worshipers of the beast.

In many Christian churches today, and in the various religions of the world, we claim with our lips that we love God. However, as in the days of the prophet, our hearts and lives are far from Him.

That is why we do not fear Him, which is why we are not departing from evil.

We will never learn to fear God by the precepts and doctrines of men. We must go to the Word of God. We must experience the pure, everlasting gospel. We must know the love of God in Christ, or we will never know God in a way that we can rightly fear Him.

> Say ye not, A confederacy, to all them to whom this people shall say, A confederacy; neither fear ye their fear, nor be afraid. Sanctify the Lord of hosts himself; and let him be your fear, and let him be your dread. (Isaiah 8:12–13)

> The Lord of hosts—regard Him as holy and honor His holy name [by regarding Him as your only hope of safety], and let Him be your fear and let Him be your dread [lest you offend Him by your fear of man and distrust of Him]. (Isaiah 8:13 AMP)

The people of this planet, religious and otherwise, readily follow the principles of men and ignore or neglect the principles of God. Therefore, men form confederacies, conspiracies of evil and rebellion, leaving God and eternal realties largely, if not totally, out of their considerations. The book of Revelation reveals to us that the last confederacy of evil will be made up of religion, politics, and money. (See Revelation 18:2–3.)

False worship will be, and is already becoming, the great separating issue between the alliances of men and those who love and fear God. The separating question is, Whom do you serve? If it is God, you will love Him, obey His law, and follow His Word. On the other hand, if the fear of man is your heart's desire, you will follow the principles and dictates of man, his philosophies, his religions, and his word. Revelation reveals that mankind is to be brought to the test: "Choose you this day whom ye will serve" (Joshua 24:15). Further, God says, "Turn you at My reproof: behold, I will pour out My spirit unto you, I will make known My words unto you" (Proverbs 1:23). As in the days of Noah, God will in a marked manner make His will and word known; yet, sadly, the reaction of most of mankind will be as we read below.

> Because I have called, and ye refused; I have stretched out my hand, and no man regarded; But ye have set at nought all my counsel, and would none of my reproof: I also will laugh at your calamity; I will mock when your fear cometh. When your fear cometh as desolation, and your destruction cometh as a whirlwind; when distress and anguish cometh upon you. Then shall they call upon me, but I will not answer; they shall seek me early, but they shall not find me: For that they hated knowledge, and did not choose the fear of the Lord: They would none of my counsel: they despised all my reproof. Therefore shall they eat of the fruit of their own way, and be filled with their own devices. (Proverbs 1:24–31)

The final confederacy of evil, revealed in the book of Revelation, will have the cooperation of most of the world, its leaders, its religion and its financial powers. (See Revelation 18:3; 17:5.) It will seem that a new day is dawning, and mankind's hopes and aspirations will be realized; yet their fear and reverence for God are based on the commandment of men. And what will be the result of this? "For you turned away from me—to death; your own complacency will kill you. Fools!" (Proverbs 1:32 TLB).

> The fear of man bringeth a snare, but whoso putteth his trust in the Lord shall be safe. (Proverbs 29:25)

God's Word and man's ways are very different. We often think that by following our cultures and traditions, our families and churches, is the way we honor God. We think our way is God's way and create religious doctrines that reflect the mind of man, not the mind of God. It all seems so good, but it is a deadly snare, a trap to lead us to eternal loss. The way of life is to trust the God revealed in the holy Bible and in the life and ministry of Christ, not the god of our own imaginations.

In the fear of the Lord is strong confidence: and his children shall have a place of refuge. The fear of the Lord is a fountain of life, to depart from the snares of death. (Proverbs 14:26–27)

A Vital Question

Who shall ascend into the hill of the Lord? or who shall stand in his holy place? He that hath clean hands, and a pure heart; who hath not lifted up his soul unto vanity, nor sworn deceitfully. He shall receive the blessing from the Lord, and righteousness from the God of his salvation. This is the generation of them that seek him, that seek thy face, O Jacob. (Psalm 24:3–6)

Who shall dwell in the presence of God? Revelation 14 tells us it is those who respond to the gospel, leading them to fear God and give glory to Him. This leads to separation from Babylonian religious confusion and compromise, and instead leads us to live lives of patience and consistent endurance, keeping God's commandments, being empowered by the faith of Jesus. (See Revelation 14:12.) Revelation 14 is all about preparing to live with God and the consequences that will come to all who reject the gospel to follow the way of their own hearts.

Let us hear the conclusion of the whole matter: Fear God, and keep his commandments: for this is the whole duty of man. For God shall bring every work into judgment, with every secret thing, whether it be good, or whether it be evil. (Ecclesiastes 12:13–14)

Endnotes

1. Noah Webster, *American Dictionary of the English Language* (San Francisco, California: Foundation for American Christian Education, 1967).
2. Greek lexicon based on Thayer's Lexicon and Smith's Bible Dictionary plus others; keyed to the large Kittel and the *Theological Dictionary of the New Testament.* Online Bible CD 2.5.3 Macintosh Version 1996

Chapter Four

Give Glory to Him

And I saw another angel fly in the midst of heaven, having the everlasting gospel to preach unto them that dwell on the earth, and to every nation, and kindred, and tongue, and people, Saying with a loud voice, Fear God, and give glory to him; for the hour of his judgment is come: and worship him that made heaven, and earth, and the sea, and the fountains of waters. (Revelation 14:6–7)

The message to give glory to God knows no cultural or national boundaries. God's message to mankind is different from the ecumenical, inter-faith spirit of the age that emphasizes a coming together, largely for dealing with perceived social evils, or the popular view that says all religions are different paths to God. The New Age religion of our day increasingly emphasizes the need to come together for human and social development. Human solidarity, they claim, is what is needed to solve our problems. Certainly, this world has many troubles. However, sin in the human heart, which is at the foundation of the vast majority of man's problems, has only one cure.

Our day is one of global apostasy and great spirituality, yet one where anything goes in the area of religion, so long as you are trying to find your own fulfillment. We have adopted the idea that man can seek God on his own terms.

Yet God's message declares, "Fear God, and give glory to Him" (Revelation 14:7). To give glory to God is to make heaven's principles our own by faith as we receive and partake of the everlasting gospel. This means following God's Word and the principles of His law in our lives. We are to make known the glory of God by our words and by our lives, by the surrender of our minds and our bodies. It is as we make known the righteous principles of heaven, living by His Word, that we truly glorify God.

In contrast, humanity tends to glorify self or other men. We almost deify our fellow human beings. Politicians, sports stars, men and women in the entertainment industry, some religious leaders, and men of finance and business are but a few of the classes of people who are glorified and praised by millions. God is calling the world to give glory to Him because He is the Creator. For when we give glory to men and to ourselves we in essence are denying the true and only God.

Today, despite a world full of religion, man is glorifying everything but God. "For though there are so-called gods both in heaven and earth, gods and lords galore in fact" (1 Corinthians 8:5 Phillips), and a great deal of spirituality, yet we are not glorifying the true God. Thus, there is a warning message, a call to cease from this glorying in men and to understand and recognize Jehovah alone as Creator.

To give glory to God means to give an honorable and correct representation of God. God is warning the world, and the religions of the world, and their followers, many of whom are seeking a god in the force of the cosmos. "You say you love Me, yet you do not glorify Me, because you are misrepresenting Me. I am not a God you can approach in any way, following various paths and holy books, doctrines and philosophies."

There is no plurality of saving truth; there is but one truth, and one means of salvation. Mankind has a multitude of gods and a multitude of ways of getting to heaven or paradise or eternal bliss, or so he thinks.

This world is filled with many types of spirituality, for mankind is often quite religious except when it comes to biblical truth. Many people want to avoid or ignore biblical truth. They want to set aside the gospel or put something in its place. The world is seeking some kind of accommodation with God. We think we are remembering and honoring God, but in reality we are forgetting Him. In response to mankind seeking God on our human terms,

God declares with a loud voice through His messengers, "Fear God, and give glory to Him" (Revelation 14:7).

God will never force obedience or worship. His call is one of warning and compelling in love. That is why He has set forth the gospel as the center of this message, as we see God manifest in the flesh, in Jesus Christ hanging upon the cross as a substitute and sacrifice. At the cross we see how God is both just, upholding His law, yet the justifier by forgiving us. Sadly, most of mankind does not want that. Man rejects the gospel and substitutes ritual, religion, churches, and the doctrines and commandments of men.

In contrast, those who receive the gospel will be obedient to the will, word, and law of God. The rest of the world follows philosophy, materialism, sensual indulgence, and the religious leaders and gods of the new age who propagate salvation in sin or salvation by human works.

Let's look at what the Scripture says so that we might understand what it means to give glory to God.

> For ye are bought with a price: therefore glorify God
> in your body, and in your spirit, which are God's.
> (1 Corinthians 6:20)

Both in our bodies and in our spirits, we are to give glory to God so that in our thoughts, words, and actions we properly represent God. We cannot do that by simply being a good Mormon, Catholic, or Baptist, or even being a good Hindu or Muslim. No, my friend, we cannot truly glorify God unless we know His Son, Jesus Christ. Now, that may sound narrow-minded in this broad-minded world. However, that is why God gives this last message with a loud voice to the entire world.

There is no accommodation in God's message with the World Council of Churches, or the United Religious Initiative, or the World Parliament of Religions. Truly, the religions of men, as much as they try to glorify God as far as they conceive Him, will never succeed. We can only give God glory by receiving His life, His Spirit, and the Lord Jesus Christ as our Savior and Master. Otherwise, our view of God is incomplete and distorted.

Many adherents of religion try to discipline their bodies in the hopes of developing spirituality. However, that is not what it means to "glorify God in your body."

Others are involved in various forms of prayer techniques or meditation and mental development, trying to find God or "the god within." That is not what it means to "glorify God in your spirit."

God is calling for true worship, which is based upon heart surrender and obedience. To glorify God in our bodies includes what we eat, what we drink, our dress, our words, our leisure time. The body is a channel or a medium to the mind and thus must be guarded and kept from debasement and sensual indulgence in order to truly give glory to God. To follow God's Word with body and spirit can never gain merit with God, though many religions teach that it can. We are saved "by grace ... through faith; and that not of yourselves: it is the gift of God: not of works, lest any man should boast" (Ephesians 2:8–9).

We are told to glorify God in our spirit. The spirit is the mental and spiritual; this affects our thoughts and our attitudes, our character. Therefore, we can glorify God in our spirits by what we read and see and listen to, what we think and dwell upon, when done according to the counsel of His Word. The spirit or mind is to be the kingly power holding dominion over the body. Moreover, the spirit, the mind, is to be under the control of God, directed by His word and Holy Spirit.

The world says we can do anything we want with our bodies so long as we worship God with our minds, but God says, "No. I want your body and your mind to be dedicated in heart service and surrender," because "the love of God is shed abroad in our hearts by the Holy Ghost which is given unto us" (Romans 5:5).

There are many religious followers who give all their lives, all their efforts, to their gods and their religions, which is commendable. They can be admired for their tenacity and dedication. Yet it will merit nothing in the sight of God. There is only one means of salvation, and that is through the gospel. The gospel alone is "the power of God unto salvation to every one that believeth" (Romans 1:16), and it enables us to truly give God glory with mind and body.

Glorify God in Your Bodies

> I beseech you therefore, brethren, by the mercies of God, that ye present your bodies a living sacrifice, holy, acceptable unto God, which is your reasonable service. (Romans 12:1)

The Spirit of God revealing to our hearts "the goodness of God" is what leads us to repentance (Romans 2:4). The mercy of God perceived, understood, and experienced is the motivating factor that leads us to want to glorify God.

Living in such a way that we present our bodies "a living sacrifice" is not a means by which we gain merit with God. We do not fast or pray or discipline our bodies or change our diets so that we can develop some kind of inner spirituality. However, there are people trying to develop a spirituality within. They seek by physical means to recommend themselves to God, or be in harmony with the godhood within or with the forces of nature or the forces of the cosmos. However, this will never glorify God.

> And so, dear brothers, I plead with you to give your bodies to God. Let them be a living sacrifice, holy—the kind he can accept. When you think of what he has done for you, is this too much to ask? (Romans 12:1 TLB)

When you think of what Christ has done for you, is it too much to fear God and give glory to Him? No, it is not. Do you find yourself saying, "God, why are You asking me to do this? Why do I have to do that? Surely if I do this or that, it will not keep me from heaven, will it?" If so, you should question whether you have experienced the everlasting gospel, for Jesus taught that he who has been forgiven much loves much, and true love serves and obeys. (See Luke 7:47.) It is in the recognition and acceptance of forgiveness, and experiencing that forgiveness, that motivates us to glorify God in our bodies and in our spirits.

And this becomes a reasonable service. It becomes part of our spiritual worship, not because we are trying to eat our way to heaven or dress our way to heaven or trying to avoid doing certain things to gain merit with God so we can go to heaven. We do what we do even if it puts us outside the mainstream of the world and the mainstream of worldly Christianity because it pleases God.

We have wives, husbands, children, friends, and family we love, and we sometimes do things for them that we would rather not do. Why? Because it will please them, and we are motivated by love. And when we truly love God, we are going to want to please Him; we are going to want to give glory to Him.

Religion is a motivating factor in the lives of many human beings. Hindus are motivated, Buddhists are motivated, and Muslims are motivated, to name a few. But the only motivation that matters, and that will change our hearts and bring us into a willing service to the true God, is in His mercy perceived, understood, and sought for. The mercy of God is most clearly demonstrated on Calvary. It is in rejecting, distorting, or following substitutes for the gospel that distort the glory of God in man, despite mankind's religious aspirations.

Understanding God's mercy motivates us to give our bodies, indeed every aspect of our lives, to the service of God—what we eat, what we drink, what we do. And why? It is our spiritual worship. You see, my friend, the service we render to God is to be the service of love. The source of that love is God, and it will be returned to Him as we glorify Him with our lives, as body and mind are surrendered to Him.

> Neither yield ye your members as instruments of unrighteousness unto sin: but yield yourselves unto God, as those that are alive from the dead, and your members as instruments of righteousness unto God. (Romans 6:13)

This verse is teaching us not to offer any part of our bodies to the service of sin in the cause of unrighteousness, but to give ourselves wholly and totally to God. This is what it means to glorify God in the body. We do not give glory to God by our pilgrimages to shrines or temples or holy sites. We do not glorify God by our sacrifices and gifts or by religious pageantry and ritual while we go on giving our lives to the indulgence of sin.

> Do not let any part of your bodies become tools of wickedness, to be used for sinning; but give yourselves completely to God—every part of you—for you are back from death and you want to be tools in the hands of God, to be used for his good purposes. (Romans 6:13 TLB)

Our bodies are to be used for the glory of God, giving a right representation of Him. Each individual, by his or her life, demonstrates the principle and philosophy that controls him or her. The question is, Who in your life are you most representing? We are called to represent God, whose image we were created in. God is inviting us back to our true purpose, which is to give glory to our Creator.

> I speak after the manner of men because of the infirmity of your flesh: for as ye have yielded your members servants to uncleanness and to iniquity unto iniquity; even so now yield your members servants to righteousness unto holiness. (Romans 6:19)

As you once yielded your body to impurity and ever-increasing lawlessness, so now yield your bodily members as servants to righteousness, to the glory of God. We cannot change our actions, appetites, and passions simply by religion. The gospel is the source and the power of the radical change in the human spirit that God requires if we are to have any hope of heaven.

"Therefore if any man be in Christ, he is a new creature: old things are passed away; behold, all things are become new" (2 Corinthians 5:17). That is why I do not smoke marijuana anymore. That is why I don't go out to night clubs anymore and stay up to the early morning hours drinking beer and listening to rock 'n' roll, and all the things that go with that lifestyle.

I did not understand the glory of God and the mercy of God when I was a young man. I thought living for the hour, living for the moment, living for sensuality and pleasure, was what life was about. That is what millions live for, and most who do so have some kind of religious ideology or practice.

The message for the last days is to give glory to God. The world is giving glory to themselves, doing what they want with their bodies and their minds, seeking a religion of human works, seeking gods that will accommodate their desires. This, however, leads to Babylonian confusion; it leads to separation from God.

There is not one way to God in the West through the Christian churches of established religion and another way in Asia through the Buddhist religion and another way to God in India through the Hindu religion and another way to God in the Middle East through Islam. Jesus said, "I am the way, the truth, and the life" (John 14:6). It is only in Him that we can be changed and transformed and rightly glorify God.

> Whether therefore ye eat, or drink, or whatsoever ye do,
> do all to the glory of God. (1 Corinthians 10:31)

All that we do in life is to be centered on God, and many people do center their lives on Him. In fact, billions of people are seeking to glorify God. However, which god are you glorifying? It makes a difference, my friend, what you believe and who you serve and what god you are giving glory to. God is not saying, "Glorify Me in the way you think best."

Can God rightly be concerned about what we eat and drink? Yes. We live in a world where millions have ill health and sickly spiritual capacities largely because of what and how they eat and drink and what they do with their bodies.

If we would eat and drink according to God's Word and council, much of the disease and physical problems we have would be greatly lessened or not exist. "And put a knife to thy throat, if thou be a man given to appetite" (Proverbs 23:2). This verse shows us how dangerous it is to be controlled by appetite. Further, when we are controlled by appetite and passion, we cannot glorify God in our minds and spirits, regardless of our religious profession. Some may ask, "Have I not the right to do as I please with my own body?" No. You have no right to defile the body and mind by lustful habits of appetite and passions. God is the owner of the whole man. Mind and body are His. They belong to Him by creation and by redemption, and when we abuse our bodies through neglect of the laws of health or sinful sensual indulgence, we rob God of the honor due Him.

Glorify God in Your Spirit

> And be not conformed to this world: but be ye transformed by the renewing of your mind, that ye may prove what is that good, and acceptable, and perfect, will of God. (Romans 12:2)

The word *conformed* means "to follow a pattern," "to become like." God is saying, "Do not follow the pattern of the world; do not become like the world." In spiritual terms there is the world and its principles and ways, and then there is God's way; they are mutually exclusive.

The word *transformed* is related to the word *metamorphosis*. As you may remember from high school biology classes, metamorphosis is when the caterpillar builds a cocoon around itself and in a few weeks out comes a beautiful flying creature that looks very different from the caterpillar. One bound to the earth, one able to fly; one rather ugly and one beautiful. That is metamorphosis. The physical world teaches something of the spiritual.

Unlike the transformation of caterpillar to butterfly, our minds and lives are to be transformed day by day, by the surrender of the will to God's law and Word. When your mind is being transformed, and you are giving glory to God in your spirit as well as in your body, you will prove or seek the acceptable ways of God.

This transformation of mind is not found in religion. It is not found in meditation, spiritual exercises, or adoration of the Host, in mysticism or pilgrimages or ceremonies or any religious ritual that man can be involved in. This renewing of the mind is the fruit of the gospel, and only by the renewing of the mind can we give glory to God.

Satan understands this battle for the mind of man. He works through false religion and philosophy to gain the control of the mind. The book of Revelation reveals he will be largely successful. For his tool of religion, Babylon "made all nations drink of the wine of the wrath of her fornication" (Revelation 14:8).

There are many sincere, zealous people who are trying to serve God, but the only way we can serve Him is by being transformed. Christ alone is the power of a changed mind. Religion can markedly affect people's minds and attitudes , but religion has no saving virtue.

> Wherefore gird up the loins of your mind, be sober, and hope to the end for the grace that is to be brought unto you at the revelation of Jesus Christ; As obedient children, not fashioning yourselves according to the former lusts in your ignorance: But as he which hath called you is holy, so be ye holy in all manner of conversation; Because it is written, Be ye holy; for I am holy. (1 Peter 1:13–16)

Mental discipline and self-improvement may provide short-term benefits for this life. However, to give God glory requires the surrender of our will, leading us to be circumspect and morally alert and sober-minded. Giving glory to God in our spirits or with our minds leads us to be obedient children. Many believe all men are children of God; however, God's children are obedient by virtue of a new mind, which knows, understands, and desires to follow His requirements. This new mind leads to a life of holiness, a reflection of the character of our Father. This life of holiness is to enter every aspect of our conversation, our manner of life, our conduct and behavior. With so many religious adherents seeking holiness, what does this word really mean?

True holiness is wholeness in our service to God. It is unreserved consecration and undivided service. To give glory to God demands all the heart, mind, soul, and strength. It is a willing service desirous to seek His will and obey His word. To be holy and give God glory is constant agreement with God, so that we live by His will and are empowered by His grace.

To Give God Glory Is to Seek Heaven's Principles

If ye then be risen with Christ, seek those things which are above, where Christ sitteth on the right hand of God. Set your affection on things above, not on things on the earth. (Colossians 3:1–2)

If then you have been raised with Christ [to a new life, thus sharing His resurrection from the dead], aim at and seek the [rich, eternal treasures,] that are above, where Christ is, seated at the right hand of God. And set your minds and keep them set on what is above (the higher things), not on the things that are on the earth. (Colossians 3:1–2 AMP)

Many people in this world, including religious people, are trying to better themselves and trying to improve this world, and admirably so. However, so much of this attempt at personal and planetary improvement is following the misguided ways of man. Religion is often reduced to that which seems to help us without strict adherence to sound moral principles. However, the Word of God declares that His true followers, those who give Him glory, set their minds and their affections on things above. This is not some sort of otherworldly make-believe life that has no practical application in the here and now. Far from it.

We have a developing new-world religion today that is called in the book of Revelation "Mystery Babylon." Religion, with the kings of the earth and the merchantmen of Revelation, are trying in vain to bring global harmony, peace, and development. Here we find mankind seeking to deal with its problems based solely on man's religion, politics, and economics. In contrast, the people of God live and plan, work and worship, according to the principles of heaven found in the Word of God. Their minds and understanding look beyond that which is found with man to the eternal knowledge that is found with God. It is the knowledge of heaven, not the knowledge of earth, that holds the key to our problems. For mankind's many personal and international problems are the results of sin. However, man, in rejecting the fear and glory of God, is "defiled with their own works" and separated from God by following "their own inventions" (Psalm 106:39). God calls this whoredom. Mankind in the last days, by virtue of following his own way, comes under the delusive deception of the "great whore that sitteth upon many waters" (Revelation 17:1).

> Having therefore these promises, dearly beloved, let us cleanse ourselves from all filthiness of the flesh and spirit, perfecting holiness in the fear of God. (2 Corinthians 7:1)

> With these promises ringing in our ears, dear friends, let us keep clear of anything that smirches [to soil] body or soul. Let us prove our reverence for God by consecrating ourselves to Him completely. (2 Corinthians 7:1 Phillips)

Reverencing God and giving Him glory means yielding body and soul to Him. The book of Revelation reveals the worshipers of the beast receive the mark on the forehead, indicating they have yielded heart and mind to this system. Receiving the mark on the hand indicates an attitude of "going along to get along," even though in heart and mind they may not be truly submissive. Both classes believe they are serving God, for it is believed that allegiance to the religious political system of Mystery Babylon and "the beast that carrieth her" (Revelation 17:7) is the right thing to do.

However, let us note what Corinthians is teaching us in regard to giving God glory. We find that the body and spirit and mind are to be consecrated and given fully to God. This is not something that is worked up in man. The change in man that enables him to willingly and with pleasure render God service is based not on what man can do but on the promises of God. The promises of God, found in the holy Bible, when accepted into the heart, have the ability to cleanse our lives from sin. This brings a change to what we do with our bodies, and a change of our character, the thoughts and feelings, our minds or spirits.

It is by the precious promises of God's love and grace that we are drawn to Him. "Being born again" (1 Peter 1:23) is to have one's mind changed so that we live a new life conformed to the will of God. And how is this? It comes "not of corruptible seed, but of incorruptible, by the word of God, which liveth and abideth for ever" (1 Peter 1:23b).

It is the word of the Lord and His precious promises that has the power to change man. Therefore, as we receive "with meekness the engrafted word," it "is able to save your souls" (James 1:21).

The commandments and doctrines of men also have the power to change and transform the life and the mind. And what is the result? "Because they received not the love of the truth, that they might be saved," they come under "strong delusion, that they should believe a lie" (2 Thessalonians 2:10–11).

We Are to Teach and Learn the Glory of God

> If any man speak, let him speak as the oracles of God; if any man minister, let him do it as of the ability which God giveth: that God in all things may be glorified through Jesus Christ, to whom be praise and dominion for ever and ever. Amen. (1 Peter 4:11)

When we speak for God, our words must be according to His Word. The religious teachers of this world are teaching many things, but if we are truly going to give glory to God, our teaching must be according to His Word, the holy Bible; it cannot be our opinions or creeds.

We find today many superstar religious leaders, and much attention is drawn to them, but their philosophy and teaching are not according to God and His Word. What is often the source of their popularity? "For the time will come when they will not endure sound doctrine; but after their own lusts shall they heap to themselves teachers, having itching ears" (2 Timothy 4:3).

In the last days, people shall desire teachers who tickle their ears with falsehood and confusion and half-truths. The call to give glory to God includes what we teach as religious leaders and what we receive as learners. The only religious teaching that is acceptable to God is "the oracles of God" as found in the holy Bible. The new world religion of the last days accepts all religions as having some degree of light and truth and therefore there should be no exclusiveness. But God can never be glorified by such a philosophy.

Truth must go forth to the world; the religious teachers of this world, if they are truly glorifying God, are going to teach, "the difference between what is holy and what is secular, what is right and what is wrong" (Ezekiel 44:23 TLB).

We cannot glorify God if we are following the teachings and commandments of men. You may say, "I am following the Word of God; I am following the counsels of God." This can only be true so far as we follow the Bible and bring its far-reaching principles into our lives and judge all things according "to the law and to the testimony: if they speak not according to this word, it is because there is no light in them" (Isaiah 8:20).

The religion of Satan is Babylon, and it has room for every belief and every ideology. However, this is not God's way. He calls the world to give glory to Him, which includes what is being taught and received and followed regarding religious matters.

Glorifying God Rightly Will Bring Forth Evidence or Fruit in the Life

Herein is my Father glorified, that ye bear much fruit; so shall ye be my disciples. (John 15:8)

God is glorified when we bear fruit. But what is this fruit? "But now being made free from sin, and become servants to God, ye have your fruit unto holiness, and the end everlasting life" (Romans 6:22).

We can never be made free from sin by pilgrimages, prayers, alms-giving, or belonging to a church or religious community. We are made free from sin by the grace of Jesus Christ alone.

Further, we are to become servants to God. Many people claim to serve God. However, we cannot truly serve God if we ignore, reject, or substitute the gospel for our own ideas. The gospel is the means by which we are made free from the guilt and condemnation of sin. Many people believe they serve God, and they are sincere and zealous. However, we cannot truly give service to God until we have been made free by the gospel of Jesus Christ, bearing fruit by a changed and transformed life. Then we can rightly begin to give glory to God.

> For ye were sometimes darkness, but now are ye light in the Lord: walk as children of light: (For the fruit of the Spirit is in all goodness and righteousness and truth;) proving what is acceptable unto the Lord. And have no fellowship with the unfruitful works of darkness, but rather reprove them. (Ephesians 5:8–10)

To give glory to God is only possible as we separate from the darkness. Darkness is sin and falsehood; it is error and misunderstanding regarding God, His character, Word, and law. Sadly, darkness in varying degrees is the religion of mankind. It is the religion of Mystery Babylon, which seeks to mix "righteousness with unrighteousness" and "light with darkness" (2 Corinthians 6:14). This state of affairs can never give God glory.

To give God glory is to live as children of light. This is possible only as our understanding is open to the truth of God and the way of salvation through the cross. To become children of light is only possible as we turn away in heart and mind "from darkness to light, and from the power of Satan unto God," accepting the gospel so that we "may receive forgiveness of sins, sanctified by faith" in Jesus Christ. (Acts 26:18). To be children of light is the restoration of the soul, leading us to live lives of moral goodness and righteousness, following God's truth as found in the Bible. To give glory to

God is to live a life seeking the will of God in every endeavor of life and worship, and separating from all forms of darkness.

A Correct Knowledge of God Gives Him Glory

> Thus saith the Lord, Let not the wise man glory in his wisdom, neither let the mighty man glory in his might, let not the rich man glory in his riches: But let him that glorieth glory in this, that he understandeth and knoweth me, that I am the Lord which exercise lovingkindness, judgment, and righteousness, in the earth: for in these things I delight, saith the Lord. (Jeremiah 9:23–24)

The inhabitants of the world who are considered the wise, the mighty, and the rich will all be a part of the Babylonian mystery religion of the last days. (See Revelation 18:3.) However, this religion is largely man-centered and therefore cannot rightly glorify God.

To know God is to not follow just any god or lord. We can only truly know God through Jesus Christ. Jesus said, "He that hath seen Me hath seen the Father" (John 14:9). Basically, He is saying, "I have come forth from the Father; My teachings and My character are a revelation of God." All the religions of this world that despise the gospel of Jesus Christ, or ignore the gospel, or substitute the gospel, no matter how sincere or honest they might be, cannot truly glorify God. For only knowing God rightly brings Him glory, not just knowing about a god or a lord, but knowing the true God, not only intellectually but in the heart. A heart experience, a transformation experience, is the result of knowing God. The transformation of character through the gospel leads to purity of life. Further, it leads to a correct adherence to the Word of God and true moral principles. This is the result of the right knowledge of God.

We have many types of religious schools in this world and lots of indoctrination in religion. However, such things do not lead us to know the truth; they are all for nothing. Jesus said, "This is life eternal, that they might know thee the only true God, and Jesus Christ, whom thou hast sent" (John 17:3).

There is no eternal life in Taoism, Buddhism, Confucianism, Catholicism, Mormonism, or the Watchtower Society. There is no eternal life in Jainism, Sikhism, or any of the world's religions. That may be a shock, and it ought to shock us, because the last message of Revelation 14 is intended to awaken our minds to the reality that there is but one road to salvation, and that is the gospel of Jesus Christ. God's judgment-hour message to give glory to Him cannot ignore Jesus.

Many religions say that Jesus was a good man. Well, that is a good start. However, Jesus was more than a good man. And consider this: if we say Jesus was merely a good man or a prophet, as many religions do, how can we ignore His word? He said, "I am the way, the truth, and the life: no man cometh unto the Father but by Me" (John 14:6). He said further, "I am the door" (John 10:7) to salvation. In other words, "I am the means to eternal life." Jesus further taught that all other attempts to gain merit and acceptance with God and eternal life are robbing mankind's hope, and a "thief cometh not, but for to steal, and to kill, and to destroy" (John 10:10). Jesus said, basically, "If you have seen Me, then you have seen what God is like, His character and His mercy." (See John 14:9.)

Knowing God results in a life that gives Him glory, "because the darkness is past, and the true light now shineth" (1 John 2:8) in our hearts, leading us to fear God and give glory to Him.

Having a Knowledge of God's Will and Living it Brings Him Glory

> For this cause we also, since the day we heard it, do not cease to pray for you, and to desire that ye might be filled with the knowledge of his will in all wisdom and spiritual understanding; That ye might walk worthy of the Lord unto all pleasing, being fruitful in every good work, and increasing in the knowledge of God; Strengthened with all might, according to his glorious power, unto all patience and longsuffering with joyfulness. (Colossians 1:9–11)

Living a life that desires to please God in all things, steadily growing and increasing in the knowledge of God, gives Him glory. God's will is that we would have a growing insight into His ways and purposes, and that happens only through the Bible. This is more than simple Bible knowledge; this knowledge is experiential, relationship based. The true knowledge that will glorify God teaches us and motivates us to live and conduct ourselves in a manner worthy of the Lord.

As we increase in the knowledge of God, we will have a fuller, deeper insight and recognition of Him. God's knowledge is different from man's knowledge. Rather than simply a strong intellect, God wishes to strengthen us through the knowledge of Himself, which leads to patience and long-suffering and joyfulness. In other words, true knowledge is to know God. This develops a character after the image of Him who created us, thus leading us to love and trust and serve Him.

Give unto the Lord the glory due unto his name; worship the lord in the beauty of holiness. (Psalm 29:2)

Truly, the world is filled with many people worshiping a god or gods, believing they are giving God glory by so doing. However, only a life of holiness truly gives God glory. Many religious people aspire for holiness. But what is the holiness that gives God glory? Holiness is purity of heart and sanctified affections; it is moral goodness. And the standard by which holiness is measured is "the measure of the stature of the fulness of Christ" (Ephesians 4:13).

To live to God's glory is "to be strengthened with might by His Spirit in the inner man. That Christ may dwell in your hearts by faith; that ye, being rooted and grounded in love, may be able to comprehend with all saints what is the breadth, and length, and depth, and height; And to know the love of Christ, which passeth knowledge, that ye might be filled with all the fulness of God" (Ephesians 3:16–19).

Blessed be the God and Father of our Lord Jesus Christ, who hath blessed us with all spiritual blessings in heavenly places in Christ: According as he hath chosen us in him before the foundation of the world, that we should be holy and without blame before him in love: Having predestinated us unto the adoption of children by Jesus Christ to himself, according to the good pleasure of his will, To the praise of the glory of his grace, wherein he hath made us accepted in the beloved. (Ephesians 1:3–6)

God has blessed us with all spiritual blessings in Christ. Not through the many gods and lords of this world but in Christ alone. God desires to save all mankind, regardless of race, culture, or nationality. Before the foundation of this world, God saw you and wanted to save you; that is the amazing love of God.

You do not have to work your way into heaven. God is on your side, and He wants to save you. It gives God glory to save sinful men and women, and to free us from the bondage of sin and death. The devil has another idea, however, and that is to present to mankind the beautiful side of evil through false religion that claims to serve God but in fact denies Him.

There are two spiritual powers in this world vying for the hearts and minds of men. In the last days, this battle for the mind of man will climax in what the book of Revelation calls the seal of God and the mark of the beast. It is the final test as to whom man will follow: Christ or Satan. That decision is being determined today. To give God glory is to allow Him to change our hearts so that we might come back to the high destiny for which we were created. I pray that you might discern and desire that which goes beyond the transitory things of this life to eternal realities, and that you would understand the words of the prophet:

In God is my salvation and my glory: the rock of my strength, and my refuge, is in God. (Psalm 62:7)

Chapter Five

For the Hour of His Judgment Is Come—Principles of Judgement

Saying with a loud voice, Fear God, and give glory to him; for the hour of his judgment is come: and worship him that made heaven, and earth, and the sea, and the fountains of waters. (Revelation 14:7)

The messages of Revelation 14 are judgment-hour messages, for what the people do with the message will determine their destiny while they are yet living. These messages will climax at the time of the mark of the beast, when the living shall be judged. It will be just like in the days of Noah.

The door of mercy shuts for most people when they die, for God's long-suffering love seeks to draw people as long as there is any hope. For some individuals the door of mercy shuts while they are yet living, having grieved the Spirit of God in hardness of heart; this is called the unpardonable sin. However, for the vast majority of people, there is still hope for their salvation until the day they die.

The messages of Revelation 14 develop two classes of people. In Revelation 14:14 we find a harvest, separation, and rewards given. In highly symbolic language, the results of our choices are described. There will be a separation between the unrighteous and the good, and a reward of eternal life or eternal death.

The judgment-hour message ties in with a warning not to receive the beast's mark, and there is a call to worship God, who made heaven and earth and sea and the fountains of waters. This is clearly taken out of the fourth commandment of God's moral law. This is a call back to the commandments of God. Revelation 14:12 depicts a people who keep God's moral law, distinct from the worshipers of the beast who follow the commandments of men.

One of the central issues of this message, which makes it a separation message, a judgment-hour message, is the call to worship God. God is calling the world back to obedience to His commandments—not to merit salvation, for the gospel is salvation by grace through faith. However, as we partake of the gospel, we are going to fear God, love Him, and reverence Him, leading us to give glory to God and obey His Word and law.

"The hour of His judgment is come" is not a judgment way off in the future, as depicted in Revelation 20, when the wicked of the ages arise from the grave to stand before the great white throne judgment to receive the consequences of the deeds done in this life and to be cast into the lake of fire. That will be an execution of judgment.

Revelation 14 is a judgment-hour message similar to that given in the days of Noah, for Jesus said, basically, "Before I come, it will be like the days of Noah." (See Matthew 24:37–39.) The wickedness, the unbelief, the misuse of God's gifts are all repeated in our own day, and it's only going to get worse. As it was in the days of Noah, there is coming a time when the door of mercy will suddenly shut.

The acceptance or rejection of Noah's message determined who was saved and who was lost. Profession was not enough. Salvation required faith that obeyed. Today there is much profession of religion, but the judgment message that separates reveals those who have faith and those who exercise unbelief. Genuine faith is shown by obedience, and the standard of obedience is the Ten Commandments as God gave them, not as interpreted or changed by man.

What is the central message of the angels (messengers) who give the warning to the world with a loud cry? It is the everlasting gospel. Those who substitute the gospel, those who reject or ignore it, follow the commandments of men; they honor and fear men; they glorify themselves or human institutions. They do not really worship God as many claim to do.

Revelation 14 reveals that the religions of the world have become Babylon, fallen from God despite all their religiosity. Religious apostasy will lead to setting up a global system of worship called the mark of the beast. Thus, the judgment-hour messages of Revelation 14 warn about the beast and his mark, calling people out of Babylon.

This is not something way off in the future, my friend. We know from Daniel and Revelation who the beast is. And God has a people who are telling the world who the beast is and warning others before these events take place. This is a time of separation, an hour of choosing.

The apostle Paul did not give this message; the reformers did not give this message. This message, in its embryonic form, was first sounded in the 1800s, in the midst of the great awakening. At the end of time it is to be given with a loud cry by a people who have an experience with Jesus. They are described in the Scriptures as "the remnant of her seed, which keep the commandments of God, and have the testimony of Jesus Christ" (Revelation 12:17). They are represented in Revelation as having the "Father's name written in their foreheads" (Revelation 14:1) rather than the mark of the beast. Further, they are "not defiled with women; [apostate and false religion] for they are virgins" (true and faithful to God). "These are they which follow the Lamb whithersoever He goeth" (Revelation 14:4).

Let us look at some biblical principles regarding judgment. First, can anyone escape the judgment?

> But why dost thou judge thy brother? or why dost thou set at nought thy brother? for we shall all stand before the judgment seat of Christ. For it is written, As I live, saith the Lord, every knee shall bow to me, and every tongue shall confess to God. So then every one of us shall give account of himself to God. (Romans 14:10–12)

Every person through all time is going to have to answer to God. The "hour of His judgment" in Revelation 14 indicates that the whole planet will be called to accountability by a separation message, just like in the days of Noah. Every human being will give an account of himself to God; there is no escaping that. However, the accountability is not only someday standing before God; it is also now. God's message is calling us to make a decision that will lead us to being either sealed or marked. What is it that we are judged by?

> He that rejecteth me, and receiveth not my words, hath one that judgeth him: the word that I have spoken, the same shall judge him in the last day. (John 12:48)

Jesus says His word will judge us. The book of Revelation is the revelation of Jesus Christ. (See Revelation 1:1–3.) The Word and counsel of God to man through the ages culminate here in Revelation 14 as a judgment-hour message. The Word and law of the Lord will bring all nations to accountability, to a time and point of decision. The final separation, the judgment, is over God's Word and law versus man's religious laws and doctrines. That is why these messages are depicted as angels who go to the whole world, to every nation, kindred, tongue, and people.

> A good man out of the good treasure of the heart bringeth forth good things: and an evil man out of the evil treasure bringeth forth evil things. But I say unto you, That every idle word that men shall speak, they shall give account thereof in the day of judgment. For by thy words thou shalt be justified, and by thy words thou shalt be condemned. (Matthew 12:35–37)

Jesus said we are going to be held to account by our words. Our words reveal what is in our hearts. Those who gain the victory over the beast and his mark, and who accept the message of Revelation 14 and are sanctified by it, are described as those who "in their mouth was no guile" (Revelation 14:5).

God sets forth the word of truth, while Babylon sets forth lying, deceptive words that may sound good, even religious, yet lead us away from truly fearing God and giving Him glory. Two confessions shall be made: one in truth and righteousness, thereby honoring God; the other will be lying words coming from those who "received not the love of the truth, that they might be saved" (2 Thessalonians 2:10). This class "believed not the truth, but had pleasure in unrighteousness" (verse 12). They will accept the words of the beast, "speaking great things and blasphemies" (Revelation 13:5). Sadly, most of mankind shall confess with their words, willingly or by the fear of men, an allegiance to the apostate powers of earth. Thus, by their words and actions they shall be judged. Truly, it is the word of truth and the word of error that separates and judges "between the righteous and the wicked, between him that serveth God and him that serveth Him not" (Malachi 3:18).

> Let us hear the conclusion of the whole matter: Fear God, and keep his commandments: for this is the whole duty of man. For God shall bring every work into judgment, with every secret thing, whether it be good, or whether it be evil. (Ecclesiastes 12:13–14)

Obedience to God has always been the standard that separates those who serve Him and those who do not. James gives us further insight regarding God's standard, for he says, "So speak ye, and so do, as they that shall be judged by the law of liberty" (James 2:12). The law of liberty is the moral law, the Ten Commandments. The law and the Word of God make distinct who truly worships Him. "For not the hearers of the law are just before God, but the doers of the law shall be justified" (Romans 2:13). As we open our hearts to the everlasting gospel, we can receive the "faith of Jesus" and thereby "keep the commandments of God" (Revelation 14:12).

The law of God is at the heart of the three angels' messages. There is given the call to "worship Him that made heaven, and earth, and the sea, and the fountains of waters" (Revelation 14:7). Here is a message calling the world back to the commandments of God and to the worship of the true God on His holy day, the true Lord's day, the seventh-day Sabbath. And why such a message? Because we are going to be judged by the law of God, and Babylon has substituted the commandments of men for the commandments of God. Thus, God says with a loud voice, "Fear Me and worship Me."

In response to this judgment-hour message, those who have made Jesus their own by faith, allowing the life of Jesus to be worked out in them, keep the commandments of God, while Babylon uplifts the commandments and religion of men. The beast will mark them as his, for they follow human institutions. In contrast, God has a people who worship Him, keeping His commandments, and they shall be sealed as His own.

Truly serving God in our age of apostasy requires consistent endurance. However, God says, "I will have a people. These are they who keep the commandments of God and have the faith of Jesus. Here is the patience of the saints." (See Revelation 14:12.) And why do they have this consistent endurance? It is not by trying hard, nor by being religious, but by accepting the everlasting gospel, which by faith and love leads to obedience to God's law.

Obedience will never buy salvation, but obedience proves whether we have really accepted the gift of Jesus and made His life our own in faith and love. In contrast, the worshipers of the beast and those who make up part of the mystical Babylonian religion of the last days have fallen from God, for they have exalted the word and commandments of men.

Jesus taught in the Sermon on the Mount in Matthew 5 that the law is not simply our outward actions; it affects our motives, our hearts, out thoughts. In the end, the law separates between those who have the "Father's name written in their foreheads" (Revelation 14:1) and those who receive "a mark ... in their foreheads" (Revelation 13:16). Obedience or disobedience to the law of God, inclusive of the fourth commandment as given by God, declares our allegiance; therefore, the law will judge and separate.

> But we are sure that the judgment of God is according to truth against them which commit such things. And thinkest thou this, O man, that judgest them which do such things, and doest the same, that thou shalt escape the judgment of God? In the day when God shall judge the secrets of men by Jesus Christ according to my gospel. (Romans 2:2–3, 16)

God is going to hold us accountable, not to the "word of men, but as it is in truth, the word of God" (1 Thessalonians 2:13). Jesus prayed, "Sanctify them through thy truth: thy word is truth" (John 17:17). Falsehood and error can never sanctify the soul, leading to the renewing of the mind and dedication to God. Falsehood and error may please the senses and dedication to error may give us a hope, but it is a false hope.

We are not held accountable to the claims of the Catholic Church or to the claims of the book of Mormon. We are not accountable to the Watchtower Society and their publications. There is no accountability to the prophet Muhammad and the Koran, or to the writings of Buddha, or to the Hindu gods and goddesses and mystics. We are accountable and judged by the truth of God, which is found in the holy Bible. However, the religions of Babylon have substituted the commandments and religion of men for the gospel and truth of God, thereby deceiving man with the false hope of being saved by works or saved in sin. Yet it is God's truth that we shall be judged by. Regardless of our profession, all sin and wrong will be judged.

God is going to judge the secret intents and thoughts of our hearts. Revelation 14 is a judgment-hour message that prompts us to ask ourselves, "Do we really love God?" Almost all the world claims to love God, or a deity as they conceive it. However, in these last days, as in the days of Noah, there is a testing message from God calling for obedience, worship, and commitment, and it is judging the hearts and showing whether we really love Him.

Before the flood God extended to the world 120 years of mercy. (See Genesis 6:3.) Noah, "a preacher of righteousness" (2 Peter 2:5), declared God's judgment message. In our day God is giving a message before the coming destruction, a time Jesus said would parallel the days before the flood. As it was before the flood, two classes of people will develop: those who are renewed by the everlasting gospel and settling into the truth of God so they cannot be moved, and those who are settling into a life of falsehood, error, and sin. During the final controversy between truth and error, between the faith of Jesus and the religion of Babylon, between the mark of the beast and the seal of God, the hour of judgment will come, when men are judged for eternal life or eternal loss while yet living. Even now that judgment has begun.

> When the Son of man shall come in his glory, and all the holy angels with him, then shall he sit upon the throne of his glory: And before him shall be gathered all nations: and he shall separate them one from another, as a shepherd divideth his sheep from the goats: And he shall set the sheep on his right hand, but the goats on the left.
>
> Then shall the King say unto them on his right hand, Come, ye blessed of my Father, inherit the kingdom prepared for you from the foundation of the world: For I was an hungred, and ye gave me meat: I was thirsty, and ye gave me drink: I was a stranger, and ye took me in: Naked, and ye clothed me: I was sick, and ye visited me: I was in prison, and ye came unto me.
>
> Then shall the righteous answer him, saying, Lord, when saw we thee an hungred, and fed thee? or thirsty, and gave thee drink? When saw we thee a stranger, and took thee in? or naked, and clothed thee? Or when saw we thee sick, or in prison, and came unto thee? And the King shall answer and say unto them, Verily I say unto you, Inasmuch as ye have done it unto one of the least of these my brethren, ye have done it unto me. (Matthew 25:31–40)

Our treatment of others will be considered in the judgment, and Satan is subtle and sophisticated, because the fallen religions of Babylon often do charitable works. However, charitable works cannot substitute for the gospel of Jesus Christ and obedience to God's Word and His commandments. Many churches, individuals, and religions are working for human health and welfare. At the same time, they are rejecting the gospel. Often our apparent love and compassion for man is at the sacrifice of love and obedience to God, and the two must be united.

Charity can never be a substitute for obedience to God. It will never merit anything in God's sight. Our sin is so great that only the blood of Jesus Christ can pay the penalty. You see, that's part of fallen Babylon's confusion, believing that good works will merit something before God. The idea that working for the benefit of man will somehow make us acceptable in God's sight is an error. Our sins have created our problems, and the uniting of the forces of religion for human welfare, while neglecting or rejecting God's cure for our souls in the gospel, is part of Satan's plan. You see, he is working to unite the religions of the world against God, and one of the means he uses is human development and welfare, which itself is good but often becomes a means of neglecting the call to "fear God, and give glory to Him" (Revelation 14:7).

> A fiery stream issued and came forth from before him: thousand thousands ministered unto him, and ten thousand times ten thousand stood before him: the judgment was set, and the books were opened. (Daniel 7:10)

This judgment scene in Daniel 7 comes after the rise and fall of Babylon, Medo-Persia, Greece, and pagan Rome, and after the rise and apparent though temporary fall of the little horn. The little horn came out of pagan Rome and is a church-state system, existing from the collapse of the pagan Roman Empire until the coming of Christ. The judgment scene the prophet Daniel sees takes place after the rise of the little horn power. This judgment ends in the vindication of God's truth, His saints, and the destruction of the apostate powers of evil embodied in the little horn. The judgment that Daniel saw is the same hour of judgment John wrote of in Revelation 14. Both Daniel and John foresaw the judgment that takes place before Christ comes to redeem His "called, and chosen, and faithful" (Revelation 17:14).

Let us take a moment here and look at the books that are being considered in the judgment.

> He that overcometh, the same shall be clothed in white raiment; and I will not blot out his name out of the book

of life, but I will confess his name before my Father, and before his angels. (Revelation 3:5)

The book of life contains the names of all those who ever entered into the service of God. Jesus bade His disciples to "rejoice, because your names are written in heaven" (Luke 10:20). Paul speaks of those "which laboured with me in the gospel, ... whose names are in the book of life" (Philippians 4:3).

Daniel said, "There shall be a time of trouble, such as never was since there was a nation even to that same time: and at that time thy people shall be delivered, every one that shall be found written in the book" (Daniel 12:1).

The apostle John says of the citizens of New Jerusalem, "there shall in no wise enter into it any thing that defileth, neither whatsoever worketh abomination, or maketh a lie: but they which are written in the Lamb's book of life" (Revelation 21:27).

The judgment that Daniel sees when the books are opened is going to consider who is worthy to be in the book of life. For not all who make a profession of God truly serve Him. Jesus taught this in Matthew 7. He said:

Not every one that saith unto me, Lord, Lord, shall enter into the kingdom of heaven; but he that doeth the will of my Father which is in heaven. Many will say to me in that day, Lord, Lord, have we not prophesied in thy name? and in thy name have cast out devils? and in thy name done many wonderful works? And then will I profess unto them, I never knew you: depart from me, ye that work iniquity. (Matthew 7:21–23)

Iniquity is lawlessness and sin. Here is a class of people who were religious, who were zealous, who thought they served Jesus. They claimed to believe the gospel, but they did not keep God's commandments. They did not really fear God, they did not truly give Him glory, because they were part of fallen Babylon, and Jesus says, "I do not know you."

The judgment will determine who is really on God's side, with punishment meted out to false professors as well as those who make no profession of religion. If we are not really God's children by grace through faith, our profession is vain and our works of lawlessness will remove us from the book of life. If we are not obedient to God because of "faith that works by love" (Galatians 5:6), we are going to be outside the city of God.

As we look further at the books considered in the time of judgment, we read:

> Then they that feared the Lord spake often one to another: and the Lord hearkened, and heard it, and a book of remembrance was written before him for them that feared the Lord, and that thought upon his name. (Malachi 3:16)

A book of remembrance is written before God, which contains records of the good deeds of those who loved and reverenced the Lord. Their acts of faith and love are all registered in heaven.

Nehemiah refers to this when he says, "Remember me, O my God, concerning this, and wipe not out my good deeds that I have done for the house of my God" (Nehemiah 13:14). In the book of God's remembrance, every deed of righteousness, every temptation resisted, and every victory gained through the fear of God is recorded. Every sorrow endured for Christ is also recorded. Says the psalmist, "Thou tellest my wanderings: put thou my tears into Thy bottle: are they not in Thy book?" (Psalm 56:8).

> I have spread out my hands all the day unto a rebellious people, which walketh in a way that was not good, after their own thoughts; Behold, it is written before me: I will not keep silence, but will recompense, even recompense into their bosom, Your iniquities, and the iniquities of your fathers together, saith the Lord, which have burned incense upon the mountains, and blasphemed me upon the hills: therefore will I measure their former work into their bosom. (Isaiah 65:2, 6–7)

There is a book of life and there is a book of remembrance, and there is a record of the sins of men. All these are going to be considered in the judgment.

> And the Lord said unto Moses, Whosoever hath sinned against me, him will I blot out of my book. (Exodus 32:33)

Those who continue in sin will be blotted out. That's why Jesus says to those in Matthew 7, "I don't know you." He cannot plead His blood in their behalf because they have been blotted out of the book of life. This principle is further confirmed:

> And the lord said unto Moses, who so ever has sinned against me him will I blot out of my book. (Exodus 32:33)

If we continue in sin, we are going to be blotted out of the book of life, for the record of our sins will be against us. We need Jesus to stand as our advocate, our intercessor. That is why the great centrality of this judgment-hour message is Jesus Christ and Him crucified, the everlasting gospel.

We read in Daniel 12 that there is deliverance and a reward for those who are found in the book and sealed before Jesus comes. Further, when Michael, the great prince, stands up, there will be a time of trouble such as never was. This is the pouring out of the seven last plagues, after the door of mercy has shut. And who shall be delivered? "Every one that shall be found written in the book" (Daniel 12:1). When the plagues begin to be poured out, after the door of mercy is shut, there will be but two classes of people: those who have followed the beast and received his mark and whose record of sin stands against them, and those who have been sealed with the Father's name and have made the atoning blood of Jesus their own by faith.

The message of Revelation 14 at the end of time helps make the final determination between those who obey God and those who obey Satan, the seal of God and the mark of the beast, the commandments of men and the commandments of God, the worship of the true God and the religion of fallen Babylon.

Those are the issues that even now are determining our eternal destiny.

This is why the judgment-hour message of Revelation 14 identifies who the beast is and warns of his mark. For the beast sets forth a counterfeit system of worship, which all the world shall wonder after. (See Revelation 13:3.)

The result of this judgment is that Jesus shall cease His work as intercessor; He shall take up His garments of kingly power to come and put down the rule of evil.

Jesus taught through the parable of the tares (Matthew 13) the lesson of separation at the time of harvest. The harvest message is Revelation 14, for we find at the end of this message there is indeed a harvest, a final separation.

Two angels come out of the temple: one is depicted as reaping the righteous and one is depicted as cutting down the wicked. (See Revelation 14:15–20). It is judgment time, my friend. What will you do with the truth? What will you do with the gospel? What will you do with God's plea to you to serve Him, to love Him? Will you hear the voice of Jesus this day and take your stand on the side of God and come out of Babylon? It does not matter what your religious profession is (or lack thereof); whoever you are, God is calling you to come out of error, sin, and falsehood. God is saying to the people of this planet, "In vain do they worship Me, teaching for doctrines the commandments of men" (Mark 7:7).

I hope and pray that you will allow the good news of the gospel and the blood of Christ to be your vindication; for the hour of His judgment is come.

Chapter Six

Worship Him—The Nature of False Worship

S aying with a loud voice, Fear God, and give glory to him; for the hour of his judgment is come: and worship him that made heaven, and earth, and the sea, and the fountains of waters. (Revelation 14:7)

Part of God's message, as given by three angels, declares, "Worship Him that made heaven, and earth, and the sea, and the fountains of waters" (Revelation 14:7).

The whole world worships. Almost everyone has some kind of spiritual philosophy, a spiritual outlook and religion, even if they do not call it religion. Indeed, the whole world worships something or someone.

Evolutionary psychologists have been puzzled as to why this is so. Is the religious nature of mankind due to evolution? Perhaps because of our superstitions of long ago, we started looking for something bigger and more powerful than ourselves to explain life's mysteries and our own short existence. Is that why humanity has gods many and lords many? No, that is not it at all.

The Bible reveals, "God hath dealt to every man the measure of faith" (Romans 12:3). God has given to every man the ability to exercise faith, a desire hidden in the heart to seek after Him. This is why man worships. Now, God did not intend that man would worship the lords and gods that he does. Further, there are not many pathways to God and eternal life. It is because of the sinful and rebellious heart of man that "we … walk after our own devices, and … every one [follows] the imagination of his evil heart" (Jeremiah 18:12). This evil heart, though not seen as such, is one of the reasons man has so many religious ideas and forms of worship.

Mankind's diverse religious ideas and practices are not based on the superstitions of men; rather, they are an indication that God does truly exist. The Bible indicates that there exists spiritual error and darkness as well as light and truth. There is good and evil, sin and righteousness. Why do these opposites exist? Because there is a holy God and there is Satan, the enemy of all mankind. Because of the lying influence of Lucifer and man's own fallen nature, mankind follows diverse spiritual ideas, in contrast to the truth of God.

The world has rejected and ignored the gospel, and has substituted various religious practices and beliefs in the place of the gospel. However, man is still religious. That is why God's message declares, "Worship Him that made heaven, and earth, and the sea, and the fountains of waters" (Revelation 14:7). It does matter, for eternity, who and what we worship.

Now, true worship can never be forced. The religion of Mystery Babylon will in the end use rewards and inducements and intimidation and force to gain allegiance and worship. However, God does not work that way. You see, we cannot serve God out of hope of reward or fear of punishment; we can only serve God because His love has been awakened in our hearts. Indeed, "we love Him, because He first loved us" (1 John 4:19).

Revelation 13 reveals that the crisis at the end is over the issue of worship: will we obey God or obey man? Now, what does *worship* mean? It means "to prostrate oneself in homage (do reverence to adore)."[1] Further, it means "to respect; to honor; to treat with civil reverence" or "civil deference." It is "the act of paying divine honors to the Supreme Being; or the reverence and homage paid to him in religious exercises, consisting in adoration, confession, prayer, thanksgiving and the like."[2]

Thou, even thou, art Lord alone; thou hast made heaven, the heaven of heavens, with all their host, the earth, and all things that are therein, the seas, and all that is therein, and thou preservest them all; and the host of heaven worshippeth thee. (Nehemiah 9:6)

We worship God because He is the Creator. Now, there are many people who might acknowledge a creator God or a designer of this world. But if that belief does not lead them to fear God, to give Him glory, and to obey His commandments, that philosophy or religion is vain; it has no saving virtue.

False Worship Is Based on the Ideas and Doctrines of Man

> This people draweth nigh unto me with their mouth, and honoureth me with their lips; but their heart is far from me. But in vain they do worship me, teaching for doctrines the commandments of men. (Matthew 15:8–9)

Here is described a class of worshipers with specific character-istics. Many religious adherents draw near to their god and their religion with their mouths and make a lot of professions. However, when the heart is far from the true God, none of our zeal, earnest-ness, and sincerity in our religious endeavors will accomplish any eternal good. This is true whether you say you are Christian or a Bahai, whether you are a Taoist or a Buddhist or a follower of any other religion or spiritual philosophy.

If our hearts are far from the true God, and His truth as re-vealed in the holy Bible, and far from the acceptance of Jesus as Lord and Savior, what religion takes its place? The commandments of men. Jesus says such worship is vain; this means it is "folly, to no purpose."[3] Further, it is "without effect; having no substance, value or importance."[4]

The message of Revelation 14 is a call to worship God and to put aside the commandments and religions of men and center our faith on Him who made the heavens, the earth, the seas, and the fountains of waters. The order and complexity of creation tell us of the order and complexity of God. How could a God of order leave man to find Him any way he chooses, through the countless conflicting ideas of man and his religions?

The Bible is specific who this creator God is. "In the beginning was the Word, and the Word was with God, and the Word was God.

The same was in the beginning with God. All things were made by Him; and without Him was not any thing made that was made. In Him was life; and the life was the light of men" (John 1:1–4).

It is by Jesus alone that "we have redemption through His blood, even the forgiveness of sins" (Colossians 1:14). And the power of redemption is because "by Him were all things created, that are in heaven, and that are in earth, visible and invisible whether they be thrones, or dominions, or principalities, or powers: all things were created by Him, and for Him" (Colossians 1:16). He who saves is He who creates, and thus all true worship recognizes "Him who made"; apart from Him we are involved in false worship.

If we try to get to heaven other than through Jesus, the gospel of John says we are thieves and robbers. (See John 10:1.) The nature of the spirit and religion of Babylon is futile, as it is stealing mankind's hope of eternal life by providing a false hope. As sincere as the followers of the world's religions and philosophies are, deception and falsehood is causing people to worship God in vain, taking them down a false path.

False Worship Professes God But Does Not Live for Him

Hear ye this, O house of Jacob, which are called by the name of Israel, and are come forth out of the waters of Judah, which swear by the name of the Lord, and make mention of the God of Israel, but not in truth, nor in righteousness. For they call themselves of the holy city, and stay themselves upon the God of Israel; The Lord of hosts is his name. (Isaiah 48:1–2)

One principle of false worship is taking God's name in vain by claiming that we love, follow, and serve Him, yet we do not live by His Word and law. There is but one truth. The Bible, from Genesis to Revelation, is the truth and revelation of God. It is God's voice speaking to us. Further, it is the truth by which every religion, and all religious philosophies and ideologies, will be judged.

Many today, as sincere and religious as they may be, take God's name in vain by professing to be worshiping and seeking a supernatural force, a power or deity, while not living according to the truth of Scripture. All such worshipers will find in the end that such worship is useless. They are not really worshiping God at all; rather, misconceptions of God, His nature and requirements are leading into religious confusion. Despite all our religiosity and seeking God, when we are in the religious confusion of Babylon we are actually fallen from God.

Isaiah, in the above verses, is speaking of the people of Israel, and what was true long ago remains true today. Israel's false worship in claiming to serve and follow God, while in reality following their own way, led them into literal captivity. The book of Revelation reveals that this same principle of ignoring or setting aside the gospel and the fear and worship of God for man's ideas will lead people into the religion of Babylonian confusion.

To become confused and captivated by the countless religious ideas and philosophies, through seeking to be in tune with the cosmos or the latent divinity within, or saved by works or saved in sin, is the bondage of Babylon. This bondage is as real as that experienced by the Jews long ago, who were literally taken captive to Babylon.

And Babylon is not a friend of God, as religious as it may appear. For the Bible says, "Come out of her ... Babylon the great is fallen, is fallen, and is become the habitation of devils, and the hold of every foul spirit, and a cage of every unclean and hateful bird" (Revelation 18:4, 2). The confused religions of Babylon are all the ideas of men that reject, ignore, or substitute something for the everlasting gospel, and there is no salvation in false worship.

> Cry aloud, spare not, lift up thy voice like a trumpet, and shew my people their transgression, and the house of Jacob their sins. (Isaiah 58:1)

> Yet they seek, inquire for, and require Me daily and delight [externally] to know My ways, as [if they were in reality] a nation that did righteousness and forsook not the

ordinance of their God. They ask of Me righteous judgments, they delight to draw near to God [in visible ways].
(verse 2 AMP)

Isaiah's message shows the nature of false worship, and it parallels Revelation 14. Isaiah is commanded to give a loud cry, to tell
the people that they are living in sin and transgression of God's
will and law. Yet notice the attitude of the people. They say, "We
seek and inquire for God daily. We seek God in visible ways, in
forms, in ceremonies and in rituals." Oh, yes, outwardly, in many
visible ways, people are seeking God. But they are not listening to
God's voice saying, "Repent and turn away from the sins and the
errors that you are in."

As it was in Isaiah's day, so it is today. The people say, "There is
no need of rebuke. We are seeking God. Can't you see how we worship God in all our ritual and practices?" However, as in the days
of the prophet Isaiah, we are living in sin and following external
religion. There is no change of heart and no renewing of the mind,
which leads to loving obedience and service to the Word and will
of God.

You see, my friend, forms and ceremonies and religious zeal
and religious practice cannot substitute for true obedience. True
obedience comes about only by partaking of the gospel, by Jesus
becoming our Savior and His life being worked out in us by faith.

False Worship Mixes Truth with Error

Whereupon the king took counsel, and made two calves
of gold, and said unto them, It is too much for you to go
up to Jerusalem: behold thy gods, O Israel, which brought
thee up out of the land of Egypt. And he set the one in
Bethel, and the other put he in Dan. And this thing became a sin: for the people went to worship before the one,
even unto Dan. And he made an house of high places,
and made priests of the lowest of the people, which were
not of the sons of Levi. And Jeroboam ordained a feast in

the eighth month, on the fifteenth day of the month, like unto the feast that is in Judah, and he offered upon the altar. So did he in Bethel, sacrificing unto the calves that he had made: and he placed in Bethel the priests of the high places which he had made. So he offered upon the altar which he had made in Bethel the fifteenth day of the eighth month, even in the month which he had devised of his own heart; and ordained a feast unto the children of Israel: and he offered upon the altar, and burnt incense. (1 Kings 12:28–33)

Here in these verses we learn what the nature of false worship is. False worship is the mixture of the true and the false. There are those who claim to serve the true God, who claim to believe in Jesus Christ. But truth is mixed with error. And truth mixed with error is deadly and deceptive. If we compare our experience with the Word of God, and the messages of Revelation 14, we see that much of today's religion, even that which is supposedly based upon the gospel of Jesus Christ, is actually spurious.

Note the points below that bring out the principles found in false worship.

1. Seeking counsel apart from God's Word, even as Jeroboam "took counsel" (verse 28), but not from God.

2. Setting up a different system or standard for God's worship to make things easy, as with Jeroboam, who declared, "It is too much for you to go up to Jerusalem" (verse 28).

3. Two centers of worship; e.g., in Bethel, which was close to Jerusalem, and one in Dan, far from the center of true worship. Thus it often is today. There is worship closely counterfeiting the true, yet not true, and one far off from the truth, for those who totally throw off God's Word.

4. Counterfeit worship made to resemble the truth of God, "like unto the feast that is in Judah" (verse 32).

5. Jeroboam created gods of his own choosing, "sacrificing unto the calves that he had made" (verse 32).

6. As with Jeroboam, many worship and follow a religion from man's ideas, "which he had devised of his own heart" (verse 33).

7. Today we have priests and other religious leaders called by men, even as with Jeroboam, for he "made priests of the lowest of the people, which were not of the sons of Levi." Further, "he placed in Bethel the priests of the high places which he had made" (verses 31–32). A professional priesthood takes the place of a calling from God. Those who are truly called of God demonstrate it by fidelity to His Word.

8. Changing God's time of worship. "Even in the month which he had devised of his own heart" (verse 33).

There are eight ways brought out in 1 Kings showing how false worship is manifest.

1. Jeroboam sought counsel and wisdom, but his counsel was not from God's word or His prophets. You see, false worship ignores, despises, or neglects God's word for the commandments and doctrines of men, the philosophies and religions of men. The counsel and instruction we receive though religious is tainted by "philosophy and vain deceit, after the tradition of men" (Colossians 2:8). Though we profess to serve the true God, it is false worship.

2. Setting up a different system or standard for God's worship to make things easy is an indication of false worship. The king declared, "It is too much for you to go up to Jerusalem." God has His way, but man comes forth and says, "No. God's way is too narrow; it is too strict. It is only for those people long ago. We live in a different age and society; we need to interpret the Scriptures according to our understanding and with our theological background and knowledge." And what happens? Just like Jeroboam, the religions of today say to the people, "It is too much for you to go up to Jerusalem. It is too much for you to take God's Word literally, obey it, and follow it." What we want is easy religion so we can think we are going to heaven,

but we do not know the Lord, for our religion is crossless and Christless.

3. Two centers or types of worship were set up. There was a worship center set up in Bethel, which was close to the true worship center in Jerusalem, and one in Dan, which was far from the center of true worship. One was a worship that closely counterfeited the true; it tried to allay itself close to the truth but it was not the truth. And that is going on today, all over this planet, especially with professed Christians who claim to have the truth, who claim to believe in the gospel. There is another class of worshipers, like those in Dan, who are far off from the truth, who virtually throw off God's Word yet say they love Him and want to serve Him.

4. Jeroboam wanted to set up a feast like the feast in Judah. This was a counterfeit to the Feast of Tabernacles, held also on the fifteenth day of the month, but a month later. The attitude of the king and many today is "why trouble ourselves to do as God has said when we can do our own thing? After all, it is still worship." The king wanted it to appear that what he was doing had heaven's blessing and that he was following what God had said. Thus it is often today.

5. Jeroboam and those who followed him were no doubt zealous in their endeavors, yet they followed gods of their own choosing. He "sacrificed unto the calves that he had made." Mankind still makes its own gods. We create a god of our own imagination and build a theology to our imaginary god. We even bow down to man-made objects, declaring, as apostate Israel of old, "These be thy gods" (Exodus 32:4) that shall intercede for us and deliver us. Much of humanity serves gods that exist only in their own minds.

6. Jeroboam's ideas of worship and religion were not based on the commandments and word of God, even though there were similarities. The similarities, however, were superficial and not true at all. What was the source of the king's religion and worship? It was what "he had devised of his own heart." Sadly, much of religion today is still that way; it comes from

the hearts of men. The only religion that can ever lead to God must come from Him. God's way to life and salvation and true worship is only found in His Word, the holy Bible, and Jesus, "the way, the truth, and the life," who said, "No man cometh unto the Father, but by Me" (John 14:6).

7) Counterfeit worship and religion requires a priesthood, religious instructors, and guides. God has "set some in the church" to be prophets, teachers, pastors, and administrators. (See 1 Corinthians 12:28.) However, God's workers only obey Him, His law, and His Word.

Jeroboam's religion, as with all false religions, had priests of a human calling, for Scripture says, "He placed in Bethel the priests." In other words, the priesthood and ministry was a paid profession instead of a calling of God. Today we have plenty of ministers and religious teachers who are nothing more than religious professionals. They do not have a calling from God, and they are not faithful to the gospel of Christ or to God's Word. They are just hired servants.

8). Jeroboam changed God's time for man's. Jeroboam's counterfeit to the Feast of Tabernacles came "even in the month which he had devised of his own heart." This is why, in the warnings and messages of Revelation 14, Scripture says, "Worship Him that made heaven, and earth, and the sea, and the fountains of waters" (Revelation 14:7). This command to worship the Creator comes from the fourth commandment of the law of God. That law says that the seventh day is the Sabbath of the Lord, the day of worship that has not been changed through all time.

Truly, every day is a gift of God, and He should be served and worshiped accordingly. However, His law has set aside one day as a memorial of creation and the re-creation worked out in us by faith in Christ's redeeming grace. To set aside Friday or Sunday or any other day for the worship of God, rather than following the commandment of God as found in His law, sincere though it be, is really no different than the counterfeit worship of Jeroboam.

This is why, in contrast to the worshipers of the beast, God's people in the last days are pointed out as those "that keep the commandments of God." They do not have simply a profession of faith and religion, but "the faith of Jesus" (Revelation 14:12).

Why did Jeroboam set up his false system of worship in opposition to God, and why do men still do the same today?

> And Jeroboam said in his heart, Now shall the kingdom return to the house of David: If this people go up to do sacrifice in the house of the Lord at Jerusalem, then shall the heart of this people turn again unto their lord, even unto Rehoboam king of Judah, and they shall kill me, and go again to Rehoboam king of Judah. (1 Kings 12:26–27)

Ignorantly, in most cases, men follow and create false religions because they are separated from God and following their own hearts. Further, they are unknowingly, in most cases, following the god of this world, Lucifer, who works through man and his religions. Jeroboam's false system of worship was intended to gain sympathy and a following; it was based on jealousy, for he had tried to usurp the place of Rehoboam, Solomon's son.

The devil is seeking to repeat the history of Jeroboam on a worldwide scale, and for the same reasons: to gain sympathy and a following. Notice what Scripture says: "For thou hast said in thine heart, I will ascend into heaven, I will exalt my throne above the stars of God: I will sit also upon the mount of the congregation, in the sides of the north" (Isaiah 14:13).

Here is the secret behind all false worship. It is the devil seeking to usurp the place of the true God in man's heart. To worship falsely and to follow error is to make Lucifer our god in the place of Jehovah.

False Worship Is Based upon Man's Works or Imagination

> To whom will ye liken me, and make me equal, and compare me, that we may be like? They lavish gold out of the

bag, and weigh silver in the balance, and hire a goldsmith; and he maketh it a god: they fall down, yea, they worship. They bear him upon the shoulder, they carry him, and set him in his place, and he standeth; from his place shall he not remove: yea, one shall cry unto him, yet can he not answer, nor save him out of his trouble. Remember this, and shew yourselves men: bring it again to mind, O ye transgressors. Remember the former things of old: for I am God, and there is none else; I am God, and there is none like me, Declaring the end from the beginning, and from ancient times the things that are not yet done, saying, My counsel shall stand, and I will do all my pleasure. (Isaiah 46:5–10)

This evil people, which refuse to hear my words, which walk in the imagination of their heart, and walk after other gods, to serve them, and to worship them, shall even be as this girdle, which is good for nothing. (Jeremiah 13:10)

In the eyes of God mankind can make an idol of false doctrines and man-made theories as readily as the people in Jeremiah and Isaiah's time who were worshiping idols of wood and stone.

The nature of false worship is built upon the idolatry of human doctrines, human philosophies, human commandments, and human forms and ceremonies.

By misrepresenting the character and attributes of God, Satan leads men to conceive of Him with a false understanding. Many people in the church and the world have a man-made philosophical idea of God that is, in reality, an idol in the place of Jehovah. When this is done, the true and living God, as He has revealed Himself in the Bible, through Christ and in the works of creation, is worshiped by few. Sadly, this is the case, despite the majority of the world's people claiming to worship deity.

Millions deify nature and "Mother Earth" while denying the God of nature. Though in a different form, idolatry is as prevalent in the world today as it was in ancient times. The gods of many of today's so-called wise and great men, the philosophers, educators, politicians, and scientists, and even the gods of colleges and universities and theological institutions, are little different from Baal.

How could this be in our enlightened age? Because we make false gods of our own ideas, philosophies, and imaginations. The nature of false worship is that it sets aside the Word of God for the commandments and ideas of men.

False Worship Trusts in New Age Concepts and the Abundance of Their Possessions

> Surely [Lord] You have rejected and forsaken your people, the house of Jacob, because they are filled [with customs] from the east and with soothsayers [who foretell] like the Philistines; also they strike hands and make pledges and agreements with the children of aliens. There land is full of silver and gold; neither is there any end to their treasures. Their land is also full of horses; neither is there any end to their chariots. Their land is full of idols; they worship the work of their own hands, what their fingers have made. (Isaiah 2:6–8 AMP)

Why would God have forsaken His people, and could He forsake us? The answer to both questions is that our rebellion and sin, past and present, will separate us from God.

Why does God separate from people? More to the point, why do people separate from God? The above verses tell us. As with ancient Israel, God's people are worshiping Him falsely. They are filled with the customs of the East, taking on the philosophies of Eastern religion, humanism, and ancient mysticism in various forms and in various ways.

Many today go to modern-day soothsayers, and the churches are filled with false prophets, people claiming to speak for God. They declare, "I have a word of knowledge," "I have a word of wisdom," "I have something from the Lord," and "The Holy Spirit has said." The people in Isaiah's day, as well as our own, "strike hands and make pledges in agreement with the children of aliens." A mixture of truth and error abounds as the church walks hand in hand with the alien philosophies and principles of this world.

Even the church growth ideas used by many of the popular churches today are following business and marketing techniques. It appears to be the truth but it is based upon the commandments of men. No matter how popular it is, if something is not true to the Word of God and the gospel of Jesus Christ, it cannot be true worship.

The true worship of God will never use the marketing techniques of the world and go to advertising agencies to build up churches, using the idea of making the customer first. Such ideas will dilute the truth to gain popularity and to please the customer rather than seeking to win souls who are brought to repentance by God's Spirit and the faithful teaching of God's Word, which is to "reprove, rebuke, exhort with all longsuffering and doctrine" (2 Timothy 4:2).

The prophet declared, "Their land is full of silver and gold, neither is there any end to their treasures, their land is also full of horses, neither is there any end to their chariots" (Isaiah 2:7). In our day of globalization and increasing consumerism, people are substituting things and possessions for the worship of the true God. Many have developed a gospel masquerading as truth from God's Word, making prosperity and possessions the new gospel, the evidence of faith and God's blessing. But God declares it is the "perverse disputings of men of corrupt minds, and destitute of the truth, supposing that gain is godliness: from such withdraw thyself" (1 Timothy 6:5).

Many throughout the world are trusting and placing undue attention on the things that man has made. The acquiring or seeking of possessions is the god of many. It is all vain and false worship, just as in Isaiah's day. And God is saying, "That which you love, that which you put so much attention upon and in essence make a god, can be swept away in a moment." And it will be, according to the Bible.

And the loftiness of man shall be bowed down, and the haughtiness of men shall be made low: and the Lord alone shall be exalted in that day. And the idols he shall utterly abolish. And they shall go into the holes of the rocks, and into the caves of the earth, for fear of the Lord, and for the glory of his majesty, when he ariseth to shake terribly the earth. In that day a man shall cast his idols of silver, and his idols of gold, which they made each one for himself to worship, to the moles and to the bats; … for fear of the Lord, and for the glory of his majesty, when he ariseth to shake terribly the earth. (Isaiah 2:17–21)

Isaiah's description of false worship states, "They worship the work of their own hands, that which their own fingers have made" (Isaiah 2:8). Today this would include statues and paintings and icons that are prayed to and venerated by many diverse religions such as Hindus, Orthodox, Buddhists, Catholics, and others. It was idolatry and false worship in Isaiah's day; it remains so today.

Idolatry includes anything that we love and trust in the place of or more than we love and trust God. Every earthly thing men trust in more than God will lead us away from Him, and therefore becomes to us an idol. Whatever possession or material thing or idea or philosophy that divides our affections or takes away from supreme love for God becomes an idol that we, in essence, worship.

There are many worshipers of idols in today's world. The vast majority of the world, in fact, is worshiping idols in one form or another. Thus God's message to every nation and people is to "worship Him that made heaven, and earth, and the sea, and the fountains of waters" (Revelation 14:7).

False Worship Will Put Trust in Religious Institutions or Outward Forms while the Heart Is Estranged from God

The word that came to Jeremiah from the Lord, saying, Stand in the gate of the Lord's house, and proclaim there this word, and say, Hear the word of the Lord, all ye of Judah, that enter in at these gates to worship the Lord.

Thus saith the Lord of hosts, the God of Israel, Amend your ways and your doings, and I will cause you to dwell in this place. Trust ye not in lying words, saying, The temple of the Lord, The temple of the Lord, The temple of the Lord, are these.

Behold, ye trust in lying words, that cannot profit. Will ye steal, murder, and commit adultery, and swear falsely, and burn incense unto Baal, and walk after other gods whom ye know not; And come and stand before me in this house, which is called by my name, and say, We are delivered to do all these abominations? Is this house, which is called by my name, become a den of robbers in your eyes? Behold, even I have seen it, saith the Lord.

Therefore will I do unto this house, which is called by my name, wherein ye trust, and unto the place which I gave to you and to your fathers, as I have done to Shiloh. And I will cast you out of my sight, as I have cast out all your brethren, even the whole seed of Ephraim. (Jeremiah 7:1–4; 8–11, 14–15)

As the word of the Lord came to Jeremiah, so the word of the Lord speaks in Revelation 14, telling us to reverence and give glory in true worship to God. "Do not trust in temples," the Lord is saying, "or in outward religion and forms and ceremonies, while at the same time in heart and life you are not really living for Me."

We can attend worship services at synagogues, mosques, temples, cathedrals, churches, or home fellowships while still living in sin. God says that such worship is vain and false. That is why God's people in Revelation 14 are distinguished as those who obey Him. They believe in God's Word and follow it, enabled by the faith of Jesus.

What is God's response to the vain worship of outward works and profession while our hearts are not truly given to Him in love?

And [then dare to] come and stand before Me in this house, which is called by My Name, and say, [By the discharge of this religious formality] we are set free!—only to go on with this wickedness and these abominations? (Jeremiah 7:10 AMP)

So many people who are worshiping God think that through religious formality and ceremonies they have acceptance with God and are serving Him. Yet their hearts are far from Him. In fact, despite their religious practices, they actually hate God. As in Jeremiah's day, this is shown because they are still living in sin. The Bible says the religious but carnal, unregenerate mind "is enmity against God: for it is not subject to the law of God, neither indeed can be. So then they that are in the flesh cannot please God" (Romans 8:7–8).

Multitudes are involved in religion that has no saving virtue. They neither know God truly, nor are they pleasing Him by their religious formality. Sadder still, rather than loving God, they are actually haters of God, shown by the carnal nature's utter inability to obey God's law and Word. Friend, the only cure for sin is the gospel of Jesus Christ. Religious zeal will never save us. Religious zeal without God in the heart is false and vain worship; it is the worship of the god of this world under the guise of worshiping the God of heaven.

The Worship of Nature and Created Things Is an Element of False Worship

Who changed the truth of God into a lie, and worshipped and served the creature more than the Creator, who is blessed for ever. Amen. (Romans 1:25)

Here we read of a class of people who worship the things God has made. The false worship spoken of in this passage is manifested today by Mother Earth worship, or pantheism; this is the idea that God is in all things and all things are God. God says such worship is false. It is going to lead you away from Him. The supposed liberation from formal religion in seeking new forms of earth-centered spirituality is merely another form of false worship.

Many people, even those who grew up with a Christian background but who never knew Jesus, are accepting various forms of earth-and nature-centered worship, following ancestral spirits, trying to get in touch with nature through various forms of witchcraft, or the religion of indigenous cultures. This is not liberation but bondage.

Nature-centered worship appeals to the carnal heart that does not want to acknowledge its sin and accountability to God. The false gods of nature "promise them liberty, [yet] they themselves are the servants of corruption: for of whom a man is overcome, of the same is he brought in bondage" (2 Peter 2:19). The gods and goddesses of nature can never free us from the bondage of our sinfulness; our liberty is an illusion while we become more firmly "servants of sin" and "free from righteousness" (Romans 6:20).

People attribute spiritual power to crystals, to certain animals, or to places on the globe; this is putting a power into nature that nature does not have. The God of the universe, Jehovah, is a personal God and the creator of all things. He controls nature's power.

Sadly, even many Christians turn God's truth into a lie. How? By rejecting what God has said in His Word and choosing what is false to please their carnal hearts. In rejecting, ignoring, or changing what God has said in His Word, we are deliberately choosing to believe a lie.

The Nature of False Worship Is to Love Unrighteousness

> Now we beseech you, brethren, by the coming of our Lord Jesus Christ, and by our gathering together unto him, that ye be not soon shaken in mind, or be troubled, neither by spirit, nor by word, nor by letter as from us, as that the day of Christ is at hand. Let no man deceive you by any means: for that day shall not come, except there come a falling away first, and that man of sin be revealed,

114

the son of perdition; Even him, whose coming is after the working of Satan with all power and signs and lying wonders, And with all deceivableness of unrighteousness in them that perish; because they received not the love of the truth, that they might be saved. And for this cause God shall send them strong delusion, that they should believe a lie: That they all might be damned who believe not the truth, but had pleasure in unrighteousness. (2 Thessalonians 2:1–3, 9–12)

The very essence of false worship is the rejection of the truth. This truth is not what I make it out to be or what you may think it is. God has declared, "No lie is of the truth" (1 John 2:21). Further, truth is not "the word of men, but ... it is in truth, the Word of God, which effectually worketh also in you that believe" (1 Thessalonians 2:13).

The power and appeal of false worship is in the acceptance or love of unrighteousness; it is salvation in sin, or salvation by works. All such worship prepares our hearts for strong delusion, and we want to believe a lie. The religion of Babylon is built upon a lie, presenting the beautiful side of evil in the garb of true religion. If we remain in such a state, we will receive the mark of the beast, the mark of rebellion and sign of our allegiance to Satan's kingdom.

False Worship Uses Threats, Force, and Compulsion

Thou, O king, hast made a decree, that every man that shall hear the sound of the cornet, flute, harp, sackbut, psaltery, and dulcimer, and all kinds of musick, shall fall down and worship the golden image: There are certain Jews whom thou hast set over the affairs of the province of Babylon, Shadrach, Meshack, and Abednego; these men, O king, have not regarded thee: they serve not thy gods, nor worship the golden image which thou hast set up. Nebuchadnezzar spake and said unto them, Is it true, O Shadrach, Meshack, and Abednego, do not ye serve my gods, nor worship the golden image which I have set up? Now if ye be ready that at what time ye hear the sound of the cornet, flute, harp, sackbut, psaltery, and dulcimer, and all kinds of musick, ye fall down and worship the image which I have made; well: but if ye worship not, ye shall be cast the same hour into the midst of a burning fiery furnace; and who is that God that shall deliver you out of my hands? (Daniel 3:10, 12, 14–15)

And all that dwell upon the earth shall worship him, whose names are not written in the book of life of the Lamb slain from the foundation of the world. And he exerciseth all the power of the first beast before him, and causeth the earth and them which dwell therein to worship the first beast, whose deadly wound was healed. And he had power to give life unto the image of the beast, that the image of the beast should both speak, and cause that as many as would not worship the image of the beast should be killed. (Revelation 13:8, 12, 15)

Force is used by many of the followers of false religions to bring conformity in the group or in the home. This is seen clearly in the laws passed in some states in India, making it difficult to convert from Hinduism without passing through government bureaucracy and formality. In Saudi Arabia it is illegal to be anything but a Muslim. Even to worship in your own home contrary to Islam can mean imprisonment. Intimidation or force is used to maintain a system of false worship.

There are even so-called Christians who threaten family members with violence and intimidation if they dare change from the family's religion or church.

In many churches the words of the prophet have come true: "Yea, truth faileth; and he that departeth from evil maketh himself a prey" (Isaiah 59:15). The marginal reading for the word *prey* means "or is accounted mad." Today, to do right and follow the Word and law of God puts you in the minority among those professed Christians who want to follow their own way. Many, as Jesus foretold, are maligned and falsely accused and cast out of the synagogues; i.e., the churches. (See Luke 6:22.)

The nature of false worship as outlined in Daniel 3 seeks to please and attract the mind, just as the king of Babylon tried the power of music and outward show. If these attractions, invented by men who were inspired by Satan, failed to make men worship the image, the flames of the furnace were ready to consume them. So it is now. False religion first tries outward attraction and reward to bring conformity. If this does not succeed, false worship seeks to force the conscience of those who will not follow. This is done by intimidation, perhaps by losing church membership or church employment or positions. This can also be through shunning or cutting off social and family relations. It can then move on to other threats and eventually physical persecution.

Christ declared of the Jews, "In vain they do worship Me, teaching for doctrines the commandments of men" (Mark 7:7). This is being done today. The commandments of men are exalted, and men are trying to force their fellow men to render obedience to them. But never are we to take the word of men before the Word of God.

The king of Babylon witnessed the seemingly impossible deliverance of the faithful servants of God as they walked unhurt in the midst of the flames with the Son of God. In religious zeal the king responded to this manifestation of God's power by publishing a decree. He declared that anyone speaking a word against the God of heaven, who had saved His servants, "shall be cut in pieces, and their houses shall be made a dunghill: because there is no other God that can deliver after this sort" (Daniel 3:29). In this decree God's wonderful deliverance of His children was misinterpreted and the way of truth confused by human inventions.

The king had a right to worship the God of heaven and to do all in his power to exalt Him above other gods. But he had no right to use his authority in compelling his subjects to change from the worship of idols to the worship of the true God. The king had no right to threaten men with death for not worshiping the true God, just as he had no right to make the decree consigning to the flames all who refused to worship the golden image.

117

Today, as in the days of Babylon, men in power, be it in the world or in the church, do not realize they cannot control the minds of their fellow men and be guiltless before God. Satan will work through religion and the state in the last days to oppress the true children of God.

Revelation 13 reveals the final result of the false worship of the ages when a global system of worship is to be enforced, first by reward and privilege, and if that does not work, then by threat of death. Virtually the entire world shall be deceived and go along willingly or merely conform outwardly to get along. Satan's final counterfeit will not appear as evil and hideous but as good and necessary. The only way to be kept from the delusions of our day and the future is to "worship the Father in spirit and in truth: for the Father seeketh such to worship Him" (John 4:23). To do this means to set aside all the human "works of righteousness which we have done," and understand and accept that it is only "according to His mercy He saved us, by the washing of regeneration, and renewing of the Holy Ghost; which He shed on us abundantly through Jesus Christ our Saviour" (Titus 3:5–6).

What Happens to the Thinking of False Worshipers?

> This know also, that in the last days perilous times shall come. For men shall be lovers of their own selves, covetous, boasters, proud, blasphemers, disobedient to parents, unthankful, unholy. Without natural affection, trucebreakers, false accusers, incontinent, fierce, despisers of those that are good, traitors, heady, highminded, lovers of pleasures more than lovers of God; Having a form [appearance, semblance] of godliness, [piety, true religion] but denying [their conduct contradicts the genuineness of their profession] the power thereof: from such turn away. (2 Timothy 3:1–5)

Faith in Christ is the way of eternal life, yet the above verses reveal that many Christians in the last days will only have a form of godliness. The religion that comes from God will, by most professors, be turned into the religion of man, carnal and controlled by the flesh rather than by the Spirit. The apostle Paul, speaking of this condition in the last days, said it would be a time of peril or danger. Jesus said of our time, just before He comes, that many professed believers would be caught up in the spirit of the world. "And because iniquity shall abound, the love of many shall wax cold" (Matthew 24:12).

This is why, with so many, their worship and praise and profession seem to make little difference in their character; for as Paul has revealed in Timothy, it is a religious form devoid of true faith and love.

The apostasy spoken of in 2 Timothy in the professed church of God, in combination with the falsehood prevailing in the world and its religions, will prepare the way for the image of the beast. The only safety is to turn away from all compromise, apostasy, and sin.

> Because that, when they knew God, they glorified him not as God, neither were thankful; but became vain in their imaginations, and their foolish heart was darkened. Professing themselves to be wise, they became fools. And even as they did not like to retain God in their knowledge, God gave them over to a reprobate mind, to do those things which are not convenient; Being filled with all unrighteousness, fornication, wickedness, covetousness, maliciousness; full of envy, murder, debate, deceit, malignity; whisperers, backbiters, haters of God, despiteful, proud, boasters, inventors of evil things, disobedient to parents, Without understanding, covenantbreakers, without natural affection, implacable, unmerciful: Who knowing the judgment of God, that they which commit such things are worthy of death, not only do the same, but have pleasure in them that do them. (Romans 1:21–22, 28–32)

It is believed by many commentators that the above verses in Romans are describing the character of man just before the flood.

A careful comparison with the verses in 2 Timothy reveals a great similarity between modern Christianity and the condition of man before the deluge.

Today we have a world filled with religion and religious people, all believing they are seeking for and serving God. Why, then, is the world not better than it is? The answer is simple: it is filled with false religion. And what happens to false worshipers' thinking? They are seeking God the world over, among every race and nation; however, they are seeking God on their own terms, be they cultural, traditional, or by what appeals to them. In all this seeking for God they "do not like to retain God in ... [their] knowledge." This is shown by the fact they are still carnal and not obedient to God's law. (See Romans 8:7–8.)

The world over, professors of religion claim to know God, but their profession is in vain, for they do not really give Him glory. This is why part of God's last message declares, "Fear God and give glory to Him" (Revelation 14:7).

The general apostasy that is prevailing today in the religious world is similar to what is described in the Old Testament. We exalt human ideas, human philosophies, and doctrines above the Word of God. This is the reason our imagination and hearts become vain and dark. This is the reason the followers of religion are characterized as "being filled with all unrighteousness." The sins in the religious community, regardless of the nature of that religion, show that men, though very religious, are for the most part "haters of God" (Romans 1:30).

The book of Revelation reveals that the last confederacy of evil will be religious in nature and will bring forth a global system of religious amalgamation noted for implementing a mark of religious conformity. It will be believed and taught that this system, combining the woman (or religion) and the beast (or the state), will solve the world's problems while at the same time honoring God. Indeed, the Bible reveals, "All that dwell upon the earth shall worship ... whose names are not written in the book of life of the Lamb slain from the foundation of the world" (Revelation 13:8). However, the fact that most of the world will sincerely follow a counterfeit system of falsehood does not make it right.

Friends, everyone in this world worships something or someone, whether it be a church or a religion or some philosophy. The question is, whom or what do you worship? If it is not the Lord Jesus Christ, and if your worship is not based on the truth of God found in the holy Bible, your worship is vain. God is pleading with us to worship Him. It cannot be forced, for true worship requires that you "be renewed in the spirit of your mind; and that ye put on the new man, which after God is created in righteousness and true holiness" (Ephesians 4:23–24). All true religion and salvation comes from God; therefore, only those renewed by His grace and love can offer Him acceptable worship.

If we could perceive that God "is, and that He is a rewarder of them that diligently seek Him" (Hebrews 11:6), and if we could understand that God in Christ became a man and walked among us to show us the Father's love and to die for our sins, then with renewed spiritual vision we would want to "fear God, and give glory to Him; … and worship Him that made heaven, and earth, and the sea, and the fountains of waters" (Revelation 14:7).

God is speaking to you this day, my friend. May you give your heart and life to Jesus. If you do, "ye shall know the truth, and the truth shall make you free" (John 8:32). This freedom is from sin and guilt and falsehood. No religion or worship can do this for you, for it is a gift of God through the everlasting gospel. I pray that you might know this freedom and knowledge of the true God, which is eternal life. That is my hope and prayer in Jesus' name. Amen.

Endnotes

1. James Strong LL.D., S.T.D., *Strong's Exhaustive Concordance* (Grand Rapids, Michigan: Baker Book House, 1987).
2. Noah Webster, *American Dictionary of the English Language* (San Francisco, California: Foundation for American Christian Education, 1967).
3. *Strong's Exhaustive Concordance,* op cit.
4. *American Dictionary of the English Language*, op cit.

Chapter Seven

Worship Him Who Made the Earth, the Sea, and the Fountains of Water • Part One

S aying with a loud voice, Fear God, and give glory to him; for the hour of his judgment is come: and worship him that made heaven, and earth, and the sea, and the fountains of waters. (Revelation 14:7)

Many people believe that the universe was created with intricate design and must therefore have a designer. But that belief has no saving virtue. We need to know God not only as the Creator but also as the one who re-creates and saves us from sin through the everlasting gospel. That God is the Creator may seem a self-evident fact to some; it is, however, a fact of faith, for Scripture says, "Through faith we understand that the worlds were framed by the word of God, so that things which are seen were not made of things which do appear" (Hebrews 11:3).

Faith comes from God, for He gives to every man a measure of faith. (See Romans 12:3.) True faith, having come from God, must be directed toward Him to be saving faith. Faith means surrendering your life to God and obeying His Word. Thus, when the Scripture says that through faith we understand "the worlds were framed by the word of God," it means we need to believe God's Word. We need to entrust ourselves to the Author of that Word. It is not enough to have a theological understanding of God or a belief in a creator. You see, the faith that believes that God is, and is truly the Creator, is the same faith that leads us to "love the Lord thy God with all thy heart, and with all thy soul, and with all thy mind, and with all thy strength" (Mark 12:30).

Which shall we follow, revelation or "oppositions of science falsely so called? (1 Timothy 6:20). This is a most important question and why the message of Revelation 14 calls us to worship God as the Creator. For human speculation often seeks to replace the word of God. This leaves us rudderless in an ocean of theories to be "tossed to and fro, and carried about with every wind of doctrine, by the sleight of men, and cunning craftiness, whereby they lie in wait to deceive" (Ephesians 4:14). And thus we see it in the statements of religious leaders quoted below.

"Humani Generis," John Paul wrote, "considered the doctrine of 'evolutionism' as a serious hypothesis, worthy of a more deeply studied investigation ... Today ... new knowledge leads us to recognize that the theory of evolution is more than a hypothesis." Pius was skeptical of evolution but tolerated study and discussion of it; the statement by John Paul reflects the church's acceptance of evolution. He did not, however, diverge at all from Pius on the question of the origin of man's soul: that comes from God, even if "the human body is sought in living material which existed before it."[1]

Says father Richard P. McBrian, a liberal theologian at the University of Notre Dame, "No Scripture scholar today would say we are literally descended from two people." To such scholars and John Paul, the evolution of our bodies matters less than the evolution of our souls.[2]

More than ten thousand pastors nationwide have signed "The Clergy Letter" of support for Evolution Sunday, February 12, a day designed to bring attention to a movement that believes there is a way to bridge the gap between the theory of evolution and creation theology.

At least two local pastors are known to have signed the letter: the Rev. Wally Carlson of Melrose Chapel United Methodist Church and the Rev. Bob Morwell of Union United Methodist Church.

"Evolution can only go so far, and that is where faith comes in," Carlson said. "No one really knows what is in that gray area in between the two."

"(This movement) is an effort to enlist the help of clergy who do not find belief in evolution incompatible with the Christian faith," Morwell said.

"Whenever we think we know all of the answers, we're wrong," Carlson said. "Because we don't."

Michael Zimmerman, dean of the college of letters and sciences at the University of Wisconsin-Oshkosh, coordinates a Web site devoted to this subject. On the site, it says 10,183 pastors had signed the Clergy Letter as of Wednesday, and that 303 congregations from 47 states have signed up to take part in some sort of Evolution Sunday dialogue. For information on Evolution Sunday, go to http://www.uwosh.edu/colleges/cols/clergy_project. htm.[3]

The statements quoted above are not at all unusual. However, the Bible says, "Worship Him that made heaven, and earth, the sea, and the fountains of waters" (Revelation 14:7). And Hebrews declares, "Through faith we understand that the worlds were framed by the word of God" (Hebrews 11:3), not by the scientific pronunciations and theories of men.[4] The Word of God declares that this world and the universe were made by the power of God. And yet we have the world's leading religious leader declaring that evolution is true.

We need to either believe men or believe God's Word. That is what the whole issue of worship and the crisis over worship revealed in Revelation is all about. Shall I believe and obey God, or shall I believe and obey man?

If by faith we accept God as Creator because His Word has declared it, that faith leads us to the acceptance of Jesus Christ as Savior and Lord. It leads us to fear God and give glory to Him, because of "faith which worketh by love" (Galatians 5:6). You see, faith is not simply intellectually accepting something. True faith involves the surrender of the heart, leading us to worship Him who made all things.

In the Beginning

How did God create?

In the beginning God created the heaven and the earth. (Genesis 1:1)

In the beginning God created. He was the initiator, not some explosion somewhere long ago in the cosmos where gases inexplicably came together and exploded in a big bang.

Many people think that perhaps God started everything and from there things just evolved. There are many mysteries in this world, to be sure. But accidental creation is not one of them. The planet's system of weather, of all nature, and of every living thing is so well-designed it could not have come about by chance and accident, no matter how much time is given to accomplish it. There is nothing of any value on this planet that comes about solely by accident. All that man creates and conceives is the result of intelligent design. How then can it be that everything we see in this world is simply a matter of chance, of nothing becoming something over a long period of time?

How Did God Create?

And God said, Let there be light: and there was light. And God said, Let there be a firmament in the midst of the waters, and let it divide the waters from the waters. And God called the dry land Earth; and the gathering together of the waters called he Seas: and God saw that it was good. And God said, Let the earth bring forth grass, the herb yielding seed, and the fruit tree yielding fruit after his kind, whose seed is in itself, upon the earth: and it was so. And God said, Let there be lights in the firmament of the heaven to divide the day from the night; and let them be for signs, and for seasons, and for days, and years.

And God said, Let the waters bring forth abundantly the moving creature that hath life, and fowl that may fly above the earth in the open firmament of heaven. And God said, Let the earth bring forth the living creature after his kind, cattle, and creeping thing, and beast of the earth after his kind: and it was so.

And God said, Let us make man in our image, after our likeness: and let them have dominion over the fish of the sea, and over the fowl of the air, and over the cattle, and over all the earth, and over every creeping thing that creep-eth upon the earth. So God created man in his own image, in the image of God created he him; male and female created he them. (Genesis 1:3, 6, 10–11, 14, 20, 24, 26–27)

God spoke things into existence. He did not start things and then let them evolve over millions of years. Further, we "are ... saved through faith; and that not of yourselves: it is the gift of God: not of works, lest any man should boast" (Ephesians 2:8–9). Jesus did not die on the cross and then leave us to try to get to heaven on our own. The same God who "dwelt among us" (John 1:14), the Word that was made flesh and revealed God to us, abides with us through the Holy Spirit enabling, strengthening, and changing us day by day. God has an interest in us, not just one time on Calvary, but day by day. And in the same way, in creation, God didn't just start things and then leave them on their own. He created by speaking and bringing everything into existence by His word.

By the word of the Lord were the heavens made; and all the host of them by the breath of his mouth. For he spake, and it was done; he commanded, and it stood fast. (Psalm 33:6, 9)

The heavens and all things were created by the word of God. Jesus said, "Now ye are clean through the word which I have spoken unto you" (John 15:3). He said again, "If ye continue in my word, … ye shall know the truth, and the truth shall make you free" (John 8:31–32).

The Word declares, "Being born again, not of corruptible seed, but of incorruptible, by the Word of God, which liveth and abideth for ever. For all flesh is as grass, and all the glory of man as the flower of grass. The grass withereth, and the flower thereof falleth away: But the Word of the Lord endureth for ever. And this is the Word which by the gospel is preached unto you" (1 Peter 1:23–25).

By the word of the Lord were the heavens made, and by the Word of the Lord, accepted by faith, we are born again and transformed. We exercise faith in the Word of God, which declares to us that we are sinners and that we are doomed to death, but that Jesus is the Savior of all mankind. The Word that declares that God is the Creator is the same Word that declares that we are sinners and that God is the Creator of the new man, "in righteousness and true holiness" (Ephesians 4:24), and the Savior of our souls. We do not really believe in creation unless we believe in salvation. Both creation and redemption are accomplished by the power of God.

How Long Did it Take God to Create this Earth?

For in six days the Lord made heaven and earth, the sea, and all that in them is, and rested the seventh day: wherefore the Lord blessed the sabbath day, and hallowed it. (Exodus 20:11)

God took six days, not six million years, not six billion years, not six hundred billion years. God created in six literal twenty-four-hour days. Do you know why we have a seven-day week?

Because of what the Bible says regarding creation week. There is no scientific or astronomical reason for a seven-day week other than the creation week as recorded in Genesis. Think about that. Our week is based upon the Word of God. The length of days, months, and years all have an astronomical basis, but the seven-day weekly cycle was established in Eden at the time that God created.

And God saw every thing that he had made, and, behold, it was very good. And the evening and the morning were the sixth day. Thus the heavens and the earth were finished, and all the host of them. And on the seventh day God ended his work which he had made; and he rested on the seventh day from all his work which he had made. And God blessed the seventh day, and sanctified it: because that in it he had rested from all his work which God created and made. These are the generations of the heavens and of the earth when they were created, in the day that the Lord God made the earth and the heavens. (Genesis 1:31, 2:1–4)

At the end of creation week, God was not tired, for God is not like us. He did not need a week to create, for He could have created in just a moment of time. Nothing is too hard for God. That's why we can believe His Word. We can believe that He is able to save us, that He is able to bring about the final culmination of this world's history, and that God in His time will finally triumph over evil. The fact that God is the Creator proves it; He is in control. Further, He desires to guide and direct you, and be in control of your life. This is not a matter of God interfering with your life or using force; rather, as your Creator, He desires to guide you and lead you in love. God is the one who created man and redeemed him, and knows how you can find the greatest happiness and fullest potential, which is found only in serving Him in love.

The Word of God says that the generations of creation lasted six literal days. God did not need to take thousands, or millions, or billions of years to create. He simply spoke and it was done. Therefore, we have the choice between faith in the Word of God or the "profane and vain babblings, and oppositions of science falsely so called" (1 Timothy 6:20).

Did God Only Create this Planet?

> To whom then will ye liken me, or shall I be equal? saith the Holy One. Lift up your eyes on high, and behold who hath created these things, that bringeth out their host by number: he calleth them all by names by the greatness of his might, for that he is strong in power; not one faileth. (Isaiah 40:25–26)

> Which maketh Arcturus, Orion, and Pleiades, and the chambers of the south. (Job 9:9)

> Thus saith the Lord, thy redeemer, and he that formed thee from the womb, I am the Lord that maketh all things; that stretcheth forth the heavens alone; that spreadeth abroad the earth by myself. (Isaiah 44:24)

Before the advent of modern astronomy and large telescopes and space probes, Job identified the constellations. He did not say they were the result of the big bang but of God's word. He "alone spreadeth out the heavens" (Job 9:8).

The God "that maketh all things" is also "thy redeemer." The God who creates is the God who saves. Faith in the Word, which declares it is God who created, leads to knowing God, who re-deems, re-creates, and saves.

God did not need great expanses of time and evolution to help Him to create; He did it by His word. And just as God did not evolve things over time, time will not make you a better person. You are not going to be better unless you accept the gospel of Jesus Christ, which changes your heart, bringing you into harmony with your Maker. The purpose of the message of Revelation 14 pointing to God as the Creator is that we might be "justified by faith," having "peace with God through our Lord Jesus Christ" (Romans 5:1).

To Whom Does Nature Testify?

> But ask now the beasts, and they shall teach thee; and the fowls of the air, and they shall tell thee: Or speak to the earth, and it shall teach thee: and the fishes of the sea shall declare unto thee. Who knoweth not in all these that the hand of the Lord hath wrought this? In whose hand is the soul of every living thing, and the breath of all mankind. (Job 12:7–10)

The Word of the Lord declares that nature testifies of its Maker. "The whole creation groaneth and travaileth in pain together until now" (Romans 8:22) because of the results of sin. Yet the detail and complexity of life tells us life did not form from non-life long ago; rather, it is by the hand of a personal Creator.

Sadly, through the ages and even in our own supposedly enlightened age, millions go to nature to try to tap into what they believe is the power of the cosmos. They are worshiping nature rather than nature's God. Nature itself testifies of God, yet many deify nature—and not only native religions and indigenous peoples, but also educated and supposedly sophisticated people. However, nature is not God; the uplifting of man from his degradation caused by sin and his subsequent need of salvation cannot be found in nature. The power of the laws of nature are set and controlled by the power of God.

> He stretcheth out the north over the empty place, and hangeth the earth upon nothing. He bindeth up the waters in his thick clouds; and the cloud is not rent under them. He holdeth back the face of his throne, and spreadeth his cloud upon it. He hath compassed the waters with bounds, until the day and night come to an end. The pillars of heaven tremble and are astonished at his reproof. He divideth the sea with his power, and by his understanding he smiteth through the proud. By his spirit he hath garnished the heavens; his hand hath formed the crooked serpent. Lo, these are parts of his ways: but how little a portion is

heard of him? but the thunder of his power who can understand? (Job 26:7–14)

Job makes it plain that the force behind nature is not natural law set in motion by accident and chance. Rather, there is a personal being who stands behind nature and created nature's laws.

Though nature presents mysteries that man and all his science are still seeking to understand, it presents to the seeker of eternal truth glimpses of divinity. However, despite the great complexity of nature and thus nature's God, the created world reveals to mankind only a part "of His ways," for nature can reveal only a "little portion" of an infinite God.

> The heavens declare the glory of God; and the firmament sheweth his handywork. Day unto day uttereth speech, and night unto night sheweth knowledge. There is no speech nor language, where their voice is not heard. Their line is gone out through all the earth, and their words to the end of the world. In them hath he set a tabernacle for the sun. Which is as a bridegroom coming out of his chamber, and rejoiceth as a strong man to run a race. His going forth is from the end of the heaven, and his circuit unto the ends of it: and there is nothing hid from the heat thereof. (Psalm 19:1–6)

God speaks to mankind through the Bible and through His Holy Spirit, reproving us and guiding us. We learn in the book of Psalms that God also speaks through that which He created. This voice of creation, the heavens and the earth, transcends every language of this world. By looking upon creation all can know, if they will, that there is a God.

"Faith cometh by hearing, and hearing by the word of God" (Romans 10:17). Further, the voice of creation speaks; therefore, by faith we can believe that God is. The faith that believes that God created is the same faith that believes His Word and accepts the Lord Jesus Christ as the Master and Savior of our lives.

God Is in Control of Nature

> The day is thine, the night also is thine: thou hast prepared the light and the sun. Thou hast set all the borders of the earth: thou hast made summer and winter. (Psalm 74:16–17)

The planet's weather cycle, and the cycle of the seasons, are intricate mechanisms set in motion by design and not by chance. In the twenty-first century, with the worry over climate change and many scientists studying and researching its effects, we remain largely at the mercy of the planet's ecosystem.

However, the God who created understands all that is taking place in the environment and in our hearts. The Word of the Lord has declared that because of man's sin, the planet will come under increasing stress and decay. He speaks though the prophet and says, "Lift up your eyes to the heavens, and look upon the earth beneath: for the heavens shall vanish away like smoke, and the earth shall wax old like a garment, and they that dwell therein shall die in like manner: but My salvation shall be for ever, and My righteousness shall not be abolished" (Isaiah 51:6).

Praise God, despite sin and death and a planet reeling under the effects of the sin and selfishness of man, we need not despair. For as truly as man dies and the environment decays and the planet is growing old, even more sure is the salvation offered to each one of us. The apparent surety of the seasons provides us with but a small glimpse of the surety for all who will come to know and believe and love the God who creates and the God who has kept mankind from total destruction.

> Then the Lord answered Job out of the whirlwind, and said ... Hath the rain a father? or who hath begotten the drops of dew? Out of whose womb came the ice? and the hoary frost of heaven, who hath gendered it? The waters are hid as with a stone, and the face of the deep is frozen. Canst thou bind the sweet influences of Pleiades, or loose the bands of Orion? Canst thou bring forth Mazzaroth in

his season? or canst thou guide Arcturus with his sons? Knowest thou the ordinances of heaven? canst thou set the dominion thereof in the earth? Canst thou lift up thy voice to the clouds, that abundance of waters may cover thee? Canst thou send lightnings, that they may go, and say unto thee, Here we are? Who hath put wisdom in the inward parts? or who hath given understanding to the heart? Who can number the clouds in wisdom? or who can stay the bottles of heaven. (Job 38:1, 28–37)

The laws and mechanisms of nature can be seen and to some degree understood. However, they are not chance events or systems evolved by accident. Rather, behind the laws and mechanisms of nature and of creation stands the Master Designer.

Nature itself testifies of God. And God is in control of nature. When we speak of acts of God, when nature gets out of control, this is not blind superstition to describe uncontrollable events. Rather, God is in control and He will directly use or allow nature to afflict mankind, to bring judgment to mankind as man separates from His love and from His protection. The environment God originally created was perfect and never brought death or destruction until sin entered the world. However, after the flood, the planet was markedly changed, and now the forces of nature at God's command or His allowance is increasingly chaotic and destructive. Yet God is still in control, and He holds in check the devil and his destroying angels and nature.

Natural law and science can describe nature's destructive forces, yet it is in reality the result of an imbalance caused by the consequences of sin. We need not put our hope in science and technology or national or global government to set things right and bring the environment and nature under control. Nor do we need to hope for the best in our personal lives and get by the best we can. What we need is to know the God who created, and the God who saves man from the results of his rebellion and sin. For God reveals Himself as Creator that we might know Him as Redeemer and Father and Friend.

Did God Create and then Leave Nature to Fend for Itself?

Thou, even thou, art Lord alone; thou hast made heaven, the heaven of heavens, with all their host, the earth, and all things that are therein, the seas, and all that is therein, and thou preservest them all; and the host of heaven worshippeth thee. (Nehemiah 9:6)

Thy faithfulness is unto all generations: thou hast established the earth, and it abideth. They continue this day according to thine ordinances: for all are thy servants. (Psalm 119:90–91)

Nehemiah declared that God preserves all that He has created. The psalmist declares that all created things continue according to God's interest and tender regard and care. It is the same way with us. If God has concern regarding nature and putting a check on its destructive forces and maintaining all living things, how much more is His concern for man, who was originally created in His image?

Nature is not left to fend for itself; it has a concerned Designer who maintains it, even in a world of sin. So, too, God takes an interest in every human being. Those who allow their hearts to be drawn by His Spirit and accept Jesus Christ as their Savior from sin, He accepts as His children.

God did not simply create and let nature go on by itself. And He will not willingly leave man to himself to reap the results of sin in his surroundings and in his character, and then die without hope.

God is saying to us in these last days of increasing tension and global problems, and in a world that presents to us many religious and spiritual pathways, "Look unto Me, and be ye saved, all the ends of the earth: for I am God, and there is none else" (Isaiah 45:22).

Where Was God before Creation as We See It Today?

> Before the mountains were brought forth, or ever thou
> hadst formed the earth and the world, even from everlast-
> ing to everlasting, thou art God. (Psalm 90:2)

In this world we have many gods and lords, and philosophies
and religions and spirituality in abundance. But there is only one
true God, and He existed before creation. All things flow out from
God, "and He is before all things, and by Him all things consist"
(Colossians 1:17).

The God who existed in eternity past is the same God who
exists now, and there is but one road to the true God. We see this
in the order and design of creation; it is not haphazard. The order
of creation is the same order of salvation, for Jesus said, "I am the
way, the truth, and the life: no man cometh unto the Father, but by
Me" (John 14:6).

By one way are we saved. That is why the center of Revelation's
message is the everlasting gospel, which reveals the God of creation and re-creation and redemption. The God who is the alpha
and omega of time and eternity, and who created all things, is the
God who saves.

The concept of evolution, that everything happened by accident and chance, is the same philosophy as the religions of this
world that are fallen from God. Man believes that by reincarna-
tion, through transubstantiation in the mass, by good works and
karma, and by involving themselves in social justice and charity,
they will arrive to a place called heaven. It is salvation by chance
and accident. However, even as this world did not come about by
chance, but was created by a God who inhabits eternity, so is mankind's restoration to that Creator. It is by planned design and His
initiative through the everlasting gospel.

The last crisis of this world is religious in nature, and it will
separate those who believe and follow the Creator and those who
follow the evolution of human religion and spirituality. The end-
time government and religion of the world, revealed in the book of
Revelation, centers around worship—it is the worship of God on

our own terms. In contrast is the true worship of God, according to His Word, the Bible, the same word that created all things.

That is the bottom line, my friend. And it is up to you to make a decision for life or for death. Will you obey God or will you obey man? Will you accept the truth of God or the lying doctrines of Babylon?

We are not a result of chance and accident. And we will not get to heaven by accident. There is but one road. Jesus called it the narrow way. He said there is a broad road that leads to destruction, and many will go down that road, for it is the natural road to follow. It will accept all the religions and philosophies of men, but it is a downward path. Jesus said that straight is the gate and narrow is the road that leads to life. (See Matthew 7:13–14.)

The Fact that God Created Makes Him the Only True God

> For great is the Lord, and greatly to be praised: he also is to be feared above all gods. For all the gods of the people are idols: but the Lord made the heavens. (1 Chronicles 16:25–26)

The call to fear God and recognize Him alone as Creator has been the privilege offered to man since his creation and subsequent fall. Mankind, because of his sin, is prone to worship falsehood, for it allows him salvation in sin, and the gods he worships are much like himself. Many of the false gods of the world need icons, statues, and symbols, but the Creator transcends all that man can make or conceive. He says to us, "Be still and know I am God" (Psalm 46:10). This is made possible as His Spirit seeks to draw all men to a personal relationship of faith and trust.

> But the Lord is the true God, he is the living God, and an everlasting king: at his wrath the earth shall tremble, and the nations shall not be able to abide his indignation. Thus shall ye say unto them, The gods that have not made the heavens and the earth, even they shall perish from the

earth, and from under these heavens. He hath made the earth by his power, he hath established the world by his wisdom, and hath stretched out the heavens by his discretion. When he uttereth his voice, there is a multitude of waters in the heavens, and he causeth the vapours to ascend from the ends of the earth; he maketh lightnings with rain, and bringeth forth the wind out of his treasures. Every man is brutish in his knowledge: every founder is confounded by the graven image: for his molten image is falsehood, and there is no breath in them. They are vanity, and the work of errors: in the time of their visitation they shall perish. (Jeremiah 10:10–15)

All the images that are found in the religions of man make us brutish. They distort our minds as to who God really is. We set forth these things as devotional helps, and objects of veneration and reverence, but they take us away from God's Word. Thus, while seemingly providing a great focus of devotion, venerating images make us spiritually dull of mind regarding the truth and glory of God.

Further, many in this world worship man-made objects and things they have made or obtained. Property, education, husbands, wives, children, jobs, and possessions are some of the things men worship and place before the honor of God. When we worship a substitute in the place of the true God, neglecting His Word, no matter how sincere we may be, we become brutish in our knowledge. Whether we have a master's or doctorate degree, or are a peasant with little or no formal education, we are dull in our knowledge. And why? Because all those who worship things, ideas, or possessions become like them.

The pictures we adore, the incense we burn to statues, the images we bow down before and pray to, thinking we are honoring God or drawing closer to Him, is all falsehood. There is no life and help to be found in these images.

**The Proof that God Can Help Us Is in the Fact that
He Alone Is the Creator**

> I will lift up mine eyes unto the hills, from whence cometh
> my help. My help cometh from the Lord, which made
> heaven and earth. (Psalm 121:1–2)

Why did the psalmist know that God could help him? Because
He is the Creator. Some versions say that the "lifting up of my eyes
unto the hills" refers to the false gods of paganism that were set in
the hills. Many pagans worshiped the power of nature, the gods of
the hills, the gods of the plains, the gods of waters, and the psalmist
is saying, "I will not lift up my eyes to these pagan deities, but I will
lift up mine eyes to the creator God."

An alternative reading states that the "lifting up of mine eyes
as to the hill" refers to the hill of Mount Moriah, were the temple
was. Many people are centering their attention on churches and
religious organizations, looking to these sources for help and salvation, thinking that if they belong to such-and-such an organization, God will accept them. No, my friend, that also is a lie. I will
lift up my eyes by faith beyond the hills and that which I can see to
God alone. This is the message of the psalmist that still rings true
to our day.

> Our help is in the name of the Lord, who made heaven
> and earth. (Psalm 124:8)

Our help is not in the politicians of this world, the governments or religions of this world. The only one who can truly help
us, individually and as a world, is He who created all things and
therefore understands the blueprint and how things are designed
to work. However, instead of acknowledging this, mankind ignores
God's solutions and seeks out human solutions.

The ultimate human solution, as revealed in the book of
Revelation, is the coming together of religion and the kings of
the earth, with the economic forces in a grand coalition. This
will be done under the banner of human development, social and

environmental renewal, and religion in the name of God, while in reality forgetting Him.

Because God Is the Creator, This Is the Reason We Should Pray to Him

Thus shall ye speak to Hezekiah king of Judah, saying, Let not thy God in whom thou trustest deceive thee, saying, Jerusalem shall not be delivered into the hand of the king of Assyria. Behold, thou hast heard what the kings of Assyria have done to all lands, by destroying them utterly: and shalt thou be delivered? Have the gods of the nations delivered them which my fathers have destroyed; as Gozan, and Haran, and Rezeph, and the children of Eden which were in Thelasar? Where is the king of Hamath, and the king of Arpad, and the king of the city of Sepharvaim, of Hena, and Ivah?

And Hezekiah received the letter of the hand of the messengers, and read it: and Hezekiah went up into the house of the Lord, and spread it before the Lord. And Hezekiah prayed before the Lord, and said, O Lord God of Israel, which dwellest between the cherubims, thou art the God, even thou alone, of all the kingdoms of the earth; thou hast made heaven and earth. Now therefore, O Lord our God, I beseech thee, save thou us out of his hand, that all the kingdoms of the earth may know that thou art the Lord God, even thou only. (2 Kings 19:10–15, 19)

King Hezekiah heard the proud boast of the king of Assyria and how king after king had fallen before him. Hezekiah was brought face to face with the probable destruction of his kingdom and people. Humanly speaking, his situation looked hopeless. At best, Hezekiah's options were not pleasant. He could put up a fight and die, or he and his nation could become subjects and slaves to the king of Assyria. In our own lives we face many problems

140

with no apparent favorable solution. However, we, like Hezekiah, must look to and pray to the God of creation, for He who made all things can provide help and answers to our seemingly insurmountable problems.

"Through faith we understand that the worlds were framed by the word of God, so that things which are seen were not made of things which do appear" (Hebrews 11:3). If God created all that we see from nothing, simply by speaking it, can He not help us? Though we see no human answers, God can provide the help you need. His power as Creator stands behind His ability to hear our prayers if we will but acknowledge Him and give Him the glory.

Man's Salvation Is Assured by the Fact that God Is Creator

For God, who commanded the light to shine out of darkness, [at creation] hath shined in our hearts, to give the light of the knowledge of the glory of God in the face of Jesus Christ. (2 Corinthians 4:6)

The God who spoke everything into existence is the same God who sends His Spirit to speak His light, truth, and love into our hearts. This demonstrates that the power of salvation is the same as the power of creation, for both are by the will and word of God. God is more than an impersonal force that stands behind creation, for though He is a spiritual being, He desires a personal relationship with man. Further, the light of heaven, which is a revelation of God's love for mankind, and for you, is seen in Jesus. He said, "I am the light of the world: he that followeth Me shall not walk in darkness, but shall have the light of life" (John 8:12).

As "the earth was without form, and void; and darkness was upon the face of the deep" (Genesis 1:2), so our hearts are in spiritual darkness. The darkness would have remained had not God intervened and said, "Let there be light: and there was light" (Genesis 1:3). And the spiritual darkness and confusion of man will remain until Jesus, the "true Light, which lighteth every man that cometh into the world," is made ours (John 1:9). And how will this be? "But as many as received Him, to them gave He power to become the sons of God, even to them that believe on His name" (John 1:12).

The Judgment of Babylon In the Past and of Spiritual Babylon Is by Virtue of God's Creative Power

> Thus saith the Lord; Behold, I will raise up against Babylon, and against them that dwell in the midst of them that rise up against me, a destroying wind. O thou that dwellest upon many waters, abundant in treasures, thine end is come, and the measure of thy covetousness. He hath made the earth by his power, he hath established the world by his wisdom, and hath stretched out the heaven by his understanding. When he uttereth his voice, there is a multitude of waters in the heavens; and he causeth the vapours to ascend from the ends of the earth: he maketh lightnings with rain, and bringeth forth the wind out of his treasures. (Jeremiah 51:1, 13, 15–16)

The ancient kingdom of Babylon was the superpower of its day. It was "the glory of kingdoms" (Isaiah 13:19). Despite its power and influence, the God of creation decreed its demise. God had used Babylon to afflict His apostate people and other rebellious nations; however, Babylon became "proud against the Lord, against the Holy One of Israel" (Jeremiah 50:29).

So too in the last days God will allow spiritual Babylon to arise, largely as a result of the apostasy of the people of this world. Babylon's final constituency will be the uniting of religion, with the Vatican as the head, in conjunction with the kings of the earth and the merchantmen. Babylon's influence in the world is described as follows:

"For all nations have drunk of the wine of the wrath of her fornication, and the kings of the earth have committed fornication with her, and the merchants of the earth are waxed rich through the abundance of her delicacies" (Revelation 18:3).

Despite all the apparent benefits of this confederacy, it is an enemy of God. Babylon is a mixture of truth and error, light and darkness; in essence, it is the beautiful side of evil. It is the culmination of Satan's long rebellion against God and his desire to be the undisputed god of this world. When the world's religious and political systems seemingly have found the answer to many of mankind's problems and have presented to the world a religion that professes God but actually denies Him, then the God of Creation "ariseth to shake terribly the earth" (Isaiah 2:21).

The proof that this world of sin will someday end can be seen in God's destruction of Babylon, despite its greatness. In a world of confusion and turmoil, violence and strife, behind it all is the Lord of creation, and He desires to guide you through this world of sin. Will you let Him?

Endnotes

1. "Vatican thinking evolves, the Pope gives his blessing to natural selection—though man's soul remains beyond science's reach." by James Collins, Time magazine, November 1996.
2. Ibid.
3. Steve Eighinger, "Movement hopes to bridge the gap between evolution and creationism." Quincy *Herald-Whig*, online edition, January 21, 2006. http://www.whig.com/353447938366589.php.
4. Creation is not simply a matter of religious faith and ignorant superstition. Therefore, the author would direct you to the following Web sites for scientific evidence of creation: www.answersingenesis.org; www.evolution-facts.org.

Chapter Eight

Worship Him Who Made the Earth, the Sea, and the Fountains of Water • Part Two

For the Lord is great, and greatly to be praised: he is to be feared above all gods. For all the gods of the nations are idols; but the Lord made the heavens. O worship the Lord in the beauty of holiness: fear before him, all the earth. (Psalm 96:4–5, 9)

Because Jehovah alone is Lord, He is worthy of worship and is to be the focus of all adoration, praise, and prayer. In contrast, those who make up Babylon and who receive the mark of rebellion are those "in whom the god of this world hath blinded the minds of them which believe not, lest the light of the glorious gospel of Christ, who is the image of God should shine unto them" (2 Corinthians 4:4; see also 2 Thessalonians 2:14; 1 Timothy 1:15). Unless the spiritual blindness is removed, we shall all fall with Babylon.

The majority of mankind is not building their lives on the Rock, a representation of God's Word and salvation that is in Jesus Christ; rather, they are building upon a foundation of sand. (See Matthew 7:26.) Many, like the people in Christ's day, build their religious hopes on the foundation of human ideas and opinions, and outward forms, pageantry, and the ceremonies of man-made religion. Further, many seek acceptance with God and salvation by works that they can do independently of the grace of Christ. All such are erecting their structure of character and their hope of eternity upon shifting sand.

In contrast, true worshipers make Jesus Lord and Master. They hear the words of Christ and do them. (See Matthew 7:24; James 1:25.)

The land also is full of idols; they worship the work of their own hands, that which their own fingers have made. (Isaiah 2:8)

Today, as in Isaiah's day, many worship the work of their own hands; that is where they are putting their trust and hope. This can be bank accounts, investment funds, and cherished possessions, be they little or much. Other man-made things we trust in more than God include our governments, our churches, religious icons and statues, and pictures that we worship as devotional aids and pray to.

Revelation 14 clearly contrasts those who worship God and those who worship the beast. There is a contrast between those who keep God's commandments and those who follow man's commandments, between those who fear and reverence God and those who fear and reverence man. There is a distinction between those who give glory to God and those who give glory to men.

Many people throughout the world worship a god of their own making. However, in Revelation we find a clear call to "worship Him who made the heaven, and earth, and the sea, and the fountains of waters" (Revelation 14:7).

But the Lord is the true God, he is the living God, and an everlasting king: at his wrath the earth shall tremble, and the nations shall not be able to abide his indignation. (Jeremiah 10:10)

God is a loving God. That's why He has given the messages of Revelation 14. He knows the time is almost over, and those who do not accept the offer of salvation will be left in their sins to perish for eternity. If we are still in our sins, we will be consumed. This is no arbitrary act of an angry, revengeful God; this is simply the outworking of the principles of justice and mercy. Sin and rebellion must eventually be destroyed, and thus God gives this message to a planet that is involved in idolatry of all kinds.

Now, God will never force worship or love; indeed, it cannot be forced and be true. That is why He sets forth the gospel as the center of the message. His love and His Spirit seek to draw people to the cross of Christ, to accept the sacrificial death of Jesus in their place. For you see, my friend, with all our religious zeal, all our religious sincerity, we can never gain acceptance with God, because sin is too terrible and it can only be paid by death. Either we accept the death of Jesus, which paid the penalty of sin for all men, or we will die our own deaths. We cannot gain God's favor by our works or by our zeal or by any means other than the gospel of Jesus Christ.

"The hour cometh, and now is, when the true worshipers shall worship the Father in spirit and in truth: for the Father seeketh such to worship Him" (John 4:23). What is it to worship in spirit and truth? It is to be "renewed in the spirit of your mind," putting "on the new man, which after God is created in righteousness and true holiness" (Ephesians 4:23–24). It is to seek with the whole heart Him who is "the way, the truth, and the life" (John 14:6). It is to live by the Word of truth, which is everlasting. It is to walk in obedience to the commandments of truth. (See Matthew 4:4; Psalm 119:142.)

We are called to "worship God in the spirit, and rejoice in Christ Jesus, and have no confidence in the flesh" (Philippians 3:3), in human ideas, inventions, doctrine, and might. Rather, we are to rejoice in the confidence of Jesus Christ, our "hope of glory," "who of God is made unto us wisdom, and righteousness, and sanctification, and redemption" (1 Corinthians 1:30). This is worshiping in spirit and truth. We must be born again of the divine Spirit. This will purify the heart and renew the mind, giving us the desire to know and love God. We will thereby be enabled and desirous to give willing obedience to all His requirements. This is true worship. It is the result of the acceptance by faith of the everlasting gospel.

God will not make us love Him; love is born in our hearts as we perceive the love of God made known to us by His Spirit. The Bible reveals that we love God because He first loved us. (See 1 John 4:10.) Many people in the world claim to love God, but if we despise the gospel, ignore it, or reject it, we cannot truly love God. For the Bible says we love God only because He first loved us.

How do we know God loves us? "God commendeth His love toward us, in that, while we were yet sinners, Christ died for us" (Romans 5:8). The greatest demonstration of the love of God is in Christ, and if we ignore it, we are fallen from God. Thus, in the message "Babylon is fallen" (Revelation 14:8), Babylon represents all the religions and institutions and people of this world who have rejected the everlasting gospel or put something in its place. Therefore, they fear and give glory to men and his institutions, rendering obedience to man's commandments.

O ye sons of men, how long will ye turn my glory into shame? How long will ye love vanity, and seek after leasing? (Psalm 4:2)

God is asking a question to the ancient people of Israel that He could just as well be asking the people of the twenty-first century: "How long will you turn My character, My mercy and love, into the shame and confusion of disgrace? How long shall you continue to wound and hurt Me? How long will you have affection for the vain things of this world that perish with the using? How long will you search out and seek the falsehoods of human imaginations? How long will you in your vain worship seek falsehood in your idols?" That is what God is saying to us.

But this thing commanded I them, saying, Obey my voice, and I will be your God, and ye shall be my people: and walk ye in all the ways that I have commanded you, that it may be well unto you. But they hearkened not, nor inclined their ear, but walked in the counsels and in the imagination of their evil heart, and went backward, and not forward. (Jeremiah 7:23–24)

Babylon is going backward as well, for "Babylon is fallen, is fallen." Fallen from the grace of God. Fallen because of the rejection of truth and the rejection of the gospel.

The first angel calls to all who "dwell on the earth, and to every nation, and kindred, and tongue, and people ... saying with a loud voice, Fear God, and give glory to Him" (Revelation 14:6–7), and to worship Him as the Creator of the heavens and the earth. In order to do this, we must obey His law. Says the wise man, "Fear God, and keep His commandments: for this is the whole duty of man" (Ecclesiastes 12:13). Without obedience to His commandments, no worship can be truly pleasing to God. "This is the love of God, that we keep His commandments" (1 John 5:3). "He that turneth away his ear from hearing the law, even his prayer shall be abomination" (Proverbs 28:9).

The duty to worship God derives from the fact that He is the Creator; therefore, it is ultimately by Him that all men exist. The Bible declares that God alone is worthy of reverence and worship; the reason for this is that He is the Creator of all things. "All the gods of the nations are idols: but the Lord made the heavens" (Psalm 96:5). "To whom then will ye liken Me, or shall I be equal? saith the Holy One. Lift up your eyes on high, and behold who hath created these things, that bringeth out their host by number: He calleth them all by names by the greatness of His might, for that He is strong in power; not one faileth" (Isaiah 40:25–26).

"For thus saith the Lord that created the heavens; God Himself that formed the earth and made it; He hath established it, He created it not in vain, He formed it to be inhabited: I am the Lord; and there is none else" (Isaiah 45:18). Says the psalmist, "Know ye that the Lord He is God: it is He that hath made us, and not we ourselves" (Psalm 100:3). The inhabitants of heaven declare, "Thou art worthy, O Lord, to receive glory and honor and power: for Thou hast created all things, and for thy pleasure they are and were created" (Revelation 4:11).

In Revelation 14, men are called to worship the Creator. This message develops a people who are keeping the commandments of God. (See Revelation 14:12.) One of these commandments points to God as the Creator. Revelation 14 calls upon every nation, kindred, tongue, and people to "worship Him that made heaven, and earth, and the sea, and the fountains of waters" (Revelation 14:7). This message is drawn from the fourth precept of the Decalogue, which declares, "The seventh day is the Sabbath of the Lord thy

God: in it thou shalt not do any work, … for in six days the Lord made heaven and earth, the sea, and all that in them is, and rested the seventh day: wherefore the Lord blessed the sabbath day, and hallowed it" (Exodus 20:10–11). The Lord says that it is "a sign between me and you, that ye may know that I am the Lord your God" (Ezekiel 20:20). In Revelation 14:7 judgment is linked with the call to worship God as the Creator, for the Sabbath is a sign of God's authority.

Therefore, we are called to remember the Sabbath. Now, many seem to think and teach that God's creation memorial is somehow superseded by what we call Christ's new creation, brought about by His resurrection on Sunday. But is this true? Or does the Sabbath memorial incorporate both a commemoration of creation and the re-creative power of Christ? In this time of the great falling away and apostasy, when the amalgamation of Christianity with New Age and paganism and interfaith religion, is growing, God sets forth a judgment-hour message. A call to worship "Him who made heaven and earth and the sea and the fountains of waters." The Sabbath memorial is an invitation to fellowship with a personal God. It is a reminder that God is the Creator and is alone worthy of worship.

Revelation 14 is calling the planet back to obedience to the Word and commandments of God. This in no wise is a means of salvation or gaining merit with God. Rather, it is the fruit and evidence of experiencing the everlasting gospel, being renewed by the power of Christ. Making Jesus Lord and Master, and truly reverencing and fearing God and giving Him glory, results in obedience to all the commandments of God.

Now, many people say that the Sabbath was simply for the Jews, but is that true? Let us see if we can determine from the Bible why the Sabbath was given. Further, we want to understand if this judgment-hour message is indeed a call back to obedience to God's Word, and to His commandments, one of which says, "Remember."

Why Was the Sabbath Given?

> And on the seventh day God ended his work which he had made; and he rested on the seventh day from all his work which he had made. And God blessed the seventh day, and sanctified it: because that in it he had rested from all his work which God created and made. (Genesis 2:2–3)

> For in six days the Lord made heaven and earth, the sea, and all that in them is, and rested the seventh day: wherefore the Lord blessed the sabbath day, and hallowed it. (Exodus 20:11)

The Sabbath is a sign or a memorial of creation. Is there creation in the gospel age to commemorate? People often say, "Sunday is a memorial of the new creation worked out for us in the sacrificial death and resurrection of Jesus." I praise God that Jesus has been raised from the dead and that we can have life in Him. However, where does the Bible say that Sunday is a memorial of the new creation through the gospel in Christ?

> Therefore if any man be in Christ, he is a new creature: old things are passed away; behold, all things are become new. (2 Corinthians 5:17)

We accept the gospel of Jesus Christ, and we accept His death as our own, when the Holy Spirit brings us to the cross of self-surrender. As our hearts are convicted of sin, righteousness, and judgment, and we surrender to Christ, His death is credited to our account. We are no longer held guilty; we have passed from death unto life. As we surrender to Christ day by day, walking with Him by faith, He begins to work out His perfect life in us. This is the new creation. That is why Revelation 14 describes a people who keep God's commandments and who fear Him and give Him glory.

This transformation comes about not from New Age religion or religious works or zeal; it is the gift of God, and it is the power of re-creation. Thus we learn that if any man is in Christ and surrendered to Christ, he becomes a new creature. "Old things are passed away, behold all things have become new." We no longer live in sin, but we seek to live for righteousness.

> For God, who commanded the light to shine out of darkness, hath shined in our hearts, to give the light of the knowledge of the glory of God in the face of Jesus Christ. (2 Corinthians 4:6)

In the above verse, we find terminology lifted right out of the book of Genesis. "And God said, Let there be light: and there was light" (Genesis 1:3). The same God who spoke light into existence now shines the light of the gospel, the light of truth, into our sin-darkened hearts. And as we accept the light of the knowledge of the glory of God as seen in Jesus, it illuminates our minds, leading us to worship and serve the true God. Salvation and the change from sinner to saint is a process of re-creation.

> And be renewed in the spirit of your mind; and that ye put on the new man, which after God is created in righteousness and true holiness. (Ephesians 4:23–24)

The God who created this world is He who, through the Lord Jesus Christ, transforms the human heart. Through the power of the gospel and the mystery of redemption, God actually re-creates us. By changing our hearts as He draws us by His love, and we become willing and desirous to serve and know Him, He begins to work out in us a renewing of the mind, and it is likened to creation.

> And be not conformed to this world: but be ye transformed by the renewing of your mind, that ye may prove what is that good, and acceptable, and perfect, will of God. (Romans 12:2)

When our minds are renewed, this leads us to want to obey God, to seek God's truth and follow it. We learned in Genesis and in Exodus that the Sabbath was given as a memorial of creation. And we find that creation is the very essence of the gospel.

The gospel is the power of God; it is the creative power of Christ. And the only day in Scripture that has been set aside as a day of worship and as a memorial of creation is the seventh day. The seventh day is a memorial of creation, showing God as the Creator, and God is also the re-creator of our hearts.

Redemption is the power of God unto salvation. It is creation once again. Thus the Sabbath is not simply a memorial of creation past; it is a memorial of creation now, in a renewed heart and mind. Revelation's judgment message is to every nation, calling all to "worship Him that made heaven, and earth, and the sea, and the fountains of waters" (Revelation 14:7). We are being called to remember the long-forgotten fourth commandment that honors God as the Creator of all and as the re-creator of our lives. It is the only Lord's Day in Scripture. The Bible is clear we are called to worship Him who made, and true worship must be based upon obedience to God's Word and law.

The Rest We Need

We have learned from Exodus 20 and from Genesis 2:2–3 that in the Sabbath there is a call to rest. But is there a rest to be experienced in the gospel?

> There remaineth therefore a rest to the people of God. For he that is entered into his rest, he also hath ceased from his own works, as God did from his. Let us labour therefore to enter into that rest, lest any man fall after the same example of unbelief. (Hebrews 4:9–11)

> So then, there is still awaiting, a full and complete Sabbath-rest reserved for the [true] people of God; for he who has once entered into [God's] rest has also ceased from [the

weariness and pain] of human labors, just as God has rested from those labors which are peculiarly His own. (Hebrews 4:9–10 AMP)

The book of Hebrews, written decades after Jesus died and ascended to heaven, declares that for the people of God, there remains a rest that we must enter into. Here is a call to a spiritual experience with God, to rest from our human endeavors to save ourselves or gain merit with God. We are to trust in God and make Jesus Christ our righteousness and the only means of our salvation, and the memorial of this rest is the Sabbath. A rest that will be fully experienced only when this corruptible puts on incorruption, and this mortal puts on immortality and death is swallowed up in life. (See 1 Corinthians 15:53–54.) Will we rest from our works even as God rested from His works on the seventh day of creation week?

Come unto me, all ye that labour and are heavy laden, and I will give you rest. Take my yoke upon you, and learn of me; for I am meek and lowly in heart: and ye shall find rest unto your souls. For my yoke is easy, and my burden is light. (Matthew 11:28–30)

One of the purposes given in the Scriptures for the Sabbath is that we would rest, and righteousness by faith is that rest. Rest from our sins, rest from our burdens, rest from the guilt and condemnation of sin, is by faith. Our rest is in Jesus Christ, who has taken our sins and in turn offers us His life.

Jesus never said that He was going to bring forth a new memorial, a new day of worship. The book of Hebrews says that the covenant comes into force after the death of the testator. Further, there can be no change in the testament or covenant after the death of the testator. (See Hebrews 9:16–17.) Therefore, Jesus would have to declare in His teachings that there would be a new memorial after His death. However, He was silent, as were the apostles. Why? Because the Sabbath unites the rest and creation memorial with God's spiritual rest through righteousness by faith.

The Sabbath has not been swept away. It is a memorial of the rest in Christ and the rest from sin. In Revelation 14, God is calling upon the world to worship Him who made; it is right out of the fourth commandment. This is why Revelation 14:12 reveals a people who keep His commandments and have the faith of Jesus and have consistent endurance, for they have found rest in Christ through union with Him. This is why they are obedient to the moral law.

Deliverance from Egypt

> And remember that thou wast a servant in the land of Egypt, and that the Lord thy God brought thee out thence through a mighty hand and by a stretched out arm: therefore the Lord thy God commanded thee to keep the sabbath day. (Deuteronomy 5:15)

Many may read the above verse and say, "See? The Sabbath is for the Jews. It was given as a memorial of their deliverance from Egypt, and this has no application to new-covenant Christians." It is true we were not physically taken out of the bondage of Egypt. However, before we make any conclusions, let us note what the Bible has to say about Egypt and what it represents.

> Woe to the rebellious children, saith the Lord, that take counsel, but not of me; and that cover with a covering, but not of my spirit, that they may add sin to sin. That walk to go down into Egypt, and have not asked at my mouth; to strengthen themselves in the strength of Pharaoh, and to trust in the shadow of Egypt! (Isaiah 30:1–2)

The rebelliousness of ancient Israel finds its parallel in the Babylon mentioned in Revelation 14. They are religious and spiritual, but they do not follow God's Word. They ignore it, despise it, or put substitutes in its place.

Israel looked to Egypt for help in times of difficulty instead of looking to the God who had sustained and delivered them in the past. They did not seek God's strength but the strength of the arm of flesh. This is the same Egyptian bondage that you and I need to be delivered from. As with ancient Israel, the people and religions of this world are rebellious in God's sight and fallen. We need to be delivered spiritually from the bondage of Egypt. That is why God is calling you and me to worship Him.

> And I will set the Egyptians against the Egyptians: and they shall fight every one against his brother, and every one against his neighbour; city against city, and kingdom against kingdom. And the spirit of Egypt shall fail in the midst thereof; and I will destroy the counsel thereof: and they shall seek to the idols, and to the charmers, and to them that have familiar spirits, and to the wizards. And the Egyptians will I give over into the hand of a cruel lord; and a fierce king shall rule over them, saith the Lord, the Lord of hosts. (Isaiah 19:2–4)

We learn in the above verse that the spirit of Egypt is manifested by separation from God; thus, there is fighting. The spirit of Egypt does not recognize the pleading and judgments of God but continues to seek after idols and counsel from demon spirits and wizards. Today we have many idols as well, much of it the idolatry of human opinion and philosophy that contradicts and denies the counsel of the Lord. We often follow New Age falsehood and ancient mysticism rather than the Word of God. Truly it can be said that many are in bondage to Babylon; it is the same spirit of Egypt.

> Woe to them that go down to Egypt for help; and stay on horses, and trust in chariots, because they are many; and in horsemen, because they are very strong; but they look not unto the Holy One of Israel, neither seek the Lord! Yet he also is wise, and will bring evil, and will not call back his words: but will arise against the house of the evildoers,

and against the help of them that work iniquity. Now the Egyptians are men, and not God; and their horses flesh, and not spirit. When the Lord shall stretch out his hand, both he that helpeth shall fall, and he that is [helped] shall fall down, and they all shall fail together. (Isaiah 31:1–3)

What was Israel trusting in? The strength of Egypt, not God's strength. Nothing has changed, for human nature doesn't change; rather, "evil men and seducers shall wax worse and worse, deceiving, and being deceived" (2 Timothy 3:13).

Israel lacked faith and had more confidence in the armies of Egypt for deliverance than in the God of creation. Jesus asked a question in His day that is a warning to us: "When the Son of man cometh, shall He find faith on the earth?" (Luke 18:8).

As with ancient Israel, many today, religious though they may be, seldom trust in God but put their trust in the help of men. It is the spirit of Egypt putting man where God should be.

And Pharaoh said, Who is the Lord, that I should obey his voice to let Israel go? I know not the Lord, neither will I let Israel go. (Exodus 5:2)

We find in the above verse that the spirit of Egypt is one of unbelief and denial of God.

And their dead bodies shall lie in the street of the great city, which spiritually [figuratively] is called Sodom and Egypt, where also our Lord was crucified. (Revelation 11:8)

We find here that Egypt represents unbelief and denial of God, rebellion, and false religion. It represents trusting in man and his wisdom. It represents backbiting and discord. It represents the cloak of carnal security and self-righteousness. Though the children of Israel had been physically removed from Egypt, yet through the centuries, in spirit, they in essence remained in Egyptian bondage, all because of unbelief. They did not have the faith of Abraham, thereby becoming a friend of God. They were never delivered from Egypt in the spiritual sense. This was especially true of those who wandered in the desert. They did not separate from the spirit of Egypt, the carnal, unconverted nature; therefore, in crisis after crisis, they sought Egypt's aid instead of turning to God.

Does the everlasting gospel deliver us here and now in the twenty-first century? It certainly does, my friend! The power of the gospel delivers us from the spirit of Egyptian bondage.

> And, having made peace through the blood of his cross, by him to reconcile all things unto himself; by him, I say, whether they be things in earth, or things in heaven. And you, that were sometime alienated and enemies in your mind by wicked works, yet now hath he reconciled in the body of his flesh through death, to present you holy and unblameable and unreproveable in his sight. (Colossians 1:20–22)

We who were alienated and enemies in our minds by wicked works, Christ has delivered through the power of the gospel. He has delivered us, as it were, from the bondage of Egypt, representing sinfulness and rebellion.

> Know ye not that the unrighteous shall not inherit the kingdom of God? Be not deceived: neither fornicators, nor idolaters, nor adulterers, nor effeminate, nor abusers of themselves with mankind, Nor thieves, nor covetous, nor drunkards, nor revilers, nor extortioners, shall inherit the kingdom of God. And such were some of you: but ye are washed, but ye are sanctified, but ye are justified in the name of the Lord Jesus, and by the Spirit of our God. (1 Corinthians 6:9–11)

These sins and many more will keep us out of the kingdom. They are the sins of unconverted human nature, the sins that are the very spirit of bondage. The only cure for these sins is the deliverance found in Jesus Christ.

For the grace of God that bringeth salvation hath appeared to all men, teaching us that, denying ungodliness and worldly lusts, we should live soberly, righteously, and godly, in this present world; Looking for that blessed hope, and the glorious appearing of the great God and our Saviour Jesus Christ. (Titus 2:11–13)

The grace of Jesus Christ delivers us from bondage. It teaches and empowers us to deny ungodliness and worldly lusts. It enables us and gives us the desire to live soberly, righteously, and godly in this present world. This was God's intent for Israel as well, if they would have lived by faith after their deliverance from Egypt. The Sabbath was not a sign to Israel of physical deliverance alone; it was to be a sign of God's power to deliver spiritually as well. And the Sabbath remains even to this day as a sign of God's power to deliver all who will accept His grace and live by faith. Further, "faith cometh by hearing, and hearing by the word of God" (Romans 10:17). In contrast, Sunday has no authority from God's Word as a sign of rest, deliverance, or sanctification.

Be ye not unequally yoked together with unbelievers: for what fellowship hath righteousness with unrighteousness? and what communion hath light with darkness? And what concord hath Christ with Belial? or what part hath he that believeth with an infidel? And what agreement hath the temple of God with idols? for ye are the temple of the living God; as God hath said, I will dwell in them, and walk in them; and I will be their God, and they shall be my people. Wherefore come out from among them, and be ye separate, saith the Lord, and touch not the unclean thing; and I will receive you, And will be a Father unto you, and ye shall be my sons and daughters, saith the Lord Almighty. (2 Corinthians 6:14–18)

God's purpose in delivering Israel from Egypt is that they would be His people. Thus is God's purpose today as He calls us out of the darkness of sin and error into the light of His love and truth. To experience the gospel is to experience separation. The children of God are no longer to live "in the vanity of their mind, having the understanding darkened, being alienated from the life of God through the ignorance that is in them, because of the blindness of their heart" (Ephesians 4:17–18).

Though citizens of the various nations of the world, the children of God are above all citizens of the kingdom of grace, and heirs of an eternal kingdom and a heavenly society. Therefore, we live not according to the dictates and standards of the world, but according to the will and Word of God. This requires separation from the ideas and philosophies and ways of man that contradict and undermine the Word of God and biblical faith. To not separate leaves us still in bondage, and the gospel will be made of no effect in our lives.

In contrast to the principle of separation, Babylon wants to join all the religions, for the betterment of human society and to bring human solidarity. Eventually all who live in this world by reward, inducement, or threat will be brought to worship in a particular way, to receive the mark of the beast. For the whole crisis at the end of time is over worship. Who has your allegiance? God's last message is calling the world to worship Him who made the heavens, the earth, the sea, and the fountains of waters.

"I will be their God and they shall be my people. Wherefore come out from among them, and be ye separate." That is part of the last message. "Come out of Babylon, My people. Come out of this religious confusion. Separate from following the commandments of men."

The Sabbath unites the memorial of physical deliverance from Egypt with the spiritual deliverance from Egypt's sin. The Sabbath is a memorial of God's power to transform us from living in the flesh and the carnal, unconverted nature to being truly the sons and daughters of God. This memorial of deliverance from Egypt is not only for the Jews thousands of years ago. For we are delivered from all that Egyptian bondage symbolizes through the power of the gospel.

A Sign of Sanctification

Why was the Sabbath given? It was given as a sign of sanctification.

> Speak thou also unto the children of Israel, saying, Verily my sabbaths ye shall keep: for it is a sign between me and you throughout your generations; that ye may know that I am the Lord that doth sanctify you. (Exodus 31:13)

> Moreover also I gave them my sabbaths, to be a sign between me and them, that they might know that I am the Lord that sanctify them. (Ezekiel 20:12)

The Sabbath did not and could not sanctify a single Jew; neither can the Sabbath sanctify anyone today. Sanctification has always been by faith in a relationship with the living God. We cannot be sanctified, changed, and transformed by any human endeavor, "for it is God which worketh in you both to will and to do of His good pleasure" (Philippians 2:13).

Are we still in need of sanctification is this gospel age? The answer is surely yes. The gospel is the means to sanctification, and the Sabbath is a memorial of this blessed experience, for each is a matter of faith and belief in God's Word. The Sabbath doesn't save you. We are saved by grace through faith in Jesus; however, the Sabbath is a memorial or reminder of the power of God to re-create, of the rest that we have in Christ and the deliverance from the bondage of our sins.

Speaking of Christ's church, Scripture says, "That He might sanctify and cleanse it with the washing of water by the word ..." (Ephesians 5:26).

We are sanctified and cleansed by obedience to God's Word. Jesus said, "Now you are clean through the words that I have spoken unto you" (John 15:3).

Jesus declared, "Sanctify them through Thy truth, Thy word is truth" (John 17:17). No sanctification is possible by following the commandments and doctrines of men, no matter how sincere we may be.

> Elect according to the foreknowledge of God the Father, through sanctification of the Spirit, unto obedience and sprinkling of the blood of Jesus Christ: Grace unto you, and peace, be multiplied. (1 Peter 1:2)

When we are truly sanctified, this experience leads us to be obedient to God's Word and God's law. This is the result of the blood of Christ shed for us and made ours by faith. As we surrender to Him, and His life becomes ours, we are accounted righteous by His grace. Further, by grace we are sanctified, set apart, and made righteous.

The Sabbath is a weekly object lesson of God's power to re-create and deliver and sanctify the soul that is yielded to Him. The Sabbath is not a shadow of ceremonies past; it is the reality and sign of a living experience of righteousness by faith. Therefore, the first angel's message concludes with a call to "worship Him who made." It is a call to keep the Lord's day, the memorial of God's creative work, in Eden and in our hearts.

May you worship God in spirit and truth this day, my friend. May you follow God's commandments in love, and may He seal you in the truth of Scripture, that you will "follow the Lamb whithersoever He goeth" (Revelation 14:4). This is my hope and prayer, in Jesus' name. Amen.

Section Two
The Denunciation

Chapter Nine

Babylon Is Fallen—The Mystery of Babylon Through the Ages, a Biblical Sketch

And there followed another angel, saying, Babylon is fallen, is fallen, that great city, because she made all nations drink of the wine of the wrath of her fornication. (Revelation 14:8)

Babylon, that Great City

Throughout the previous chapters I have been speaking about Babylon. In the next three lessons we will study the Scriptures to understand the spirit and nature of who and what Babylon is.

Revelation declares that Babylon is "fallen" from God. It has no relationship with God, though much of the spirit and the institutions that make up Babylon are religious. Babylon's description of being fallen would indicate that there are those in Babylon who once walked with God, who once knew God, who once made a profession of God. But now, it "is fallen, that great city."

In ancient times, Babylon was both a city and a kingdom. It was one of the prophetic kingdoms described in the book of Daniel. The prophets Isaiah and Jeremiah also describe the rise and fall of this kingdom.

In the book of Revelation, Babylon is not a literal city or kingdom. There are actually two cities spoken of in the book of Revelation: New Jerusalem and Babylon. New Jerusalem represents the kingdom of God and the eventual home of the redeemed. Babylon represents religious error and apostasy, and the religious and political system of the last days.

Revelation 14 reveals that there will be two classes of people. Even now each person on this planet is in the process of aligning on one side or the other. These two classes are described in Revelation as a small remnant of earth's teeming billions who truly follow God. Those who follow the religion, philosophies, and commandments of men are part of the kingdom of Babylon.

The book of Revelation reveals that these two classes of humanity will be made distinct in the final crisis of the ages, just before Jesus comes the second time in the clouds of heaven. Humanity will be divided by the messages of God. One class is described as those who are sealed with the "Father's name written in their foreheads" (Revelation 14:1). This means that by faith and the acceptance of the everlasting gospel, they have learned to love and fear God and thereby live to give Him glory. This class is settling into the truth of God with heart, mind, and strength and thus will not be moved from their allegiance to God and His word and His law. They have accepted the sign or seal of God's creative and redemptive power, as they "worship Him that made heaven, and earth, and the sea, and the fountains of waters" (Revelation 14:7).

The second class, who will make up most of this world's inhabitants, are those who will "worship the beast and his image, and receive his mark" (Revelation 14:9). These people have ignored the everlasting gospel or put in its place substitutes, the doctrines and commandments of men. This class is even now settling into falsehood, error, and sin with heart, mind, and strength, often in the name of God. All such people will come to a place where they cannot and will not be moved from their allegiance to falsehood in all its forms.

Revelation presents the world as being divided into two camps, represented by two cities: Babylon and New Jerusalem, representing truth and error, the glory of God and the glory of men.

"Babylon is fallen, is fallen, that great city, because she has made all nations drink of the wine of the wrath of her fornication" (Revelation 14:8). This fornication is spiritual idolatry. Babylon, through her doctrines and her teachings, causes the world to become spiritually drunk and mad. Therefore, many do not understand and perceive spiritual truth and thus have set aside the gospel. They have made the fear of men their fear, the commandments of men their commandments, and the religion of men their religion.

We are going to do a brief biblical overview, beginning in Genesis, and look at the spirit of rebellion and apostasy that has been developing from the earliest ages of time on this planet. The book of Revelation reveals that God will allow apostasy to fully develop before the harvest, which leads to the final separation. And that which shall separate is the sealing or marking of "him that serveth God and him that serveth him not" (Malachi 3:18).

The development of evil and the subsequent apostasy and rebellion over the ages had its beginnings with Lucifer.

Babylon's Beginnings

> Thou wast perfect in thy ways from the day that thou wast created, till iniquity was found in thee. (Ezekiel 28:15)

Here, in a few words, the Bible reveals the source of evil that has so terribly ravaged Planet Earth. The history of this planet after the fall of Lucifer has been the working of evil against good, the truth of God against error. Now, it often appears to our human eyes that evil has mostly triumphed over good. However, God has always had His witnesses for truth, and His knowledge has never been fully extinguished. God will allow Satan and his followers to fully develop their counterfeit system, known in the book of Revelation as Babylon. Babylon is a spirit that encompasses churches, governments and organizations, philosophies, and individuals. Babylon is a state of mind, a mind that is against God, either openly or more insidiously in professing to know God while in reality it rejects Him.

In essence, all that constitutes Babylon obscures the truth and character of God. In Hebrew *Babylon* means "confusion." In the New Testament it is known figuratively as "a type of tyranny."[1] This confusion and religious tyranny is the result of the rejection of God's truth as found in Scripture. This is accomplished through some form of falsehood that results in making God's truth of no effect or of no saving virtue.

The Bible reveals that in the days of Noah, which will parallel the history of the last days, they "changed the truth of God into a lie" (Romans 1:25). One way this is done is by obscuring God's truth and character so that it is not seen or properly recognized. How does this happen?

Babylon Is Blindness

> In whom the god of this world hath blinded the minds of them which believe not, lest the light of the glorious gospel of Christ, who is the image of God, should shine unto them. (2 Corinthians 4:4)

In the rejection of the gospel by substitution or distortion, by outward ignoring or despising, we become part of Babylon, and thus we become spiritually confused. Now, much of the world believes in a god or gods, or follows some kind of spirituality. Virtually the whole world in that sense is religious, but that is part of the blinding nature of Satan. He works upon all "them which believe not." Mankind believes many things, of course, but we don't believe the truth of Scripture, the truth of Christ as our Savior, the only means of salvation. This spirit of blindness is often manifested by outward rejection of God's truth and character while maintaining a form of religion.

Forgetting God, the Real Spirit Behind Babylon

> And even as they did not like to retain God in their knowledge, God gave them over to a reprobate mind, to do those things which are not convenient. (Romans 1:28)

Humanity takes pride in their supposed intellectual and spiritual enlightenment, while they are ignorant, both of the Scriptures and the Spirit of God. Not following God's Word and His Holy Spirit, mankind must have some means of quieting his conscience. This is often done by seeking religion, philosophies, and spirituality that are contrary to biblical truth.

Bible truth, known and accepted by faith, leads to a willing surrender to the Lord Jesus Christ. In such a life of faith and love, Jesus works out in the believer His righteousness, leading us to fear God and to give Him glory. In contrast, what most people desire is a method of forgetting God. This often appears as deep spirituality, enlightenment, or religious fervor. It is religion without the true God as its source. And that is the essence of Babylon. The nature of Babylon is an attempt, through religion, philosophies, and human ideas, to forget God. We may think we are honoring Him, but our hearts are far from Him.

Satan, the Hidden God or Spirit behind Babylon

How art thou fallen from heaven, O Lucifer, son of the morning! how art thou cut down to the ground, which didst weaken the nations! For thou hast said in thine heart, I will ascend into heaven, I will exalt my throne above the stars of God: I will sit also upon the mount of the congregation, in the sides of the north: I will ascend above the heights of the clouds; I will be like the most High. (Isaiah 14:12–14)

This was Satan's boast, Satan's aspiration. And here is where we find the true spirit behind Babylon. Satan is the mystery god, the hidden one behind the religion and philosophy of Babylon. He is the one leading most of mankind. And what do we find as the main characteristics of Lucifer, who has fallen from God? His experience was one of self-exaltation, self-serving, self-worshiping; this is the spirit of Lucifer. Lucifer's spirit is abundantly manifested in mankind, as everything is focused toward man while forgetting and neglecting God. Sadly, much of this neglect of God passes under the name of religion, even in professed Christianity.

For thousands of years Satan has being conditioning the mind of man, and in these last days he has been abundantly successful. He is so working in the hearts of men that his voice and spirit are heard and followed more often than the voice of God through His Word. Thus Satan, through a rebellious but religious humanity, is in the process of placing his throne first in the minds of man, then eventually he will openly appear, claiming to be God. The religions and institutions who make up Babylon are in the process of becoming Satan's congregation, by which he believes he shall be "like the most High."

> Now the serpent was more subtil than any beast of the field which the Lord God had made. And he said unto the woman, Yea, hath God said, Ye shall not eat of every tree of the garden? And the woman said unto the serpent, We may eat of the fruit of the trees of the garden: But of the fruit of the tree which is in the midst of the garden, God hath said, Ye shall not eat of it, neither shall ye touch it, lest ye die. And the serpent said unto the woman, Ye shall not surely die: For God doth know that in the day ye eat thereof, then your eyes shall be opened, and ye shall be as gods, knowing good and evil. And when the woman saw that the tree was good for food, and that it was pleasant to the eyes, and a tree to be desired to make one wise, she took of the fruit thereof, and did eat, and gave also unto her husband with her; and he did eat. (Genesis 3:1–6)

God said, "You can eat of every tree of the garden except one." Notice how the serpent distorted God's word and command. "Can it really be that God has said, You shall not eat from every tree of the garden?" (Genesis 3:1 AMP). That is not what God said.

Further, the serpent's response raised doubts as to the reliability of God. Here is found the spirit and character of Babylon. It appears to be close to the truth. It appears to offer spirituality. It seems as if it will take us to God, but it does not.

The only means by which we can recognize the lies of the serpent and the lies of Babylon is by the word of God. Eve responded to the serpent by repeating God's command, "We may eat of the fruit of the trees of the garden: but of the fruit of the tree which is in the midst of the garden, God hath said, Ye shall not eat of it, neither shall ye touch it, lest ye die." Then "the serpent said unto the woman, you shall not surely die." Here is an absolute contradiction of God's word.

Eve could have known that the serpent was lying to her if she would have given heed to God's word, but she did not. The serpent said, "For God doth know that in the day ye eat thereof, then your eyes shall be opened," another lie "and ye shall be as gods, knowing good and evil."

"And when the woman saw that the tree was good for food, and that it was pleasant to the eyes, and a tree to be desired to make one wise, she took of the fruit thereof and did eat and gave also of her husband with her and he did eat."

God warns us, "Love not the world" (1 John 2:15). The love of the world separates us from the love of God, the pride of life, the lust of the flesh, and the lust of the eyes. Love for the world will replace love for God. This is what took place with Eve.

What is the nature of the controversy revealed here in this encounter between the serpent and Eve, this early development of the Babylonian spirit that is fallen from God? We find there is a distrust of God's love. There is doubt regarding God's word and His wisdom. There is a changing of God's word and distortion of His character by the serpent and Eve's acceptance of that lie.

In this encounter in the Garden of Eden, we find humanity breaking God's commandments, followed by the acceptance of the serpent's lie that eternal life and fulfillment is available inherently in man without any need of God. The lies the devil presented to Eve, and thus to following generations, declares that sin and rebellion are really God's attempt to keep from us forbidden and mysterious knowledge that is actually for our benefit. Such knowledge is nothing more than the mystery of iniquity and will lead to the worship of man above God, and man beginning to look to himself as god. This is demonstrated as man disregards God's law and word and ignores his accountability to Him.

Further, as with Eve in her quest to seek a new and wonderful experience, so mankind lives for and often worships God largely by that which pleases the senses rather than by obedience and faithfulness to His counsel.

The apostasy described in Genesis has been increasing in mankind through the ages and is culminating in our own day. As we continue with our biblical sketch, noting how step by step this spirit of apostasy has been developing, we will look next at the story of Cain and Abel.

Babylon Is a Religion that Follows God on Human Terms

And in process of time it came to pass, that Cain brought of the fruit of the ground an offering unto the Lord. And Abel, he also brought of the firstlings of his flock and of the fat thereof. And the Lord had respect unto Abel and to his offering: But unto Cain and to his offering he had not respect. And Cain was very wroth, and his countenance fell. And the Lord said unto Cain, Why art thou wroth? and why is thy countenance fallen? If thou doest well, shalt thou not be accepted? and if thou doest not well, sin lieth at the door. And unto thee shall be his desire, and thou shalt rule over him. And Cain talked with Abel his brother: and it came to pass, when they were in the field, that Cain rose up against Abel his brother, and slew him. (Genesis 4:3–8)

God was not playing favorites in His treatment of these two brothers. The issue at hand was that Abel obeyed God while Cain followed his own path. In the same way, God, in His warnings in the New Testament against false religion and the fall of spiritual Babylon, is not arbitrarily condemning man's sincere religious beliefs and practices. Like Cain, the falsehood of Babylon appears to be religious and zealous for God; yet, like Cain, it is religion that goes its own way. It is religious belief and practice that ignores, rejects, or substitutes something in the place of the Word of God.

God was happy with Abel, for Abel in faith and love was obedient to His will. Abel placed his trust in the substitute that God would provide as an atonement for sin. The offering of the "firstling of the flock" showed this.

Cain, on the other hand, sought to go his own way. He was determined to set up human standards in the place of God's commands. Despite this, he expected God to accept him for his religious zeal, for he brought the choicest offerings from the fruits of the field to lay upon the altar.

Thus we read, "For Cain and his offering He had no respect or regard. So Cain was exceedingly angry and indignant, and he looked sad and depressed. And the Lord said to Cain, Why are you angry? And why do you look sad and depressed and dejected? If you do well, will you not be accepted? And if you do not do well, sin crouches at you door; its desire is for you, but you must master it" (Genesis 4:5–7 AMP).

Cain did not gain the victory over his willful disregard of God's word and law. Therefore, he did not gain victory over the sin in his heart. The evil surmising and disregard of God's word was a seed of evil sown in Cain's heart, and he soon reaped what he had sown. This led to the murder of his brother.

What can we learn from the lesson of these two brothers regarding the apostasy and religious rebellion that finds its counterpart in the religion of Babylon? What are the issues? Salvation in human works: I can approach God my way; I can worship God my way. There are many roads to God. I don't have to be strictly obedient to what He has said.

Apparently Cain was a religious man, for he brought an offering to God. But it wasn't according to God's truth; it was not according to God's commandments. He had religious zeal and a desire for form and ceremony; however, he disregarded God's word. That is the nature of Babylon, whether professedly Christian, Catholic, non-Christian or pagan. "Mystery Babylon" at the end of time incorporates all these religions and thus most of the world.

We find in the story of Cain and Abel how the commandments of men are cherished above God's revealed will. Then we find religious persecution. The children of disobedience persecuting the children of God because they will not join them in religious apostasy and rebellion.

That is what the book of Revelation reveals as well. Babylon, a system of worship in apostasy, will draw in the kings of the earth, the merchants of the earth, and the religions of the earth, and will eventually persecute the true children of God.

The Spirit of Babylonian Rebellion
Before the Flood Is Repeated in Our Day

> And God saw that the wickedness of man was great in the earth, and that every imagination of the thoughts of his heart was only evil continually. (Genesis 6:5)

Here we find a situation that Jesus said will be repeated at the end of time. (See Luke 17:26.) God looked upon the world and saw that the wickedness of man was great in the earth, and that his imagination, his purpose, his desires, and the thoughts of his heart were only evil continually. What is the nature of evil? How do we define evil? Evil is everything that is contrary to the will and the word of God and His law.

> For the wrath of God is revealed from heaven against all ungodliness and unrighteousness of men, who hold the truth in unrighteousness. (Romans 1:18)

What happened in the days of Noah is happening again today. They held the truth, but it was unrighteousness. The religions of Babylon pervert the truth; in other words, they mix truth with error. By sin and compromise and disregard of God's Word, they make the truth of no effect.

> Because that, when they knew God, they glorified him not as God, neither were thankful; but became vain in their imaginations, and their foolish heart was darkened. (Romans 1:21)

The first angel's message is "Fear God, and give glory to Him" (Revelation 14:7). The people and religions that make up Babylon often claim to know God and may even claim to serve Him; however, they do not glorify Him. This is because they misrepresent His character and the truth of His word.

> Professing themselves to be wise, they became fools, and changed the glory of the uncorruptible God into an image made like to corruptible man. (Romans 1:22–23)

The above verse describes what man is doing today in science and politics, education and the arts, and indeed at every level of society and even with religion. Babylon is setting before the people a corrupt understanding of God. This understanding of God is made in the likeness of men. We make God and His truth like ourselves.

> Who changed the truth of God into a lie, and worshipped and served the creature more than the Creator, who is blessed for ever. Amen. (Romans 1:25)

Virtually all religion has some truth; therefore, some think all religions must eventually lead to God. However, it is not truth that commends most religions. Rather, it is the error that makes truth of no effect, which condemns them. To follow error rather than the truth will cause us to serve the creature, which is man's idea about God, rather than serving the true Creator God.

> And even as they did not like to retain God in their knowledge, God gave them over to a reprobate mind, to do those things which are not convenient. (Romans 1:28)

Eventually God is going to step back and leave us to the sin and rebellion we have chosen. He is going to give us up, just like He gave the people up in the days of Noah. They became so wicked, so perverse, so rebellious in nature that God said, "I can do nothing more for you." That is what is described in the book of

Revelation. God is going to give us up; He is going to allow the seven last plagues to fall on us because we have so fully rejected Him. Yet much of this rejection is done in His name, in the name of religion. That's what makes the final deception so deadly, for it turns the truth of God into a lie.

What are the principles that are revealed in Genesis 6:5 and again in Romans chapter 1, which parallel the spirit of Babylon today? The plans and purposes of men had no thought of God in them, for His word and law did not guide them. Though claiming to know God, they do not give Him glory; therefore they became unthankful toward God in their hearts, and their minds became spiritually dark by the rejection of truth.

They changed the character of God into a representation of themselves, as man's philosophies and ideas took precedence over God's Word. They changed God's truth into a lie. They called light darkness and darkness light. They worshiped the gifts of God more than the Giver.

As we go through the Bible, we see the development of error, sin, and apostasy that has been transpiring for centuries, even millenniums. It will culminate in a grand apostasy at the end of time. This is why God gives this message of warning, "Babylon is fallen, is fallen." Our only safety will be to give heed to the "voice from heaven, saying, Come out of her, My people, that ye be not partakers of her sins, and that ye receive not of her plagues" (Revelation 18:4).

Babylon After the Flood

> And Cush begat Nimrod: he began to be a mighty one in the earth. He was a mighty hunter before the Lord: wherefore it is said, Even as Nimrod the mighty hunter before the Lord. And the beginning of his kingdom was Babel, and Erech, and Accad, and Calneh, in the land of Shinar. And they said, Go to, let us build us a city and a tower, whose top may reach unto heaven; and let us make us a

name, lest we be scattered abroad upon the face of the whole earth. (Genesis 10:8–10; 11:4)

After the flood Nimrod began to draw other men to himself in the place of God. Here we see the beginning of the mystery of iniquity, in which man, instead of being accountable to God, becomes accountable to other men. The beginning of Nimrod's kingdom was Babel. He then established many other cities, trying to draw the people into the cities, where they could be more completely controlled and manipulated.

Now, once again, in the early twenty-first century, the majority of mankind lives in urban areas. City life certainly provides many apparent benefits. However, in the final crisis, having the majority of earth's inhabitants in the cities will make it much easier to draw the majority into conformity, willingly or not, and into the final confederacy of rebellion against God and His law.

After the flood the people began to build a city and a tower. The idea was that the top would reach unto heaven. With most of the descendents of Noah, we see early on a rejection of God's word. They were concerned about another flood. God said He would never send a flood again to destroy the earth. (See Genesis 9:15.) However, many disbelieved God. They wanted to make a name for themselves instead of glorifying Him. These Babel builders were determined to keep their communities united in one body, and to establish a kingdom that would eventually embrace the whole earth, a new world order.

This magnificent tower, reaching to heaven, was intended to stand as a monument to the power and wisdom of its builders. However, there is only one thing that is eternal, only one thing that is lasting in this world, and that is the word of God.

The whole undertaking was designed to exalt the pride of its builders, to turn the minds of future generations away from God and lead them into idolatry. This confederacy was founded in rebellion; it was a kingdom established for self-exaltation. It was a kingdom in which God was to have no rule or honor.

What can we learn from this narrative in Genesis that will help us see the parallels in today's age of apostasy? We find that God's word and His authority was supplanted, exalting human authority and looking to men for guidance and protection. There was a plan to develop a universal government or religion that was to replace the knowledge of the true God. There was self-exaltation, an exalting of the laws of nature above nature's God. Further, man and his institutions were put in the place of God.

Lessons from the Babylonian Captivity

The word that came to Jeremiah concerning all the people of Judah in the fourth year of Jehoiakim the son of Josiah king of Judah, that was the first year of Nebuchadrezzar king of Babylon; The which Jeremiah the prophet spake unto all the people of Judah, and to all the inhabitants of Jerusalem, saying, From the thirteenth year of Josiah the son of Amon king of Judah, even unto this day, that is the three and twentieth year, the word of the Lord hath come unto me, and I have spoken unto you, rising early and speaking; but ye have not hearkened. And the Lord hath sent unto you all his servants the prophets, rising early and sending them; but ye have not hearkened, nor inclined your ear to hear. They said, Turn ye again now every one from his evil way, and from the evil of your doings, and dwell in the land that the Lord hath given unto you and to your fathers for ever and ever: And go not after other gods to serve them, and to worship them, and provoke me not to anger with the works of your hands; and I will do you no hurt.

Yet ye have not hearkened unto me, saith the Lord; that ye might provoke me to anger with the works of your hands to your own hurt. Therefore thus saith the Lord of hosts; Because ye have not heard my words, Behold, I will send and take all the families of the north, saith the Lord, and Nebuchadrezzar the king of Babylon, my servant, and will bring them against this land, and against the inhabitants thereof, and against all these nations round about, and will utterly destroy them, and make them an astonishment, and an hissing, and perpetual desolations. (Jeremiah 25:2–9)

God allowed ancient Babylon to overrun Israel and the surrounding nations. Why did this take place? Because they would not listen to His word through His prophets. The world's people and their religions are rejecting the word of God today and are thereby fallen. Ancient Israel rejected or neglected the word of God, as is seen in their continual disobedience. This led them into exalting the commandments and the religion of men, and into physical captivity to Babylon. And so it will be repeated at the end of time.

All those who reject, neglect, or change God's Word are going to end up in Babylon, even as the professed people of God in Israel's day. If we neglect God's word and substitute human commandments and self-will for following God, we will come under Babylonian captivity, as surely as the Jews did. In fact Israel was in subjection, to one degree or another, to all four of the great prophetic powers mentioned in Daniel. And why? Because of disobedience. Why are the earth's inhabitants becoming drunk through Babylon's wine of fornication, which is spiritual adultery? Because of disobedience—having other gods before the Lord.

We are taking a broad sweep of the Bible, looking at the nature of apostasy, which will climax in the end days with the mark of the beast and the rise of Mystery Babylon. We now come down to Jesus' day and the religion that prevailed at that time, the religion of the scribes and the Pharisees. What was that like?

Babylon Places Form and Ritual and the Traditions of Men In the Place of True Conversion

For I say unto you, That except your righteousness shall exceed the righteousness of the scribes and Pharisees, ye shall in no case enter into the kingdom of heaven. (Matthew 5:20)

The scribes and Pharisees were very religious and zealous with their forms and ceremonies, yet they rejected God's word. In the end they also rejected Christ, who was the very focus of the sacrificial service. They rejected God Himself, which is the nature of apostasy in all ages. The religion of the scribes and Pharisees was a religion of human works, human opinions, and the doctrines and religions of men in the place of true faith. The shocking words of Christ to the people of His day declared that their religious experience must be of a different nature than that of their leaders. (See Matthew 5:20.) And thus it is today. We are called to "follow the Lamb whithersoever He goeth" (Revelation 14:4), rather than religious teachers and leaders and organized religion, much of which will lead us into Babylonian captivity.

> But woe unto you, scribes and Pharisees, hypocrites! for ye shut up the kingdom of heaven against men: for ye neither go in yourselves, neither suffer ye them that are entering to go in. (Matthew 23:13)

The result of the religion of the scribes and Pharisees was, in effect if not intent, to obstruct the way to the kingdom of heaven and salvation. Though sincere, they made the way of God and the truth of God obscure. By placing the interpretations of men above divine revelation, they distorted the truth of God and made it dark and mysterious. Often, those who were impressed by the Spirit and Word of God, and who sought the liberty of righteousness by faith, were hindered and blocked. Religious leaders sought to bind those seeking liberty with the cords of human religion.

> Woe unto you, scribes and Pharisees, hypocrites! for ye make clean the outside of the cup and of the platter, but within they are full of extortion and excess. (Matthew 23:25)

The everlasting gospel renews us in the spirit of our minds by the power of re-creation. (See Ephesians 4:23-24.) However, the religion of the scribes and Pharisees, which finds its counterpart in the modern religion of Babylon, merely makes clean the outside of the cup. While religion presents much that is attractive, perhaps even spiritual, many followers remain unconverted. Jesus said that unless a man is born again he shall not see, perceive, or experience the kingdom of God. (See John 3:3.)

> Woe unto you, scribes and Pharisees, hypocrites! for ye are like unto whited sepulchres, which indeed appear beautiful outward, but are within full of dead men's bones, and of all uncleanness. (Matthew 23:27)

As we look upon the ritual and ceremony, the exuberance and the song and the praise found in the religions of the world, it looks wonderful—much as it was in the days of Christ. The religion prevailing in His day is the same as in our own day. It appears "beautiful outward, but ... within [it is] full of dead men's bones, and of all uncleanness." In the book of Revelation, Jesus declares that the same religion will prevail just before He comes. Babylon, and thus its people, religions, and institutions, will "become the habitation of devils, and the hold of every foul spirit, and a cage of every unclean and hateful bird" (Revelation 18:2).

Despite Christ's assessment, Babylon as an organization, which also reflects to some degree the attitude of her adherents and the leaders of the world that unite with her, "saith in her heart, I sit a queen, and am no widow, and shall see no sorrow" (Revelation 18:7).

In some parts of the world, the most beautiful landscapes can be found in cemeteries. But under the grass, behind all the beauty, is death and decay. Thus it is with the religions that make up Babylon; it is filled with death. And all who are part of Babylon, unless they repent and come out of her, will experience eternal death.

> Then the Pharisees and scribes asked him, Why walk not thy disciples according to the tradition of the elders, but eat bread with unwashen hands? He answered and said unto them, Well hath Esaias prophesied of you hypocrites,

as it is written, This people honoureth me with their lips, but their heart is far from me. (Mark 7:5–6)

What is the religion of Babylon, which was also the religion of the scribes and Pharisees? It is the traditions of men that are exalted above the Word of God. With our songs and prayer and praise, we honor God. Yet the heart is not guided by God and thus cannot truly fear Him and give glory to Him.

Those who follow Christ will not be "defiled with women; for they are virgins" (Revelation 14:4). The women represent false religion and the philosophies of men. In contrast, the people of God have experienced the power of the gospel, the power of Jesus' love.

In the religion of the scribes and Pharisees, human creeds supplanted the Word of God. It was a religion that sought God's favor and merit by the works they could do. The religion of the leaders was based on human righteousness rather than righteousness by faith. Thus there was no power of love in the heart, leading to true service and obedience. The priesthood was separate; their goal was to keep believers in subjection to themselves. While outwardly religious they were inwardly corrupt. They rejected the truth, and by precept and doctrine, threat and intimidation, they kept the truth from others also.

Apostasy in the Church: A Sign of the Rise of Babylon

This know also, that in the last days perilous times shall come. For men shall be lovers of their own selves, covetous, boasters, proud, blasphemers, disobedient to parents, unthankful, unholy, Without natural affection, trucebreakers, false accusers, incontinent, fierce, despisers of those that are good, Traitors, heady, highminded, lovers of pleasures more than lovers of God; Having a form of godliness, but denying the power thereof: from such turn away. (2 Timothy 3:1–5)

Paul declared that the last days would be dangerous times. While we are familiar with the dangers of the development and proliferation of weapons of mass destruction, environmental degradation, terrorism, war, economic disparity, and disease, these are not the dangers the Bible says we should be most concerned with. These problems and more find their root cause in the sinful heart of man. It is spiritual danger that should concern us most, the falling away from truth and sound doctrine and true faith. We have come to a time where the ideology and practices of the church often parallel that which is in the world. "They will maintain a façade of 'religion,' but their conduct will deny its validity" (2 Timothy 3:5 Phillips).

Apostate religion often claims the name of Jesus and the name of God, but it has substituted ritual, mysticism, marketing, psychology, and the doctrines of devils in the place of God's Word. Much of religion is a rejection of the truth, while seeking the world and its pleasures. The spirit of Babylon, which is fallen from God, is a deviation from the path of virtue taught by Christ. It is man worshiping human ideas instead of God.

Babylon Deceives the World

> And I saw three unclean spirits like frogs come out of the mouth of the dragon, and out of the mouth of the beast, and out of the mouth of the false prophet. For they are the spirits of devils, working miracles, which go forth unto the kings of the earth and of the whole world, to gather them to the battle of that great day of God Almighty. (Revelation 16:13–14)

Revelation 16 reveals the threefold religious union that makes up the final confederacy of Babylon. This union leads the world in revolt against God through the false philosophies and teachings of men. It will be a unity of religion based on social and human needs, not on God's truth. Miracles will be used to establish and confirm the deception. This is already developing right before our eyes. This system of the beast, the dragon, and the false prophet will draw the world's inhabitants into deception, to receive a lie. And why do people receive a lie? Because they did not have a love of the truth; rather, they take pleasure in unrighteousness. (See 2 Thessalonians 2:10–12.)

The entire world will eventually give allegiance to the system of Mystery Babylon. This allegiance will extend to the world government, controlled by this woman.

Economic prosperity will be the promise to the followers of Mystery Babylon, while economic boycott and persecution will be the fate of all those who, for conscience's sake, cannot follow the beast or receive his mark. The followers of false religion will persecute the true children of God. Jesus has told us, "The time cometh, that whosoever killeth you will think that he doeth God service. And these things will they do unto you, because they have not known the Father, nor Me" (John 16:2–3).

What will be Babylon's final end? "And the great city was divided into three parts, and the cities of the nations fell: and great Babylon came in remembrance before God, to give unto her the cup of the wine of the fierceness of His wrath" (Revelation 16:19).

The system of Babylon and its myriad religions may seem to be the way to God. However, God's people are different. They walk the narrow road, the road that Jesus said was difficult to enter. (See Matthew 7:13–14.) God is not trying to keep us out of heaven and away from eternal life. Rather, the narrow road to heaven can only be walked with Jesus. And we can gain entrance to that narrow road only through the blood of Jesus Christ, leading to self-surrender and obedience. In contrast, the broad road leads to Babylon, with room for whatever you wish to believe and practice.

Babylon's final end is destruction. The ultimate end of God's people is eternal life. The message therefore to separate from Babylon is a life-and-death message. Obedience to God's Word and His law is the dividing line between those who will follow the apostate principalities and powers of earth and those who truly worship Him.

The New Jerusalem is not only symbolic; it is also literal. Those who follow Jesus with heart. mind and soul, and who surrender to

Him, will experience the earth made new. The residents of New Jerusalem will have been made citizens of that great kingdom by the blood of Jesus Christ through the new covenant.

> And I saw a new heaven and a new earth: for the first heaven and the first earth were passed away; and there was no more sea. And I John saw the holy city, new Jerusalem, coming down from God out of heaven, prepared as a bride adorned for her husband. And I heard a great voice out of heaven saying, Behold, the tabernacle of God is with men, and he will dwell with them, and they shall be his people, and God himself shall be with them, and be their God. And God shall wipe away all tears from their eyes; and there shall be no more death, neither sorrow, nor crying, neither shall there be any more pain: for the former things are passed away. (Revelation 21:1–4)

There are many tears shed in this world: tears of pain, grief, sorrow, and disappointment. As we consider what sin is doing to this planet and to God, there are many tears to shed. But praise God, He is going to wipe away all tears from our eyes, and there shall be "no more death, neither sorrow, nor crying, neither shall there be any more pain." Physical, emotional, and spiritual pain will all be gone, "for the former things are passed away."

"And He that sat upon the throne said, Behold, I make all things new" (Revelation 21:5). Only those who are made new, Jesus said, shall experience and see this kingdom. (See John 3:3.)

"And He said unto me, It is done. I am Alpha and Omega, the beginning and the end I will give unto him that is athirst of the fountain of the water of life freely" (Revelation 21:6). Soon all the things foretold in Revelation shall be accomplished. We are nearing the end of this world's history. Where will you stand? Who will have your allegiance? This is the vital and all-important question.

A Call to Separate from Babylon

> And after these things I saw another angel come down from heaven, having great power; and the earth was lightened with his glory. And he cried mightily with a strong voice, saying, Babylon the great is fallen, is fallen, and is become the habitation of devils, and the hold of every foul spirit, and a cage of every unclean and hateful bird. For all nations have drunk of the wine of the wrath of her fornication, and the kings of the earth have committed fornication with her, and the merchants of the earth are waxed rich through the abundance of her delicacies. (Revelation 18:1–3)

Babylon will end up being wholly filled with death, separated from God, looking beautiful but inwardly full of destruction and dead men's bones. This includes individuals of all nations. Is it you? What are you drinking today? Have you drunk of the wine of the wrath of fornication? Or are you drinking the word of life? Are you receiving spiritual life day by day, moment by moment, from Jesus because you are surrendering to Him? Or are you partaking of the spirit of the age, the spirit of Babylon?

> And I heard another voice from heaven, saying, Come out of her, my people, that ye be not partakers of her sins, and that ye receive not of her plagues. For her sins have reached unto heaven, and God hath remembered her iniquities. (Revelation 18:4–5)

God is going to bring Babylon to accountability. While this judgment is yet in the future, the message that Babylon is fallen is for the present. This fall from truth and God will deepen until heaven declares, "We would have healed Babylon, but she is not healed: forsake her, … for her judgment reacheth unto heaven, and is lifted up even to the skies" (Jeremiah 51:9). We must make our separation now, taking a stand for God and for His truth, separating from the corruptions of this world, the corruption of our own hearts. God will remember Babylon's iniquities and reward her accordingly. He will also remember and reward His people.

I pray that God will give you the grace and the willingness to choose Him. The true and everlasting God loved the world so much that "He gave His only begotten Son, so that whoever believeth in Him should not perish, but have everlasting life" (John 3:16). Will that be your experience today, my friend? I pray it will be.

Endnotes

1. James Strong LL.D., S.T.D., *Strong's Exhaustive Concordance* (Grand Rapids, Michigan: Baker Book House, 1987).
2. To learn more about these prophetic chapters in Daniel, secure the free e-book or order the bound book *Let Daniel and Revelation Speak* at www.inspirationspeaks.com.

Chapter Ten

Babylon Is Fallen—A Personal Application

A nd there followed another angel saying, Babylon is fallen, is fallen, that great city, because she made all nations drink of the wine of the wrath of her fornication. (Revelation 14:8)

Babylon takes in virtually every individual and every religion that has no connection with the true God, who has not made Jesus Savior and Lord. Babylon and all it religious adherents seek heaven and God. While this sincerity is commendable, many are seeking wrongly. God spoke to ancient Israel, "O ye sons of men, how long will ye turn My glory into shame? how long will ye love vanity, and seek after leasing?" (Psalm 4:2). These words still ring true today. Through the messages of Revelation 14, God is asking, "How long shall man love that which is empty, vain, and useless?" Most of mankind worships and follows various religions or ideologies, yet it is seeking after leasing which means "a lie, untruth, falsehood, a deceptive thing."[1] Today Babylon is fallen, and it continues to fall further away from God because of the rejection of the first angel's message.

Babylon's religious organizations are made up of the beast, the dragon, the false prophet, and every individual on this planet is affiliated with or influenced by one of these components, except for those the Bible calls "the remnant." The remnant are those people who follow the Lamb, represented in Revelation 14:1–5, 12. They are not defiled by the corrupt religious systems of this world. They have no guile in their mouths. They are honest and true before God and man.

To be part of Babylon involves not only our membership or affiliation. It goes deeper than that, for we can be part of Babylon by our thoughts, motives, and actions. Babylon is ultimately the spirit of falsehood, sin, and the ways of man, in contrast to the will and word of God. Every unconverted individual, regardless of social or economic status, is on one common platform. They are all part of Babylon in God's sight and are fallen from Him.

Men regularly turn from one doctrine, philosophy, or religion to another. People may think they are Christians, but they know nothing of the meaning of the words "a new heart also will I give you" (Ezekiel 36:26). Accepting new theories does not bring true spiritual life to anyone, nor does uniting with a religion or a church, even if the church or religion is correct.

Further, connection with a church cannot take the place of conversion. A person may be a church member and a professed Christian, and may appear to work earnestly, performing religious duties from year to year, and still be unconverted. If we are unconverted, having never experienced the everlasting gospel, not having known Jesus as Lord and Savior, we are fallen from God.

You may call yourself a follower of any one of numerous spiritual ideas and religions, from Animist to Zoroastrian. However, if you are not converted, you are part of Babylon, fallen from God.

Religious teachers may draw thousands of followers yet be far from the true God and not born again. A religious leader may be exalted to the height of human greatness, but if he has never experienced the inward work of grace that transforms the character, he is still part of Babylon.

Many religious leaders, even in the Christian world, are popular and have a great name. They are in Babylon because they have rejected the gospel or perverted it. They cannot call the world to fear God and give glory to Him. They have put something in the place of the gospel and above the Word of God.

In contrast, God's remnant, scattered throughout the globe, follow Jesus. Therefore, they love and obey God and give glory to Him. This fear of God, which is the result of the everlasting gospel, leads the remnant to reverence God and love Him enough to obey Him, having a consistency to do what is right by the faith of Jesus.

Apart from that experience, every individual, religion, and institution is part of Babylon; it is fallen from God.

There is no salvation or eternal life in Babylon. God declares in Revelation 18, "Come out of her, My people." God in mercy sees those who follow Him in sincerity with the light they have. However, salvation requires a separation. Thus God calls and warns.

Even those who profess to be Christians need more than an intellectual belief in the truth if they are to be saved. For the truth must transform to have any saving virtue. When we accept truth only with the intellect, while our hearts and lives remain unchanged, even though our beliefs may be accompanied by form and ceremony, we are still in Babylonian captivity. However, when the truth is received into the heart, and we live by the grace of God and are obedient to His law and to His Word, we are set free.

> For the grace of God that bringeth salvation hath appeared to all men, Teaching us that, denying ungodliness and worldly lusts, we should live soberly, righteously, and godly, in this present world; Looking for that blessed hope, and the glorious appearing of the great God and our Saviour Jesus Christ; Who gave himself for us, that he might redeem us from all iniquity, and purify unto himself a peculiar people, zealous of good works. (Titus 2:11–14)

When God's grace is at work in our lives, it teaches, motivates, and leads us to deny ungodliness and worldly lusts. This is the experience that will separate us from Babylon. Without this experience of grace, we are part of the great Babylonian spirit of rebellion, which is the prominent characteristic of mankind in these last days.

In the pages that follow we will look at what it means to be fallen. We need to examine ourselves and see if we are fallen from God. You can be a good Baptist, a devout Hindu, or a zealous Muslim and still be fallen from God. Such people may claim to love God and to be seeking Him. However, if we are not partakers of the grace of God, we are fallen; we are in Babylon, and we have no part of God and no part of salvation. This is true regardless of our zeal or our profession of religion.

Fallen Because of Unbelief and Departing from God

> Let us labour therefore to enter into that rest, lest any man fall after the same example of unbelief. (Hebrews 4:11)

The apostle Paul said that the love of God constrained him, motivated him, and pushed him along. (See 2 Corinthians 5:14–15.) That is what it means to labor and to enter into rest. God is not looking for people who will work their way to heaven. However, when we experience the grace of God, a love develops in our hearts that cherishes God's presence and the counsel of His Word. We are to labor to enter into that rest by maintaining this connection with God. Failure to do so because of carelessness or sin will lead us into a fallen condition.

How do we become fallen? Unbelief. The writer of Hebrews says the Jewish people disbelieved God often. There was nothing particularly evil about them. They were simply a reflection of you and me, of humanity. We need to learn from the failures of the Jewish people, not because they were worse than we are, but because we are just like them. Though their example of falling in unbelief occurred long ago, humanity has not changed. They fell from God and His truth, eventually leading them into literal Babylonian captivity. They didn't really believe and trust God as they claimed to.

> Wherefore I was grieved with that generation, and said, They do alway err in their heart; and they have not known my ways. (Hebrews 3:10)

The word *err* means "to be led aside from the path of virtue, to go astray, sin, or fall away from the truth."[2] This is the experience of many. Going astray from the truth and law of God leads to a fall, and many are fallen. Though they claim to seek God, they do not know His ways. God is calling, "Let the wicked forsake his way, and the unrighteous man his thoughts: and let him return unto the Lord, and He will have mercy upon him; and to our God, for He will abundantly pardon" (Isaiah 55:7).

Man believes he can go astray from God's commandments and truth and still have salvation. However, God says through the prophet, "My thoughts are not your thoughts, neither are your ways My ways, saith the Lord. For as the heavens are higher than the earth, so are My ways higher than your ways, and My thoughts than your thoughts" (Isaiah 55:8–9). It is to His higher way that God is calling man.

What is God's way from which we so often go astray and which leaves us fallen from Him? "Yet the Lord pleads with you still: Ask where the good road is, the godly paths you used to walk in, in the days of long ago. Travel there, and you will find rest for your souls. But you reply, 'No, that is not the road we want!'" (Jeremiah 6:16 TLB).

> Take heed, brethren, lest there be in any of you an evil heart of unbelief, in departing from the living God. But exhort one another daily, while it is called today; lest any of you be hardened through the deceitfulness of sin. (Hebrews 3:12–13)

To be fallen from God and living in unbelief means we do not accept God's Word, or we claim to know it but do not live by it. Our hearts can become hardened in unbelief if we are deceived by sin. We do not need to leave religion or stop professing belief in God. On the contrary, many remain religious while their hearts disbelieve the truth of God. They become insensitive to the drawing of God and to His Spirit's work of reproof.

To be deceived by sin is to become familiar with it, to accept it and be comfortable with it. Television is one of Satan's greatest tools to make men at ease with sin, for in being entertained we become desensitized to evil. The worldview presented by the media is largely in contradiction to God's Word. This is why Jesus warned us, "Because iniquity shall abound, the love of many shall wax cold. But he that shall endure unto the end, the same shall be saved" (Matthew 24:12–13).

Entire denominations, many churches and fellowships, and hundreds of millions of religious people are being deceived by sin. We are living in sin, cherishing sin, and excusing sin, all the while claiming to believe in God. But the Bible is clear; there is no salvation in sin. There is salvation only in being delivered from sin by the blood of Jesus Christ and empowered by His grace so that we might overcome. If we are not experiencing the gospel and overcoming grace, then regardless of our religious profession, we are fallen. We are part of this great confusion of religion called Babylon.

God, in love and mercy, calls us to repent of our sins, to come out of the confusion of Babylon so that we might be delivered. To experience the everlasting gospel, leading us to fear God and give glory to Him. This leads us to "be blameless and harmless, the sons of God, without rebuke, in the midst of a crooked and perverse nation, among whom ye shine as lights in the world" (Philippians 2:15).

> While it is said, Today if ye will hear his voice, harden not your hearts, as in the provocation. For some, when they had heard, did provoke: howbeit not all that came out of Egypt by Moses. But with whom was he grieved forty years? was it not with them that had sinned, whose carcases fell in the wilderness? And to whom sware he that they should not enter into his rest, but to them that believed not? So we see that they could not enter in because of unbelief. (Hebrews 3:15–19)

Millions of people were delivered by God from Egyptian captivity, yet failed to enter the Promised Land. Sadly, this history will be repeated. The majority of this world's religious people, desirous of what they call heaven and eternal life, will fall short of their hope. Why? Because they have fallen in unbelief.

Most of the world has a variety of religious philosophies and ideologies. However, those things will not take anyone to heaven.

The Bible doesn't say that the way to heaven is being religious, having the right philosophy, believing whatever you want. The way to heaven is a narrow road that passes through one door. Jesus said, "I am the door. No one comes to the Father except by Me." (See John 10:9; 14:6.) God isn't being exclusive or narrow-minded. There simply is just one means of salvation.

You and I, regardless of the religious profession we make or the delusive philosophies we hold regarding God and eternity, are fallen if we think, live, and act in unbelief of God's Word and commands. We, like the ancient Hebrews, will find ourselves one day deprived of the Promised Land of eternity and heaven, "which God hath prepared for them that love Him" (1 Corinthians 2:9).

Today we must hear God's voice to repent, allowing the measure of faith He has placed in every human heart to grow. This takes place by listening to His Spirit's voice of reproof and invitation, and giving heed to His Word. It is only by grace we are saved through faith, and lifted up from our fall. It is through God's mercy that we are made "heirs of the kingdom which He hath promised to them that love Him" (James 2:5).

> For unto us was the gospel preached, as well as unto them: but the word preached did not profit them, not being mixed with faith in them that heard it. (Hebrews 4:2)

These religious people had the word of God preached to them. However, it did not profit them, because it was not mixed with faith. Today many people in the world preach and are propagating the Christian gospel. Many more are promoting various religious views of what they believe to be spiritual truth and the way to eternal life. However, they do not have saving faith. This is demonstrated most clearly by the fact that they are not being sanctified and cleansed "with the washing of water by the word" (Ephesians 5:26).

Jesus gave a startling warning in Matthew 7. He declared that, at the end of time, there will be those who cry out, "Lord, Lord open unto us, we are your children. Jesus, we have done wonderful works in your name." And yet the most disappointing words that could ever be heard are spoken, as Jesus says, "I don't know you. You are workers of iniquity and did not do My Father's will. I never knew you: depart from Me." (See Matthew 7:21–23.)

We can propagate the gospel and declare God's Word, but if this does not lead to obedience in love, we are fallen from God; we are in Babylon.

Hardness of Heart Makes Us a Part of Babylon

Blessed (happy, fortunate and to be envied) is the man who reverently and worshipfully fears [the Lord] at all times [regardless of circumstances], but he who hardens his heart will fall into calamity. (Proverbs 28:14 AMP)

The person who does not reverence and worship God does not seek to follow Him in all the circumstances of life. Hardening our hearts means not being receptive to the Word of God and to God's Spirit. We can be religious and still have hard hearts.

The only cure for hardness of heart, which causes us to be fallen from God, is the gospel. The prophet Ezekiel describes the intervention of God in the life of a person and the effect it will have.

Then will I sprinkle clean water upon you, and ye shall be clean: from all your filthiness, and from all your idols, will I cleanse you. A new heart also will I give you, and a new spirit will I put within you: and I will take away the stony heart out of your flesh, and I will give you an heart of flesh. And I will put my spirit within you, and cause you to walk in my statutes, and ye shall keep my judgments, and do them. (Ezekiel 36:25–27)

Unless the above experience becomes ours, we are fallen. This experience was God's purpose for all those He called from Babylonian captivity and exile. It is still His purpose for those who will come out of spiritual Babylon today.

The Workers of Iniquity Are Fallen

There are the workers of iniquity fallen: they are cast down, and shall not be able to rise. (Psalm 36:12)

The working of iniquity, which is immorality and a departure from moral rectitude, constitutes the fall of Babylon, and perhaps is our fall as well. Those who are living lives of lawlessness, who are not obedient to God's moral law, who excuse sin, live in iniquity; they are fallen from God.

O Israel, return unto the Lord thy God; for thou hast fallen by thine iniquity. (Hosea 14:1)

Israel claimed to serve God. Israel was chosen by God. You could say Israel was the true church. However, belonging to the right organization, having the proper lineage or connection with the true God through your ancestors, means nothing. Having the right profession or religion means nothing in God's sight. Israel had all this and more. Israel had the word of God. Prophets were sent from God. The sanctuary system that was given to them was the gospel in symbols. Yet even with all this, Israel was fallen from God just as Babylon is fallen from God.

The reason Israel was fallen is the same reason many who are religious are fallen today. Even if we claim to be religious, we, like Israel, are fallen in God's sight because of our iniquity. Acceptance by man or his religions does not prove our acceptance with God. Many people in Babylon have heard the everlasting gospel and claim to believe it. However, because they are living in sin, even excusing sin, and perhaps as organizations institutionalizing sin, they are fallen from God.

Those who believe that they are saved by their works are fallen and therefore part of Babylon.

Those Who Seek to Gain Merit with God by Their Works are Fallen

> Christ is become of no effect unto you, whosoever of you are justified by the law; ye are fallen from grace. (Galatians 5:4)

Some may think they can be saved by keeping God's law, or by doing certain things. They may think that religious service or zeal merits something in God's sight. They are sadly mistaken. We are saved by grace, God's unmerited favor, not through anything we do or our goodness; salvation is the gift of God. (See Ephesians 2:8–9.)

Many individuals are zealously religious, desirous to serve God, and claim to love Him. Yet they are trying to gain merit with God rather than accepting His grace. This leads to the mistaken idea that when their life comes to an end, if they have done more good than bad, God is going to grant them eternal life. Such ideas lead us away from God.

Some people make no formal profession of religion. They believe that God will accept them based on the fact that, in their assessment, their lives were more good than bad. However, that is based on their own ideas and vain hope rather than God's standard.

With all such ideologies we are fallen from grace. It is only by grace that we are saved. True grace instructs us and enables us to "live soberly, righteously, and godly, in this present world" (Titus 2:12).

> But Israel, which followed after the law of righteousness, hath not attained to the law of righteousness. Wherefore? Because they sought it not by faith, but as it were by the works of the law. For they stumbled at that stumbling-stone. (Romans 9:31–32)

> Whereas Israel, though ever in pursuit of a law [for the securing] of righteousness (right standing with God), actu-

ally did not succeed in fulfilling the Law. For what reason? Because [they pursued it] not through faith, relying [instead] on the merit of their works. [they did not depend on faith but on what they could do]. (Romans 9:31–32 AMP)

The people of Israel tried to do certain things to gain acceptance with God. Yet righteousness was never obtainable, for man can never gain God's acceptance by what he does, by his works. Many people today believe that by their good works, by the performance of certain religious duties, they are gaining God's favor. Religion becomes man-centered, and the glory of God is obscured and changed into the image of man. This mistaken notion leads to separation from God.

By grace through faith we are to have lives "filled with the fruits of righteousness," lives of zeal, works, and obedience. However, it can only be "by Jesus Christ." Then our religious service will be "unto the glory and praise of God" (Philippians 1:11).

We Become Fallen by Following Our Own Counsel

Destroy thou them, O God; let them fall by their own counsels; cast them out in the multitude of their transgressions; for they have rebelled against thee. (Psalm 5:10)

Many in this world are religious and want to do the right thing. However, instead of going to God's Word, many look to other human beings and to human institutions to find answers regarding the things of God and eternity, and the problems of this world.

If we do not follow God's will and Word, His counsels and law, and we follow our own way, we are fallen from Him. To be fallen from God is to eventually be lost and doomed to destruction. This is not an arbitrary act of God or the result of simple ignorance on our part. In following our own counsel and human religion, we have no cure for the guilt of our sin. Without God's grace in our lives, we are found living in transgression and sin. To one degree or another we are rebels against Him.

Pride Leads to a Fallen Condition

> Pride goeth before destruction, and an haughty spirit before a fall. (Proverbs 16:18)

There is a sincere attempt, even in the religious world, to build up people's self-esteem, and thus there is much feel-good religion today. Yet this is a false religion. For while there are sentimental feelings of love for God, the reproof, rebuke, and admonition of Scripture, as well as God's denunciation of sin and the call to repentance, is set aside. Such religion caters to our feelings, builds up our pride, and leads to a spiritual fall. This is why so many religious adherents, Christians included, "honoureth Me [God] with their lips; but their heart is far from Me" (Matthew 15:8).

There is much pride of opinion and pride of life in our modern society. It is cultivated in young and old, and is encouraged both subtly and openly, even as a virtue. The spirit of pride is provided to the public in the name of entertainment and used as a means of selling products. The way of man and the way of God are radically different, as we see in Proverbs. There we learn that pride leads to our downfall.

The Bible reveals that if we humble ourselves before the Lord He will lift us up. (See James 4:10.) Jesus is our example, for He humbled Himself unto death, even the death of the cross. The Bible says, Let this mind, this example that was in Christ Jesus, also be in you. (See Philippians 2:5–8.)

> And the pride of Israel doth testify to his face: therefore shall Israel and Ephraim fall in their iniquity; Judah also shall fall with them. They shall go with their flocks and with their herds to seek the Lord; but they shall not find him; he hath withdrawn himself from them. (Hosea 5:5–6)

But the pride and self-reliance of Israel testifies before his [own] face. Therefore shall [all] Israel, and [especially] Ephraim [the northern ten tribes], totter and fall in their iniquity and guilt, and Judah shall stumble and fall with them. (Hosea 5:5 AMP)

The tribe of Ephraim was eventually cut off from the children of Israel, no more to have the covenant promises with God. Why? Because they relied on themselves and their falsehoods and idols instead of relying on God, and they would not listen to His prophets.

Haughtiness and pride, be it with individuals on a personal level in our own hearts or in society, its entertainment, or its political, religious, or business institutions, leads us into a fallen condition in the eyes of God.

Losing our Love While Maintaining a Profession of Religion Causes Us to be Fallen

Nevertheless I have somewhat against thee, because thou hast left thy first love. Remember therefore from whence thou art fallen, and repent, and do the first works; or else I will come unto thee quickly, and will remove thy candlestick out of his place, except thou repent. (Revelation 2:4–5)

Here is an admonition to professed Christians, those who have the true faith, the true religion. They were fallen and were being called to repentance. Why is this so? And what was the nature of their fall? Jesus revealed much that was good in their experience; however, they had lost their first love. They were no longer motivated by faith that works through love.

They had good works, but they did not do them for the love of Jesus. The motivating power of the Spirit of Christ was being replaced by human effort. Many are in the same position today. We can have all kinds of religious programs, but when the love of

Jesus is not in our hearts and Jesus' Spirit is not motivating what we do, we are simply being religious.

Our religious life may be commendable in many respects, even as it was with the church at Ephesus. And yet we can be deficient in our love for God. Our doctrines may be correct, and we may hate false teaching and worldly practices. We may openly oppose and reject false teachers and the errors they promote. We may labor with untiring energy. But this is not sufficient. For Christ says to many, "You have left your first love."

This warning and reproof to the church in Ephesus has been written for our admonition as well. We are in danger of making a profession of the truth, even doing missionary work, yet the love of Christ has been lost. Losing our first love means falling away from Christ. Such a fall opens the door to selfishness, evil surmising, evil speaking, envy, and jealousy. These are but some of the results when our first love has grown cold. In losing our first love, religion is still there; however, there is an absence of true faith and love, which consequently leads us to be in a fallen condition. Don't let this fall happen to you.

Those Who Trust in Riches and the Things of This World Are Fallen

> He that trusteth in his riches shall fall: but the righteous shall flourish as a branch. (Proverbs 11:28)

Many people, religious and non-religious alike, are seeking riches or trusting in riches rather than the living God. That is why, in the developed world, we often find apathy to the truth of God. Nevertheless, people are seeking a spiritual experience. They are religious, but it is a religion apart from Christ, from following the narrow way.

Trusting in riches leads to a spiritual fall. Sadly, some Christian teachers and churches today preach a gospel of prosperity. The emphasis is not on the grace of God and what Jesus has done for us; rather, it is the money and prosperity that God is going to give us, or which we deserve, simply because we profess to be God's children.

Often the emphasis is on giving to God (which is often merely giving to men) so that we may receive from Him much more in return. We should not give to God in order to get back from Him, for God has already given to us abundantly through "the exceeding riches of His grace in His kindness toward us through Christ Jesus" (Ephesians 2:7).

> He who leans on, trusts in, and is confident in his riches shall fall, but the [uncompromisingly] righteous shall flourish like a green bough. (Proverbs 11:28 AMP)

Many people today serve God (or the gods of this world) in the hope of getting something in return. This is the motivation for their offerings and religious service.

God so loved the world that He gave His Son to die in our place so that we might have eternal life. Therefore, our giving and service must be based on the motivation of love, not on what we expect to gain from God.

Christian materialism, or the vain materialism of the world and the self-confidence that possessions give us, will only separate us from God. Separation from God is to be fallen from Him, and to be fallen is to be lost unless we repent.

In contrast, a life of righteousness and godliness, obtained by surrender to the grace of God, "is profitable unto all things, having promise of the life that now is, and of that which is to come" (1 Timothy 4:8).

Fallen Because of Apostasy

> Hear ye this word which I take up against you, even a lamentation, O house of Israel. The virgin of Israel is fallen; she shall no more rise: she is forsaken upon her land; there is none to raise her up. For thus saith the Lord God; The city that went out by a thousand shall leave an hundred,

and that which went forth by an hundred shall leave ten, to the house of Israel. (Amos 5:1–3)

Why were the leaders and the people of Israel in a fallen spiritual condition and suffering under the judgments of God? God was constantly calling, "For thus saith the Lord unto the house of Israel, Seek ye Me, and ye shall live" (Amos 5:4). Sadly, Israel was much like humanity today: religious and spiritual yet seeking God in falsehood and error. Therefore, God said through the prophet, "Seek not [the golden calf at] Bethel nor enter into [idolatrous] Gilgal, and pass not over to [the idols of] Beersheeba; for Gilgal shall surely go into captivity and exile, and Bethel [house of God] shall become Bethaven [house of vanity, emptiness, falsity, and futility] and come to nothing" (Amos 5:5 AMP).

Israel's fallen condition was the result of the false gods and materialism that many trusted in. False worship, or the truth merely professed but not followed, led many to "turn justice into [the bitterness of] wormwood and cast righteousness (uprightness and right standing with God) down to the ground" (Amos 5:7 AMP).

Much of Christianity in the last days is represented by Jesus in Revelation 3 as being lukewarm and in need of nothing. Revelation reveals that the state of churches in our day is largely self-satisfied, believing it is unnecessary to receive the rebuke, reproof, and admonition of the Lord. Jesus says, "As many as I love, I rebuke and chasten: be zealous therefore, and repent" (Revelation 3:19). However, many religious professors want nothing of Jesus' love if it means repentance and change. This unwillingness to receive reproof is of the same nature as fallen Israel.

They hate him who reproves in the [city] gate [holding him as an abomination and rejecting his rebuke], and they abhor him who speaks uprightly." (Amos 5:10 AMP)

The people of Israel would not receive God's counsel; they would not receive His word. Many people today do the same thing. They say, "We love God and serve Him," yet despite such profession, they will not listen to God's law, His Word, and His call to repent. While we may not make our opposition open and express it in words, it is reflected in our attitudes and in our actions.

Israel fell from God because of apostasy. Many individuals and churches today are repeating the same attitudes and actions as revealed in the writings of the prophet Amos.

Those Who Are Not Rooted and Grounded in the Truth Will Fall

> They on the rock are they, which, when they hear, receive the word with joy; and these have no root, which for a while believe, and in time of temptation fall away. (Luke 8:13)

Jesus is speaking here of a class of people who have heard God's Word and the gospel but are not rooted and grounded in truth and love. Therefore they fall away. Yet in this fall, they remain religious and maintain their profession.

The book of Revelation describes a time of trial and temptation that is to come upon the world. (See Revelation 3:10.) During this time God will not secretly rapture people out. Rather, He will give people the grace to go through the trials and temptations in order to be His witnesses. This is what God has always done, and He will do the same even in the last days. In the midst of worldwide apostasy and the setting up of the mark, God has a people with consistent endurance keeping His commandments by the faith of Jesus. (See Revelation 14:12.)

Many religious people, including Christians who are not rooted and grounded in the truth, will fall away during the final crisis and receive the mark of the beast. This is why God, in love and mercy, calls to the people of this world through the message of Revelation 14. He seeks to warn us now of our fallen state so that we, by His grace, might be lifted up from our fallen spiritual condition and practices.

God's voice through His messengers declares, "Babylon is fallen." This refers to our religion, spiritual practices, and character. If we do not listen, we are conditioning ourselves to hear the words of the religious political system of the beast, "speaking great things and blasphemies" (Revelation 13:5). If we refuse or neglect to repent, we are in danger of losing eternal life. Further, we will worship the beast with all the masses of the world, and we will do so in the name of God.

The vast majority of religious people, even Christians, are going to fall away at the crisis hour. That process is taking place even now. If you are part of Babylon, in thought and life or in religious belief and practice, you are fallen from God.

Come out of Babylon and all that it represents. This is the plea of Jesus. He is stretching forth His hand to lead you away from Babylon, away from death to eternal life. Will you let Him?

Endnotes

1. Greek lexicon based on Thayer's Lexicon and Smith's Bible Dictionary plus others; keyed to the large Kittel and the *Theological Dictionary of the New Testament*. Online Bible CD 2.5.3 Macintosh Version 1996.
2. Ibid.

Chapter Eleven

Babylon Is Fallen—
Who and What Is Babylon?

A nd there followed another angel, saying, Babylon is fallen, is fallen, that great city, because she made all nations drink of the wine of the wrath of her fornication. (Revelation 14:8)

God's declaration of Babylon's fall includes individuals who, by their thoughts, attitudes, and actions (in short, their character) are in spiritual confusion and apostasy. However, Babylon represents the religions of this world, especially the one the Bible calls "Mystery, Babylon the great, the mother of harlots and abominations of the earth" (Revelation 17:5).

Babylon is fallen because she has rejected the gospel, or distorted the gospel, or put something in its place. Babylon claims to reverence and fear God, and outwardly this appears to be true. However, as Scripture declared of ancient Israel, so it is true of Babylon. "This people draw near Me with their mouth, and with their lips do honour Me, but have removed their heart far from Me, and their fear toward Me is taught by the precept of men" (Isaiah 29:13). Babylon does not really worship God; it worships human ideologies and religion rather than following God and His Word.

As we said before, so say I now again, If any man preach any other gospel unto you than that ye have received, let him be accursed. (Galatians 1:9)

Babylon will eventually be accursed and subsequently destroyed because it has perverted the gospel; it has set up a substitute for the gospel. Human religion takes the place of the Bible and faith in Jesus. Sincere though it may be, the religion of Babylon is the vain attempt to gain salvation on human terms. Though the book of Revelation reveals one organization in particular as Babylon, it also encompasses all the planet's religions that reject, ignore, or put something in the place of the true gospel. The final confederacy at the end of time will see the political and economic powers of the world openly join with the religious institution of Babylon.

> Thus saith the Lord, Let not the wise man glory in his wisdom, neither let the mighty man glory in his might, let not the rich man glory in his riches: But let him that glorieth glory in this, that he understandeth and knoweth me, that I am the Lord which exercise lovingkindness, judgment, and righteousness, in the earth: for in these things I delight, saith the Lord. (Jeremiah 9:23–24)

Babylon is fallen because it glorifies man rather than glorifying God. Further it must be understood that glorifying God can never be forced or learned. It is the result of experiencing the gospel of Jesus Christ, of having sins forgiven and a heart renewed by the power of God's grace. There is a lot of outward religion in today's world that does not truly please and honor God.

Man takes pride in wisdom, might, and riches, whether of a religious or secular nature. Thus it is with Babylon, for we read, "How much she hath glorified herself, and lived deliciously, so much torment and sorrow give her: for she saith in her heart, I sit a queen, and am no widow, and shall see no sorrow" (Revelation 18:7).

> They have healed also the hurt of the daughter of my people slightly, saying, Peace, peace; when there is no peace. Were they ashamed when they had committed abomination? nay, they were not at all ashamed, neither could they blush: therefore they shall fall among them that fall: at the time that I visit them they shall be cast down, saith the Lord. Thus saith the Lord, Stand ye in the ways, and see, and ask for the old paths, where is the good way, and walk

therein, and ye shall find rest for your souls. But they said, We will not walk therein. (Jeremiah 6:14–16)

As it was with Israel, so Babylon is also fallen, for it teaches a peace-and-safety message during a time of judgment, when God is calling for repentance and commitment. Mankind is extremely spiritual and religious, yet this world is falling apart economically, socially, morally, even environmentally. This world is waxing "old like a garment" (Isaiah 51:6).

Now is the hour of judgment, the time of decision. And the judgment is based upon the message of Revelation 14. It will sift between the wheat and the tares. The great harvest Jesus spoke of has begun. The message of Revelation divides between the true and the false.

At this time in our world's history, when God's call (represented by the angel messengers of Revelation 14) is being given, the general belief in the churches of this world is to come together in ecumenicalism, to come together in interfaith unity, to work for the problems of humanity, to establish a global age of peace That sounds wonderful, and seeking to deal with humanity's many problems is certainly necessary, but it is largely done apart from God's will and Word.

God is calling us to His ways, to His truth, and to the everlasting gospel. He is calling us to keep His commandments. However, many say no in word and action. Our lips say that we love and serve God; however, we think we can get to heaven our own way. That is the attitude of Babylon and that was the attitude of ancient Israel. Israel's attitude led them into captivity to the Babylonian kingdom. And the same attitude exercised by the inhabitants of this world is leading us into captivity. We are bound by falsehood and error and sin, much of it done in the name of God. That is why people will be marked, showing that they have given their hearts, minds, and will to the spirit that denies the will and word and commandments of God.

There are only two classes of people. The first class is bound for New Jerusalem and are being sealed. These people are settling into the truth of God in their minds and hearts so that they cannot be moved from their faith. The other class of people, just as religious and earnest but in the wrong direction, is part of Babylon. They are settling into compromise, sin, and falsehood. They will be so convinced that they are right, they will receive the mark of the beast, which is a mark of rebellion against God. We are preparing for that day even now.

How Many Will Come under Babylonian Confusion?

> For all nations have drunk of the wine of the wrath of her fornication, and the kings of the earth have committed fornication with her, and the merchants of the earth are waxed rich through the abundance of her delicacies. (Revelation 18:3)

The book of Revelation reveals that only a remnant will truly serve God and eventually be saved. This is not because God is arbitrary or that He has limited the number of people who can be saved. Only a remnant is saved because most people have become intoxicated on the wine of falsehood and want to be saved in their own way. Thus the whole world will be deceived by Babylon. All the nations of the world have drunk of the wine of the wrath of her fornication.

The people of the world are becoming spiritually stupefied because of drinking the false doctrines and philosophies of Babylon. This wine of falsehood will lead those who imbibe it to experience the wrath of God in the seven last plagues and eventually eternal death.

We learn from Revelation 18 that the kings of the earth have committed fornication with Babylon. This speaks of an illicit union of religion and government. The nations of the world, including their people, kings, and leaders, will join with Babylon. The merchants of the earth are going to wax rich through this amalgamation of church and state. This grand coalition is the new world order, as "Mystery Babylon" will ride the beast, representing the kingdoms of this world. (See Daniel 7:17, 23 for the prophetic meaning of a beast.)

Religion, politics, and money will combine at the end of time in a confederacy done for human solidarity, human development, peace, and harmony in this world. The catalyst for such a new order will most likely come after a grave worldwide crisis. The people and leaders of the world will be clamoring for order in the midst of chaos. Thus the Scriptures reveal that a beast (a kingdom) will come out of the bottomless pit of world chaos and confusion. (See Revelation 17:8.) However, the whole system is built on the commandments of men, and it leads people away from God. That is why it is called fornication. That is why God is calling us to come out of Babylon, to come out of this system, be it churches or organizations.

> Or despisest thou the riches of his goodness and forbearance and longsuffering; not knowing that the goodness of God leadeth thee to repentance? But after thy hardness and impenitent heart treasurest up unto thyself wrath against the day of wrath and revelation of the righteous judgment of God. (Romans 2:4–5)

So many in Babylon claim to love God and worship Him, but in substituting human opinion and religion for the gospel they actually despise God, despite their claims to the contrary. Those who despise the riches of God's goodness and forbearance and long-suffering reject the gospel, ignore it, or put something else in its place.

> To them who by patient continuance in well doing seek for glory and honour and immortality, eternal life. (Romans 2:7)

Verses seven and eight reveal two classes of people, the same two classes as found in Revelation 14.

Verse seven parallels the group in Revelation 14:12, who have the patience of the saints, keeping the commandments of God and the faith of Jesus.

But unto them that are contentious, and do not obey the truth, but obey unrighteousness, indignation and wrath. (Romans 2:8)

The other class is characterized by disobeying the truth. The entire world will be divided into those who fear God and give Him glory and those who love a lie and obey unrighteousness. On what side will you stand? That is largely determined by your daily life and decisions for truth or error, light or darkness.

What Forces Make Up Babylon?

And I saw three unclean spirits like frogs come out of the mouth of the dragon, and out of the mouth of the beast, and out of the mouth of the false prophet. For they are the spirits of devils, working miracles, which go forth unto the kings of the earth and of the whole world, to gather them to the battle of that great day of God Almighty. (Revelation 16:13–14)

Demon-inspired spirits come out of the mouths of the dragon, the beast, and the false prophet. And what comes out of the mouth are doctrines and teachings and philosophies that are contrary to biblical faith and sound doctrine. In the place of God's truth the dragon, the beast, and the false prophet become channels to deceive the world with "seducing spirits, and doctrines of devils" (1 Timothy 4:1).

The leaders of the earth are going to be taken in the snare as well as the inhabitants of the world. All except a remnant are going to be deceived by these three unclean spirits.

What do these spirits represent? The dragon is the non-Christian religions of this earth. These people are sincere in their beliefs, but in rejecting the gospel they reject the only means of salvation. "For I am not ashamed of the gospel of Christ: for it is the power of God unto salvation to every one that believeth; to the Jew first, and also to the Greek" (Romans 1:16). The dragon represents the religions of this world that have a belief in a god or gods, or a higher force or power, but they substitute the gospel of Christ for human works.

The beast is the Roman church-state system. Many people in this system are doing commendable work. But the commandments of men and the traditions of the church pervert the gospel and offer men a substitute that cannot save.

The false prophet is apostate Christianity. We find false prophets throughout the Old Testament. They came from the midst of the children of Israel and claimed to speak for God. Other false prophets have come from within the Christian church. Jesus warned us of this when He said, "Many shall come in My name, saying, I am Christ; and shall deceive many" (Matthew 24:5). The false prophets claim to speak for God, claim to know Jesus, and claim to have the truth, but they are leading people away from fidelity to God's word and law.

The false prophets promise peace and safety, or life in rebellion. That is what the false prophets did in Old Testament days. They claimed to speak for God, saying, "I have a vision, God has said, I have a word of knowledge, I have a word of faith." They gave wonderful-sounding messages and the people flocked to it, but it was contrary to the word of God. It offered peace and safety in the midst of judgment. There are false prophets today throughout Christendom, and much of the church itself has become a false prophet or messenger.

What Is God's Attitude towards Babylon?

> And after these things I saw another angel come down from heaven, having great power; and the earth was lightened with his glory. And he cried mightily with a strong voice, saying, Babylon the great is fallen, is fallen, and is become the habitation of devils, and the hold of every foul spirit, and a cage of every unclean and hateful bird. For all nations have drunk of the wine of the wrath of her fornication, and the kings of the earth have committed

fornication with her, and the merchants of the earth are waxed rich through the abundance of her delicacies. And I heard another voice from heaven, saying, Come out of her, my people, that ye be not partakers of her sins, and that ye receive not of her plagues. For her sins have reached unto heaven, and God hath remembered her iniquities. (Revelation 18:1–5)

Revelation 18 describes the outpouring of the Holy Spirit. This message will come when the system of Babylon comes together with the religions of the world and the kings of the world and the merchantmen forming an alliance. God in His mercy is going to startle this planet with a message to awaken people, just as He did in the days of Noah.

The message declares, "Babylon the great is fallen, is fallen, and has become the habitation of devils and the hold of every foul spirit and the cage of every unclean and hateful bird." Here at the end, there is nothing good left in Babylon, for it is filled with death.

"All nations have drunk of the wine of the wrath of her fornication, and the kings of the earth have committed fornication with her, and the merchants of the earth are waxed rich through the abundance of her delicacies." The warning, denunciation, and call to separate are God's attempt to awaken the people before the door of mercy shuts forever. In the midst of this message, God says, "Come out of her, My people."

The wine of falsehood confuses many honest individuals who are caught up in the spirit or religions of Babylon. God sees their sincerity, zeal, and earnestness, but they are confused. Therefore, He sends messengers who are filled with the Spirit, calling them out of Babylon.

God did the same for Lot and his family. They had become confused, desensitized by the sin around them. Though Lot loved God, he was affected by the evil. Before judgment came, God called them out. Those who listen and come out of the religious confusion and apostasy to follow the Lamb will be saved.

The Angel Identifies Babylon

And there came one of the seven angels which had the seven vials, and talked with me, saying unto me, Come hither; I will shew unto thee the judgment of the great whore that sitteth upon many waters: With whom the kings of the earth have committed fornication, and the inhabitants of the earth have been made drunk with the wine of her fornication. So he carried me away in the spirit into the wilderness: and I saw a woman sit upon a scarlet coloured beast, full of names of blasphemy, having seven heads and ten horns. And the woman was arrayed in purple and scarlet colour, and decked with gold and precious stones and pearls, having a golden cup in her hand full of abominations and filthiness of her fornication: And upon her forehead was a name written, Mystery, Babylon the great, the mother of harlots and abominations of the earth. (Revelation 17:1–5)

In Revelation 17, the woman represents a church. In Revelation 12 we find a pure woman, representing God's church. The woman of Revelation 17 is beautiful. She is decked with gold and precious stones and pearls; however, the Bible declares she is a harlot. This is a false religious system that claims to serve the true God but is fallen from truth.

The apostle Paul wrote, "I am jealous over you with godly jealousy: for I have espoused you to one husband, that I may present you as a chaste virgin to Christ" (2 Corinthians 11:2). All through the Scripture this concept of women and marriage is used by God to represent a relationship that He desires to have with His people. "I have likened the daughter of Zion to a comely and delicate woman" (Jeremiah 6:2).

The woman "Mystery Babylon" represents a church that sits on many waters, which represents the nations, kindreds, tongues, and peoples of this world. (See Revelation 17:15.) This system of Babylon encompasses the world and has worldwide influence.

We learn in Revelation 17:2 that the kings of the earth have committed spiritual adultery with this woman. In this religious system's politics we find so much involvement with the governments of this world that in the end the governments will be subservient to the woman, which is why this system is also called a beast. Verse two says the inhabitants of the earth have been made drunk with the wine of her false teachings.

This global system of apostasy called Babylon will have one visible head, which is the Vatican. Though Babylon is made up of non-Christian religions, Catholicism, and apostate Christendom, all roads lead to Rome. The statesmen and leaders of the world are often found in Rome visiting the pope. More than 170 countries have ambassadors at the Vatican. Why? Rome is just a church, is it not? Yes. But it is also a state, and it deals with the world at large, both as a church and a state.

The Catholic system is involved at every level of human society, and much of it is positive and good. This involvement reaches from the UN to a little clinic in the Congo. The late Jesuit author Malachi Martin said, "In secular eyes, the Roman Church stands alone in every practical sense—and not merely among religious and ethical structures and groups—as the first fully realized, fully practicing and totally independent geopolitical force in the current world arena."[1]

Revelation 17:3 states that "Mystery Babylon" sits on the beast. Daniel 7:17 describes the beast as a kingdom in prophecy. The beast carrying her shows the political involvement this woman engages in, which will be most prominent just before the coming of the Lord.

Revelation 17:4 declares this woman is dressed in purple and scarlet, representing the colors of Caesar and of royalty, for the Roman church came out of pagan Rome and it is simply a continuation of that kingdom. Purple and scarlet were also prominent colors in the sanctuary. This woman has developed a counterfeit priesthood and ritual.

Verse 4 also states this church has a golden cup in her hands that is full of abominations. The center of this system is the golden cup of the mass and the monstrance, which is a large gold or sil-

ver container in which the Host is placed and then shown to the congregation for adoration. The golden cup represents the beautiful side of evil, for the cup's beauty draws our attention, while the doctrines and ritual inside the Lord calls abominations.

Revelation 17:5 declares that this church is named "Mystery Babylon." In other words, elements of ancient Babylon are in this system. The religion of Rome is the religion of Babylon. The doctrines and practices of the Roman church are not based on the Bible. Rather, it is paganism under the veneer of Christianity. This is why the Revelation of Jesus exposes this counterfeit system, for it is confusion and is leading many away from Him.

In the words of the Catechism, "Liturgical catechesis aims to initiate people into the mystery of Christ (it is 'mystagogy') by proceeding from the visible to the invisible, from the sign to the thing signified, from the 'sacraments' to the 'mysteries.'"[2] "Mystagogy" is at the heart of the Roman system, and thus it is identified in Revelation 17 as "Mystery Babylon."

Babylon was also a code word for Rome. In 1 Peter 5:13, Babylon represents "Rome as the most corrupt seat of idolatry and the enemy of Christianity."[3]

Revelation 17:5 states that "Mystery Babylon" is the mother of harlot daughters and therefore claims to be the mother church. The apostate Protestant and evangelical churches are her fallen daughters, and she is attempting to draw the daughters of this world's religions to herself. He who occupies the seat of Peter is recognized as the great spiritual leader of this world. This is why all the major religions of this world regularly visit the Vatican. Further, the world's religions are regularly involved with Rome in ecumenical and interfaith meetings and dialogue. In a world of chaos and increasing tension and trouble, such meetings may appear good, and no doubt they often are. However, they reveal the extent of the influence of Rome, and Revelation 17 reveals that Rome is the mother of false religion.

An example of the interreligious influence of the woman of Revelation 17 is the "Appeal for Peace," convened April 27, 2006. Many religions were represented at the International Prayer Meeting for Peace. The Archdiocese of Washington, Georgetown

University, and the Catholic University of America, and the Rome-based Community of Sant'Egidio organized this event. What religious groups were represented at this meeting?

> Religious leaders of Christians, Muslims, Jews, Buddhists, Hindus, Shintoists and Sikhs were among the more than 500 participants.

> Cardinal Theodore E. McCarrick of the Washington Archdiocese, one of the co-sponsors of the two-day gathering, told the group that by coming together they were fulfilling Pope John Paul's dream "that we would pray together for peace."[4]

Revelation 17:6 declares that this church structure is drunk with the blood of the saints, and Rome has been guilty of the murder of millions over the ages. Revelation reveals that this spirit of intolerance will once again encompass the globe when Babylon has control. All nonconformists who do not go along with its system of worship will be locked out of the world's economy and will eventually face a death decree. (See Revelation 13:15–17.) God's people are not going to be taken away by a secret rapture before that time. God is going to strengthen His people to pass through this time to His glory and to give Him honor as His witnesses and messengers.

Revelation 17:9 tells us this woman or religious system sits on seven mountains, and Rome has always been known as the city of seven hills.

Revelation 17:18 states this church structure is a great city that sits on seven mountains, where she reigns over the world. Babylon encompasses more than the seat of power in the seven-hilled city of Rome. Babylon is a spirit or mindset that is in rebellion to God's Word and law. Much of this rebellion is religious in nature. Prophecy has identified the seat of rebellion as a great city, which is also the name of the church system identified by God as "Mystery Babylon."

Why would a city be called a whore and be accused of having committed fornication with the kings or political rulers of the earth? Such an accusation could never be made against Paris, Johannesburg, New York, Tokyo, Moscow, or Beijing. These great cities and many more are filled with wickedness and vice. Then why is God pointing out one city alone?

Fornication and adultery are used in the Bible in both the physical and the spiritual sense. The Bible says of Jerusalem, "How has the faithful city become a harlot!" (Isaiah 1:21). Israel had been set apart from other people to be holy and to fulfill God's purpose as His witnesses. However, they entered into unholy alliances with the idol-worshiping nations around them. Israel, "through the lightness of her whoredom, ... defiled the land, and committed adultery with stones and with stocks" (Jeremiah 3:9). Further, "they have committed adultery, and blood is in their hands, and with their idols have they committed adultery" (Ezekiel 23:37).

It is not possible for a city to engage in literal fornication in the flesh. Therefore, the prophet John in the book of Revelation, as with the Old Testament prophets before him, is using the term in its spiritual meaning. This great city, called "Mystery Babylon," claims a spiritual relationship with God, yet has been and continues to be unfaithful to Him.

Only one city besides Jerusalem could have this charge of spiritual fornication made against it. That city is Rome. Specifically, Vatican City. The Church of Rome claims to have been the headquarters of Christianity since its beginning and maintains that claim to this day. The supreme pontiff, the holy father, by virtue of the title Vicar of Christ, is believed to be the representative of God on this earth, or at the very least first among equals. This is why we see many of the world's religious leaders and groups, and many of the world's political leaders, regularly making their way to Rome.

Why does Rome have such influence? Because she is the one who sits at the head of this global system, revealed by John in the Revelation. Not only does the pope of Rome call himself the Vicar of Christ, but the church he leads claims to be the one true church and the bride of Christ. Christ's bride, His true church, is to have no earthly ambitions. Yet the Vatican is passionately involved in earthly enterprises and political involvement with the governments of the earth, much of which appears good. However, as John foresaw in his vision, it is involved in adulterous relationships with the kings of the earth.

Babylon at the end is made up of the beast, the false prophet, and the dragon. All three religious groups will be tied in with the world's political structure, with the Vatican as the visible head of this temporary harmony and cooperation.

Babylon is a spirit and an attitude. It encompasses churches and denominations and religious structures and institutions. Babylon is a spirit of rebellion against the will of God, the Word of God, and the commandments of God, often done in His name. It teaches people to fear God by following the commandments of men. It seeks to glorify God, but it does not lead to obedience and a heart service to the Lord Jesus Christ. Babylon is fallen because it leads people away from God.

"Come out of her, My people." That is God's plea to you. The choice is clear: the religion of men, which leads to separation from Christ, or the grace of Christ, which leads to separation from the religions of this world.

No denomination is going to save you, my friend. All the denominations of this world, to one degree or another, are caught up in this spirit of Babylon. They are all affected by it.

The question is, Whom do you serve? Your answer determines your destiny. For there are only two classes of people described in the final chapters of the book of Revelation: those who fear God and give glory to Him, keeping His commandments, and those who fear men and follow the commandments and doctrines of men.

Clearly, it is decision time. Will you follow the way of Jesus or the way of men? That is the only question we need to settle. It is not a matter of choosing one denomination over another. It is not a matter of choosing one type of spirituality over another. It is not a matter of choosing what religion we should follow. The decision is truth or error.

Jesus is pleading with us, calling us to Himself, saying, "Why will you die? Come unto Me and be ye saved, all the ends of the earth." (See Ezekiel 33:11; Isaiah 45:22.)

There is room enough in the Father's kingdom for everyone, but we must be saved God's way, not our own way. It doesn't matter

whether you grew up in India, Jordan, Vietnam, or the Bible belt of the United States. The religion you grew up with wasn't good enough for our fathers and it's not good enough for us. There is only one religion that is good enough, only one that saves, and that is found only in the gospel of Jesus Christ.

Nothing in life is more important than this question: "What must I do to be saved?"

The message of Revelation 14 is one of God's last attempts to save the people of this planet, including you and me. His message separates the wheat from the tares. "Come out of her, My beloved." That is the plea of God. Will you listen? I pray, my friend, that you will let Jesus help you make the right choice for eternal life.[5]

Endnotes

1. Malachi Martin, *The Keys of this Blood* © (New York, New York: Simon and Shuster, 1990), 143.
2. *The Catechism of the Catholic Church* © (Paulines Press, Nairobi, Kenya), 281.
3. Greek lexicon based on Thayer's Lexicon and Smith's Bible Dictionary plus others; keyed to the large Kittel and the *Theological Dictionary of the New Testament*. Online Bible CD 2.5.3 1996.
4. Catholic News Service/USCCB, 2006.
5. For further study on the woman of Revelation 17, the author recommends *A Women Rides the Beast* by Dave Hunt (www.thebereancall.org), *The Two Babylons* by the Reverend Alexander Hissop, and *Let Daniel and Revelation Speak* by David Wilson (available as a free PDF e-book, or you may purchase a bound copy at www.inspirationspeaks.com).

Section Three
The Warning

Chapter Twelve

If Any Man Worships the Beast—
Preparing for the Mark or the Seal

And the third angel followed them, saying with a loud voice, If any man worship the beast and his image, and receive his mark in his forehead, or in his hand, The same shall drink of the wine of the wrath of God, which is poured out without mixture into the cup of his indignation; and he shall be tormented with fire and brimstone in the presence of the holy angels, and in the presence of the Lamb. (Revelation 14:9–10)

The above verses contain one of the most serious warnings in all of Scripture. However, we must understand that God warns us because of His love and mercy. The gospel proves that. "Herein is love, not that we loved God, but that He loved us, and sent His Son to be the propitiation for our sins" (1 John 4:10). In contrast, those who receive the mark of the beast have rejected, ignored, or perverted the gospel, or put something in its place, mixing truth and error. The Bible describes this class as those who will be deceived by the "working of Satan with all power and signs and lying wonders, and with all deceivableness of unrighteousness in them that perish; because they received not the love of the truth, that they might be saved. And for this cause God shall send them strong delusion, that they should believe a lie: that they all might be damned who believed not the truth, but had pleasure in unrighteousness" (2 Thessalonians 2:9–12).

In the last days before Jesus comes the second time in the clouds of heaven, two classes of people will be developed: those who have the seal of God and those who have the mark of the beast. The seeds of rebellion and apostasy had its beginning long ago. The great rebellion began because of the corruption in the mind of Lucifer. "Thou wast perfect in thy ways from the day that thou wast created, till iniquity was found in thee" (Ezekiel 28:15). Lucifer was the first to fall under the delusion of sin and self-ishness, and he has sought to spread his sin and rebellion to the human race.

In this chapter we want to develop a spiritual background so that we might better understand the issues regarding the mark of the beast. You see, the mark of the beast is not some technological mark on our person at the end of time, though this is the common and incomplete understanding of most people.

The mark of the beast has to do with worship and allegiance: who has our hearts, our mind, and our strength. (See Mark 12:30.) Whoever has our hearts will determine whether we are marked or sealed.

> How art thou fallen from heaven, O Lucifer, son of the morning! how art thou cut down to the ground, which didst weaken the nations! For thou hast said in thine heart, I will ascend into heaven, I will exalt my throne above the stars of God: I will sit also upon the mount of the con-gregation, in the sides of the north: I will ascend above the heights of the clouds; I will be like the most High. (Isaiah 14:12–14)

Satan's purpose was to rule the universe and subvert the au-thority of God. He says, "I will ascend into heaven; I will exalt my throne above the stars of God." What does that mean? Stars in the Bible are literal celestial bodies that we see at night. They are also used in Scripture symbolically. Revelation speaks of a third of the stars being cast down to the ground, meaning the angels who were cast from heaven with Lucifer. (See Revelation 12:4.) In Revelation, Jesus is depicted as holding the seven stars in His hand, which are the seven angels of the seven churches. Stars here represent the leaders of the seven churches. (See Revelation 1:20.)

Jude 13 speaks of wandering stars, which are apostate teach-ers. Daniel 12:3 represents the glory of the stars as the people of

God. Satan says, "I want to exalt my throne above the stars of God, above the angels, above the religious leaders of this world and over the people of God." He wants universal dominion over all of God's created beings. That is what Satan means when he says I will exalt my throne above the stars of God. He is not speaking literally, saying that he wants to have his throne somewhere in the universe. He wants dominion and rulership over intelligent beings.

Satan declares, "I will sit also upon the mount of the congregation." *Congregation*, as used in this verse, means "an appointment; i.e., a fixed time or season, by implication an assembly (as convened for a definite purpose); the place of meeting."[1] So Satan is saying, "I am going to have a congregation made up of God's subjects, who were created to serve and love Him, but I want them to serve and honor me."

This is the purpose of Satan, to mold man into his own image and to gain the allegiance of the world so that he may be their god. The people of this planet, his congregation, at the time of the mark of the beast, will be in total rebellion against God. Now, as people do this, they are not going to be devil worshipers in the strict sense of the term. The vast majority of them will be religious and would be horrified to think they are worshiping the devil. But the Bible says, "To whom ye yield yourselves servants to obey, his servants ye are to whom ye obey; whether of sin unto death, or of obedience unto righteousness" (Romans 6:16).

The worshipers of the beast will be lost, though many will be religious and sincere. They will believe that the beast is God's instrument on earth. This is why the "world wondered after the beast … and they worshipped the beast, saying, Who is like unto the beast? who is able to make war with him?" (Revelation 13:3–4).

Many people, like the angels in heaven who fell with Lucifer, will be deceived by the beast that has "a mouth speaking great things" (Revelation 13:5). Fair speeches and lofty sentiments of love, justice, and charity will come from the beast, but he also opens "his mouth in blasphemy against God" (Revelation 13:6). Why will the people of this planet be so deceived? Why are we so often deceived even now? The rejection of the truth and a love for unrighteousness sets us up to believe a lie. For the majority of this planet's inhabitants, religious or not, "there is a way which see-meth right unto a man, but the end thereof are the ways of death" (Proverbs 14:12). If you serve God wrongly, and have falsehood and sin in the place of truth and righteousness, you are already worshiping Satan and preparing for the mark of the beast.

Satan understands this; therefore, he seeks to shape the mind of man so that he actually receives worship from people who don't know it, at least not until the end, when it will be to late. Satan's purpose is to develop in man his own image and thereby gain the allegiance of the world so that he may be their god and the people his congregation.

Satan has made the claim, "I will sit also upon the mount of the congregation, in the sides of the north" (Isaiah 14:13). What does this mean? "Beautiful for situation, the joy of the whole earth, is mount Zion, on the sides of the north, the city of the great King" (Psalm 48:2).

The "sides of the north" is a symbol of the dwelling place of God. Satan is seeking to sit in the place of God. Now, he cannot physically usurp God's place and remove Him. However, if he can have the worship of this world's inhabitants, in his mind he will have succeeded in taking the place of God.

Satan is trying to reproduce his mind in the hearts and minds of the people of this planet, even religious people. In fact, so much the better if they are religious; then they will believe they are serv-ing God when they are really serving the god of this world.

Could it be that the world's inhabitants will be subjects of Satan though religions and claiming to serve God? Jesus said the following startling words of the religious leaders of His day who believed they served God:

> Ye are of your father the devil, and the lusts of your father ye will do. He was a murderer from the beginning, and abode not in the truth, because there is no truth in him. When he speaketh a lie, he speaketh of his own: for he is a liar, and the father of it. (John 8:44)

These were religious people, but they were worshipers of Satan according to the words of Jesus. They did not recognize it, and the people they where leading did not recognize it. However, by sin, disobedience, and unbelief, they made themselves subjects of Satan. And thus it will be at the end of time.

The prophecy of Isaiah 14 reveals that Satan's plan is to dethrone God from the heart of man and then to pattern human nature into his own image of deformity. Mankind has accepted Satan by neglecting God or substituting something in the place of Him, His word, and the everlasting gospel. As the people of this world accept Satan as god, they take on his attributes and become filled with his spirit. Satan's spirit controlled most of the religious leaders in Jesus' day, and his spirit controls most people today. (See Titus 3:3; Romans 3:9–18; Ephesians 4:17–19; Galatians 5:19–21.)

Notice this description of Satan in Ezekiel.

Thine heart was lifted up because of thy beauty, thou hast corrupted thy wisdom by reason of thy brightness: I will cast thee to the ground, I will lay thee before kings, that they may behold thee. (Ezekiel 28:17)

Satan's wisdom and knowledge and perception were corrupted because he looked to himself instead of to God. And this is being repeated in the hearts of man. The Bible reveals two minds that are being developed in mankind: the mind of Christ and the mind of Satan. There will be two signs reflecting which mind we have: the seal of God, because we have made God the center of our lives, or the mark of the beast. There will be two classes: those who disobey God's commandments for the commandments of men, and those who obey God's law and word.

Revelation makes it clear that there will be those who fear men and reverence his institutions and religions and principles, and there will be those who fear God, honoring and obeying Him in love. There will be a class of people who give glory to men and others who give glory to God.

There is a remnant who is developing the mind of Christ and making the life of Jesus Christ their own by faith. The gospel is becoming the power of God unto salvation in their lives. In contrast, the majority of the world's inhabitants, religious and otherwise, love unrighteousness; therefore they do not love the truth. Two minds, two images, are being formed in the hearts of men. The crisis of the last days over worship, the seal of God and the mark of the beast, makes the distinction clear.

For a short time God will allow Satan and his congregation to rule this world as a final demonstration of the futility of Satan's kingdom and principles. At the end God will humble Satan and his followers so they will know that the Most High God rules the universe.

> Son of man, say unto the prince of Tyrus, Thus saith the Lord God; Because thine heart is lifted up, and thou hast said, I am a God, I sit in the seat of God, in the midst of the seas; yet thou art a man, and not God, though thou set thine heart as the heart of God. (Ezekiel 28:2)

Tyrus was a city-state in the area of modern-day Lebanon.[2] The description of Tyrus refers not only to this one city and kingdom, which was often in rebellion against God, but symbolically describes the attributes of Satan as well.

Satan, under the symbol of the kingdom of Tyrus, declares, "I am a God … in the midst of the seas." The word *midst* means "inner man, mind, will, heart, understanding, inclination, resolution, determination (of will) conscience, heart (of moral character)."[3]

The seas, while having a literal meaning, are of no significance to Satan's purpose and plans. Rather, for him to be "in the midst of the seas" means to control the thoughts, feelings, and minds of the people of this world. The seas represent the people and nations of this world. (See Revelation 17:15.)

How will Satan gather the people to worship him, to be as God to them? He will not do it in the character that some people attribute to him, with a tail, pitchfork, and horns. Oh, no. Satan is a beautiful angel, though fallen. He comes across in sophistication and in beauty. Remember how he worked in the Garden of Eden?

He did not appear as some hideous monster; he came with great subtlety and attraction. When Satan appeared to Jesus just after His wilderness fasting, he did not come as a demon; he represented himself as an angel from heaven. However, his words betrayed him. This is how we can know the true from the false, by the Word of God.

Since the fall of man, Satan has been studying the properties of the human mind, and he has learned to know it well. He is a genius; he was, after all, the highest angel in heaven.

Satan works deceptively in these last days as he seeks to link the human mind with his own, instilling it with his thoughts and character. He is doing his work in such a deceptive manner that those who accept his guidance don't even know they are being led by him. Politicians, statesmen, people in the arts and media, those in education and religion, indeed all of society, high and low, are being influenced by him and know it not.

Though people claim to be free, they are actually guided by Satan, often unknowingly. The deceiver works to confuse the minds of men and women so that only his voice will be heard. When they hear and follow Satan's voice, it leads them away from the gospel into sin, compromise, self-centeredness, and manmade ideas and religion. Thus the words of Jesus are fulfilled, for He said, "He that entereth not by the door into the sheepfold, but climbeth up some other way, the same is a thief and a robber" (John 10:1).

Sadly, many of earth's billions are trying to gain heaven and acceptance with God while denying the only true way, which is through Christ. He said, "I am the door, by Me if any man enter in he shall be saved" (John 10:9).

Satan links his mind with the human mind through false religions and ideologies. In fact, anything that leads away from the truth of God's Word and from the gospel of Jesus Christ has Satan behind it. Satan gains control of minds; thus, the people of this planet reflect his attributes and hear his voice, even if unknowingly. The result is that Satan becomes god to this class of people. They are giving allegiance to him and they do not even know that's what they are doing.

This issue of the mark of the beast will make plain to the whole universe who serves God and who serves the devil. This transformation of the human mind will prepare the world for the final rebellion against God and the mark of the beast; "in whom the god of this world has blinded the minds of them which believe not, lest the light of the glorious gospel of Christ, who is the image of God, should shine unto them" (2 Corinthians 4:4). This blindness of the human heart and lack of spiritual discernment is preparing the way for the image of Satan to be formed in man.

> And God saw that the wickedness of man was great in the earth, and that every imagination of the thoughts of his heart was only evil continually. (Genesis 6:5)

Before the flood, man's heart, "the feelings, the will and even the intellect,"[4] was only evil. Jesus said this would be the condition "just before I come." (See Luke 17:26.) The world will be evil: not only murderers, rapists, and gross evildoers, but they will be evil by virtue of the fact that they do not follow the truth of God. They are not submissive to Christ; they have not made Him Lord and Savior. And without the renewing power of the gospel of Jesus Christ, every one of us, even those we may call good people, are evil. We are separated from God, not adhering to His commandments and His word. This is what makes us evil. (See Psalm 50:16–17; Jeremiah 13:10.)

According to the Genesis record of man's condition just before the flood, Satan had succeeded in reproducing his image in the minds and bodies of mankind, thus prompting the deluge from God to sweep the earth clean of its corruption.

Just prior to the coming of Christ, mankind will reach a stage similar to the days of Noah. The minds, purposes, and imaginations of the majority of mankind will again be bent toward evil. People may appear religious, or be seeking spirituality, but they are carnal; therefore, man's religion leads people away from God.

> For they that are after the flesh do mind the things of the flesh; but they that are after the Spirit the things of the

Spirit. For to be carnally minded is death; but to be spiritually minded is life and peace. Because the carnal mind is enmity against God: for it is not subject to the law of God, neither indeed can be. So then they that are in the flesh cannot please God. (Romans 8:5–8)

The verses cited above reveal two minds: the mind led by God's Holy Spirit, which is subject to His law in love, and those who are unconverted, often religious in some way, but obedient to the flesh. They are enemies of God, which is evident because they are not subject to His law. Left to ourselves in our carnal nature, we cannot please God and are really rendering Satan worship.

And he causeth all, both small and great, rich and poor, free and bond, to receive a mark in their right hand, or in their foreheads: And that no man might buy or sell, save he that had the mark, or the name of the beast, or the number of his name. Here is wisdom. Let him that hath understanding count the number of the beast: for it is the number of a man; and his number is Six hundred threescore and six. (Revelation 13:16–18)

How many are going to receive the mark of the beast? The prophecy says all. This includes the "small" in society: the vast majority of this world's common people, who have no "rank or influence."[5] It also includes the "great: "persons, eminent for ability, virtue, authority, [and] power."[6] The "rich"—those who are "wealthy, abounding in material resources"[7]—will receive the mark of the beast. This includes most people in the developed world. The mark will also be received by the "poor": those who are "destitute of wealth, influence, position, [and] honour,"[8] which is the vast majority of the world's billions.

The mark will leave no one for the "free," those who live in countries with relative or great freedoms will receive the mark. Those who will receive the mark include those under the bondage of servitude as modern-day slaves, or those who live under oppressive governments, be they religious or political.

Indeed, virtually the whole world, except for a remnant that are written in the Lamb's book of life, will receive the mark. (See Revelation 13:8.)

Whatever form the mark of the beast takes, it is ultimately an acknowledgement of who has our heart, mind, and allegiance. It will either be the God of heaven or the god of this world, Satan. Further, the mark will reveal what is already an established fact: that all along we have been developing the mind of Christ or the mind of Satan.

The mark will be enforced with increasing pressure, including economic isolation as nonconformists are cut off from buying and selling. Eventually death will be decreed for those who do not submit. The religion we claim to have will be tested, proven to be genuine or false. Then it will be seen whether Christ has all the mind, strength, and soul.

In contrast to the worshipers of the beast, who ultimately are worshiping Satan, whether knowingly or unknowingly, are those who have the patience of the saints and consistent endurance, who keep God's commandments and have the faith of Jesus. (See Revelation 14:12.)

John foresees a people who are victorious over the beast and his mark. This victory is gained by living for Christ on this earth before and during the time of the mark. Notice how these people are described: "And I looked, and, lo, a Lamb stood on the mount Sion, and with Him an hundred forty and four thousand, having His Father's name written in their foreheads" (Revelation 14:1).

Again speaking of God's people we read, "And they shall see His face, and His name, [God's character] shall be in their foreheads" (Revelation 22:4).

In all that we do, our thoughts and purposes should be, "Is this the way of the Lord? Will this please my Savior?" Jesus gave His life for us. Our hearts belong to God, and a surrendered heart is all He requires. The name of God is to be written on our foreheads, because God is the center of our lives. It is to such people that the seal of God is promised.

The Seal or the Mark?

The seal of God is a settling into the truth spiritually: our thoughts, our feelings, our moral character, and our intellect, which is our understanding of God's word and law. We will not be moved from our allegiance if we have made the truth of God our own by faith. It will change us, leading us to "follow the Lamb whithersoever He goeth" (Revelation 14:4).

Those who will eventually receive the mark of the beast are even now settling into falsehood, the commandments of men, the rejection of God's Word, and sin and compromise. They are preparing for the mark unless they hear the Spirit's voice and God's call to repent.

At the end of time the seal of God and the mark of the beast will be the final revelation of the mind and spirit of Christ or the mind and spirit of the devil.

What Is God's Purpose for Man?

For whom he did foreknow, he also did predestinate to be conformed to the image of his Son, that he might be the firstborn among many brethren. (Romans 8:29)

According as he hath chosen us in him before the foundation of the world, that we should be holy and without blame before him in love. (Ephesians 1:4)

God's eternal love is not just for a select few, but for all mankind, for His desire is that all would be saved and be conformed to the image of His Son. Before God created this world, He had already chosen us in Christ. That is why we read that Jesus was "the Lamb slain from the foundation of the world" (Revelation 13:8). As soon as there was sin, there was a Savior. "For God so loved the world, that He gave His only begotten Son, that whosoever believeth in Him should not perish, but have everlasting life" (John 3:16). That love did not begin when Christ was born into

235

this world, or at Calvary when He died for our sins. Long before you and I were born, God's love for us and His eternal purpose for us were in His heart and mind.

If we grasp the awesomeness of the love of God, why would we want to serve the beast? Why would we want to go against God's will and commandments? Why would we want to seek to save ourselves by some other gospel, some other religion, some false hope of salvation?

The Image of the Beast

In Daniel chapter 2 we see a vision of a great metal man, representing the great kingdoms of prophecy: Babylon, Medo-Persia, Greece, Rome, and, in the last days before Christ comes, the kingdom of iron and clay. The kingdoms represented in Daniel 2 are kingdoms of men; they are the result of man's genius, planning, and invention.

Human history is but a revelation of the human heart, and the image in Daniel 2 degenerates over time from gold to iron. So with the golden dreams of man; they are no higher than man himself. Thus the image in the last days ends with the weakness of iron and clay mixed together. The image of Daniel 2 teaches us that the progress of man is not upward but downward. Where the image of man is, rather than the image of God in man, there is always degeneration.

It is the law of the intellectual and spiritual nature of man that by beholding we become changed. If we behold the doctrines and commandments of men, the way and spirit of the world, our minds will be conformed to the image of Satan, which is an image of rebellion against the will and word of God.

Regardless of the sophistication and religion that goes with it, the mind and image of Satan is simply neglecting, ignoring, or refusing God's will and way in our lives. That is what it means to worship Satan and have him as your god.

Mankind will never rise higher than the standard of purity or truth he seeks. If selfish indulgence and the pursuit of pleasure is his greatest ideal, as it is with many, he can never attain anything more exalted. Our false concepts of God, and our involvement in false worship, cannot lead us to God; thus, we are going to sink lower and lower. Such is the case in our day. Mankind is degenerating morally, spiritually, and in many other areas.

Only the grace of God has the power to exalt man. Left to ourselves, and to our own religions and devices, mankind's course must eventually be downward. That is what we are seeing today.

The Image of God

> But the path of the just is as the shining light, that shineth more and more unto the perfect day. (Proverbs 4:18)

In the image of Daniel 2 we saw how the kingdoms of men and the glory of man are degenerating lower and lower. In contrast, the lives of God's people, who are justified and cleansed by the blood of Jesus Christ, are like a light that shines brighter and brighter. There is growth, development, and a change of heart. No longer are they degenerating and being "conformed to this world," the image of Satan. Rather, they are being "transformed by the renewing of ... [the] mind, that ... [they] may prove what is that good, and acceptable, and perfect, will of God" (Romans 12:2).

The Image of the Beast

In Daniel 4:30 we learn that King Nebuchadnezzar worshiped self. This has always been the source of the degeneracy of the kingdoms of the world and the source of mankind's present degeneration.

In Daniel 4 we find that this great king was spiritual. He worshiped and had been exposed to the truth of God. However, he boasted, just like Satan. King Nebuchadnezzar exalted his own attainments while forgetting God; this led to his downfall. Thus the image of the beast is the worship of self and following false doctrines, religions, and ideas.

The Image of God

> But God forbid that I should glory, save in the cross of our Lord Jesus Christ, by whom the world is crucified unto me, and I unto the world. (Galatians 6:14)

The image of man is centered on self; the image of God in man is centered on Christ. Our selfishness is yielded to the will and word of God. This is our highest ideal and the purpose for which we were created. The mind of Satan exalts self, human religion, and the doctrines of men. The mind of God seeks to serve God and follow His will and way.

The Image of the Beast

King Nebuchadnezzar thought he had a knowledge of God. We read this in Daniel chapters 2, 3, and 4. The king acknowledged the God of heaven but continued in his system of false worship. Despite the revelation of God's truth, the king sought to force the conscience of his subjects by his decrees in setting up a golden image to exalt his own selfishness. His intellectual understanding of the true God did not keep him from worshiping self and ultimately Satan.

Following or exalting self, human ideas, and human religions is in the end the worship of Satan. Therefore, when the crisis of the mark of the beast comes, an intellectual knowledge of the issues or of the Bible will be of no avail. We shall have no safety unless we have conformed our lives to the principles of Scripture through the enabling grace of Christ.

In Daniel 2:47 and 3:28 we read that the king had a marvelous experience. God revealed Himself to King Nebuchadnezzar, and the king made an acknowledgement of God, but it was only intellectual. The religion of men and the pride of man gained the ascendancy because he only had a superficial understanding. He didn't surrender his heart. Many in Babylon, and many who will receive the mark of the beast, believe they have an understanding of the truth. But truth that is not lived and imparted loses its life-giving power.

The Image of God

> Wherefore lay apart all filthiness and superfluity of naughtiness, and receive with meekness the engrafted word, which is able to save your souls. But be ye doers of the word, and not hearers only, deceiving your own selves. (James 1:21–22)

We are to receive the word with meekness, allowing the Word of God, by His Spirit, to be engrafted into our minds as its principles and teachings become our own. This leads to spiritual growth, thus saving us from the power and pollution of sin.

> So get rid of all uncleanness and the rampant outgrowth of wickedness, and in a humble (gentle, modest) spirit receive and welcome the Word which implanted and rooted [in your hearts] contains the power to save your souls. But be you doers of the Word [obey the message], and not merely listeners to it, betraying yourselves [into deception by reasoning contrary to the Truth]. (James 1:21–22 AMP)

Religion in the image of man acknowledges God, has an intellectual understanding of who He is, but the heart is not changed. In contrast, those who receive God's Word and surrender their hearts and minds to it and its author are empowered by the Spirit of God to be doers of the Word. These are two distinct experiences: one of intellectual ascent alone, and one of surrender of heart and mind. Only in a full heart surrender can the truth of God be lived out in our lives. Truth that is only received intellectually, while the heart is not surrendered to it, is of no saving virtue.

The Image of the Beast

In Daniel 7 we find the rise of a little horn, a political and religious power, which is called the beast in Revelation 13. This little horn had "eyes like the eyes of man, and a mouth speaking great things" (Daniel 7:8). As were the eyes or understanding of the little horn, so was its mouth. It was an image of man, the heart of man, the eyes of man, and the mouth of man. Therefore, its words, dogmas, and decrees were the doctrines and commandments of men.

So it is today. All churches, governments, businesses, and institutions that speak and teach and act according to man, contrary to God's word in the Bible, will lead us downward, for they are opposed to the principles of God.

The Image of God

The eyes of your understanding being enlightened; that ye may know what is the hope of his calling, and what the riches of the glory of his inheritance in the saints. (Ephesians 1:18)

God has a people who do not follow the way of men. The eyes of their understanding, their minds, are enlightened by the glorious gospel; therefore, they follow the will and way of God.

Jesus taught, "The light of the body is the eye, if therefore thy eye is single then that whole body shall be full of light" (Matthew 6:22). The eye represents our perception and understanding as the light of the Holy Spirit and the Word of God illuminate our minds. Wholehearted devotion to God is the meaning of the Savior's words; this indicates the image of God is being reproduced in the life and character.

The Image of the Beast

Let all bitterness, and wrath, and anger, and clamour, and evil speaking, be put away from you, with all malice. (Ephesians 4:31)

This is the spirit of the natural man, the one who does not know Jesus Christ and has not been renewed by the gospel in heart and mind.

The Image of God

Love endures long and is patient and kind; love never is envious nor boils over with jealousy, is not boastful or vainglorious, does not display itself haughtily. It is not conceited (arrogant and inflated with pride); it is not rude (unmannerly and does not act unbecomingly. Love (God's love in us) does not insist on its own rights or its own way, for it is not self-seeking; it is not touchy or fretful or resentful; it takes no account of the evil done to it (it pays no attention to a suffered wrong). It does not rejoice at injustice and unrighteousness, but rejoices when right and truth prevail. Love bears up under anything and everything that comes, is ever ready to believe the best of every person, its hopes are fadeless under all circumstances, and it endures everything [without weakening]. (1 Corinthians 13:4–7 AMP)

The above verses reveal the image of God that is formed in the lives of those who accept the gospel, as they allow Jesus to live out His life in them. The mind of man is bitterness, wrath and anger, and evil speaking. The mind of God is love, a love that endures long. It is patient and kind; it is not self-seeking or self-willed.

One of two minds or characters is being formed in the heart of every person, young or old. The question is, "Who has control of your mind?" In what direction is your life developing? Is it tending toward the image of Satan? Or are you building upon the foundation of God's Word and the gospel of Jesus Christ?

The Image of the Beast

> Now the works of the flesh are manifest, which are these; Adultery, fornication, uncleanness, lasciviousness, Idolatry, witchcraft, hatred, variance, emulations, wrath, strife, seditions, heresies, envyings, murders, drunkenness, revellings, and such like: of the which I tell you before, as I have also told you in time past, that they which do such things shall not inherit the kingdom of God. (Galatians 5:19–21)

All people, religious or not, who are controlled by the flesh, living a life more of the flesh than of the spirit, are developing a mind and character that will accept the mark of the beast willingly. There are many others who have conditioned themselves to be accommodating and noncommittal to truth and the principles of God, and they too will accept the mark. They merely go along with the new order in order to continue in their uncommitted ways.

The Image of God

> But the fruit of the Spirit is love, joy, peace, longsuffering, gentleness, goodness, faith, Meekness, temperance: against such there is no law. And they that are Christ's have crucified the flesh with the affections and lusts. (Galatians 5:22–24)

All of mankind has the mind of the flesh unless they are being renewed by the creative power of God. My friend, what mind is being formed in your life? The mind you have will determine your eternal destiny. The fruit of the Spirit is the mind of God being restored in the mind of a person who accepts the mercy of

God and "the washing of regeneration, and renewing of the Holy Ghost" (Titus 3:5).

The Mind of Satan

> Wherein in time past ye walked according to the course of this world, according to the prince of the power of the air, the spirit that now worketh in the children of disobedience: Among whom also we all had our conversation in times past in the lusts of our flesh, fulfilling the desires of the flesh and of the mind; and were by nature the children of wrath, even as others. (Ephesians 2:2–3)

Paul here is declaring that there is a class of people who live according to the principles of this world. The "prince of the power of the air guides them" meaning Satan. They are children of disobedience. The mind of Satan leads away from God and lives in disobedience to Him. Such a mind can be religious, but it is not being conformed to the will and way of God.

The Mind of Christ

> Let this mind be in you, which was also in Christ Jesus: Who, being in the form of God, thought it not robbery to be equal with God: But made himself of no reputation, and took upon him the form of a servant, and was made in the likeness of men: And being found in fashion as a man, he humbled himself, and became obedient unto death, even the death of the cross. (Philippians 2:5–8)

In Isaiah we read that Satan boasted, "I will be like God, and I will sit in the place of God and receive worship." Notice the contrast between the attitude of Lucifer, "son of the morning," the created one, and the Creator, "Jesus ... the bright and morning star" (Revelation 22:16). Christ became a man. He humbled Himself and became obedient unto death, even the death of the cross, for our salvation.

Lucifer, a created being, has exalted himself above his Creator. His spirit will be perfected in the mark of the beast, as the prideful hearts of men exalt man's religion and commandments above the commandments of the Most High God.

> Forasmuch then as Christ hath suffered for us in the flesh, arm yourselves likewise with the same mind: for he that hath suffered in the flesh hath ceased from sin; That he no longer should live the rest of his time in the flesh to the lusts of men, but to the will of God. (1 Peter 4:1–2)

Whose will are you following, your own or the will of God? This will determine whether you will be marked or sealed. To receive the mark of the beast means to come to the same decision as the beast has, which is to stand in opposition to the word and law of God. This took place in Jesus' day, and those doing so were religious. The same spirit is at work at the end of time. To be marked is a settling into error, falsehood, and sin, so that we cannot be moved, either by God's love or by His warnings.

Those who are uniting with the world and its principles and religions are preparing for the mark of the beast.

Those who are distrustful of themselves, and look to Jesus and His enabling strength for salvation, humbling themselves before God and purifying their souls by obeying the truth, are preparing for the seal of God in their foreheads. They are settling into the truth intellectually and in their experience so that they will not be moved by the threats or rewards of the beast system that will be brought to bear upon them.

The choice is yours, my friend. I pray that you will choose wisely, that you will choose the will and way of God. The way of salvation, the way of deliverance. What we are developing today in our character and in our lives determines where will be when the great harvest takes place: on the side of Christ and eternal life, or on the side of Satan and eternal death. Marked or sealed, what will it be for you?

Endnotes

1. James Strong LL.D., S.T.D., *Strong's Exhaustive Concordance* (Grand Rapids, Michigan: Baker Book House, 1987).
2. Tryus—ancient city of Phoenicia, south of Sidon. It is the present-day Sur in Lebanon, a small town on a peninsula jutting into the Mediterranean from the mainland of Syria south of Beirut. It was built on an island just off the mainland, but the accumulation of sand around a mole [causeway] built by Alexander the Great to facilitate his siege of the city (333–332 BC) has formed a causeway more than .5 miles (.8 km) wide. The date of the founding of the city is uncertain, but by 1400 BC it was a flourishing city. The maritime supremacy of Tyre was established by 1100 BC, and by that date its seamen seem to have sailed around the Mediterranean and to have founded colonies in Spain, southern Italy, and North Africa. Tyrians founded the city of Carthage in the ninth century BC. Tyre was famous for its industries, such as textile manufactures, and particularly for the purple Tyrian dye. (*The Columbia Electronic Encyclopedia*®, Copyright © 2005, Columbia University Press. Licensed from Columbia University Press. All rights reserved.
3. Hebrew lexicon is Brown, Driver, Briggs, Gesenius Lexicon; this is keyed to the *Theological Word Book of the Old Testament.* Online Bible Version CD 2.5.3, 1996.
4. *Strong's Exhaustive Concordance*, op cit.
5. Greek lexicon based on Thayer's Lexicon and Smith's Bible Dictionary plus others; keyed to the large Kittel and the *Theological Dictionary of the New Testament.* Online Bible CD 2.5.3, 1996.
6. Ibid.
7. Ibid.
8. Ibid.

Chapter Thirteen

If Any Man Worships the Beast—
The Beast Identified • Part One

And the third angel followed them, saying with a loud voice, If any man worship the beast and his image, and receive his mark in his forehead, or in his hand, The same shall drink of the wine of the wrath of God, which is poured out without mixture into the cup of his indignation; and he shall be tormented with fire and brimstone in the presence of the holy angels, and in the presence of the Lamb. (Revelation 14:9–10)

There is much speculation in the Christian world as to what the mark of the beast is. Some believe it is a myth or a symbol of evil. The number 666 associated with the mark is also open to speculation, but is usually thought of as a sign of evil, a number used in the occult. In fact, more attention is given to the number 666 and the mark than to understanding who the beast is.

It is sad when one of the most serious warnings in Scripture is so little understood by the majority of Christians and the world in general. This is all the more inexcusable since the beast can be identified using the characteristics found in Revelation 13 and Daniel 7. What comes as a surprise to most is that the beast, often referred to as the antichrist, is with us now.

There are several books, that I would recommend for the reader who desires more in-depth understanding of the subject of the beast and the number 666 than we will take time to develop in this study.[1]

What is the mark of the beast? This is a vital question and one that deserves careful study.

- Is it a super computer that is able to monitor the personal and private information of all living on the planet, believed to be located in western Europe?

- Is it global space satellites able to track and monitor every person on the planet?

- Is it a cashless economic system?

- Is it smart cards that contain all your vital personal information, such as bank records, medical records, passport and drivers license, etc.?

- Is it the Universal Product Code, those black lines with numbers found on most retail products?

- Is it the VeriChip, which is currently imbedded in new American passports, and is being used in business for inventory control and tracking? When scanned at the proper frequency, the VeriChip responds with a unique sixteen-digit number that can correlate information stored on a database. In a yet to be introduced human application it can be used for identity verification, medical records access, and other uses. The VeriChip has been used in animals for identification and tracking purposes, and is injected as simply and as painlessly as a vaccination. Once the chip is inserted, it is invisible to the naked eye.

The Bible is where we find this term "mark of the beast," and only the Bible can give us the true meaning. The first step to answering this puzzle is to identify the beast of Bible prophecy.

The beast will be a religious power. The whole issue of the mark of the beast is over worship, so it will be religious in nature. The Bible warns us that whoever receives the mark of the beast, "the same shall drink of the wine of the wrath of God" (Revelation 14:10).

Recognizing who the beast is and the nature of the mark is critical. We must understand it before these things come to pass, because the warning has been given to us for right now.

The warning regarding the beast and his mark is not only for an event and crisis in the future. God gives warning ahead of time to inform the people to prepare. He does this in love.

Now, let us go to Revelation chapter 13 and look at the characteristics that identify who the beast is.

> And I stood upon the sand of the sea, and saw a beast rise up out of the sea, having seven heads and ten horns, and upon his horns ten crowns, and upon his heads the name of blasphemy. (Revelation 13:1)

The beast coming out of the sea represents a nation or kingdom. Daniel 7:17 and 23 tell us that a beast, in Bible prophecy, represents a kingdom or a political power. The beast is not a charismatic person at the end of time, for a beast is not a person but a kingdom.

This political power or kingdom comes out of the sea. What does that mean?

> Son of man, say unto the prince of Tyrus, Thus saith the Lord God; Because thine heart is lifted up, and thou hast said, I am a God, I sit in the seat of God, in the midst of the seas; yet thou art a man, and not God, though thou set thine heart as the heart of God. (Ezekiel 28:2; the kingdom of Tyrus is a symbol of Satan's seat in the midst of seas, or people.)

> And he saith unto me, the waters which thou sawest, where the whore sitteth, are peoples, and multitudes, and nations, and tongues. (Revelation 17:15)

The beast out of the sea represents a kingdom or power coming out from the midst of a populated area. The prophetic beasts of Daniel 7 not only came out of the sea, but from the midst of the winds of war and strife, whereas the beast of Revelation 13:1 is seen coming up out of the sea in relative peace.

The beast had "seven heads and ten horns." This is symbolic. We are not to look for some hideous creature at the end of time that will take control of the world.

Revelation 12:3 says, "And there appeared another wonder in heaven; and behold a great red dragon, having seven heads and ten horns, and seven crowns upon his heads." Revelation 12:9 tells us that this dragon is Satan, the devil. However, as we study chapter 12, we learn that the devil used pagan Rome to try to attack the infant Jesus. As pagan Rome fell, Satan used another power to try to persecute Christ's church. Christ's church is represented in Revelation 12 as the woman in the wilderness. So the dragon primarily represents Satan. But he uses churches, institutions, and governments to accomplish his purposes.

This seven-headed, ten-horned dragon introduced in Revelation chapter 12 is reintroduced in chapter 13 at a different time of history. It is called a beast, meaning a kingdom.

We read in Revelation 17:3, "So he carried me away in the spirit into the wilderness: and I saw a woman sit upon a scarlet colored beast, full of names of blasphemy, having seven heads and ten horns." Here again we find a seven-headed, ten-horned beast. The beast of chapters 12, 13, and 17 is the same power. This power is introduced at different times in earth's history. Thus this beast of Revelation 13 and the beast in Revelation 14 are but a continuation in another form of the dragon beast first introduced in chapter 12. The beast of Bible prophecy, which many people refer to as the Antichrist, can be traced back to the Roman Empire.

In Daniel 7 we see a ten-horned beast. This was the pagan Roman Empire. The horns were subsequent powers that arose from it. As Rome began to decay, these ten horns or kingdoms arose in its midst, in its territory. Three of them were destroyed, and the seven that remain are the modern nations of western Europe. This beast of Revelation 13 began to develop during the last centuries of the Roman Empire. Daniel called it a little horn, and it continues to the end of time. The horns on the beast of Revelation 13 are not new powers but are political powers that assisted and came to the aid of the beast. These powers were the kingly monarchies of Europe, indicated by the crowns on the horns.

And the ten horns out of this kingdom are ten kings that shall arise.... (Daniel 7:24)

Then I lifted up my eyes and saw, and behold, four horns [symbols of strength]. And I said to the angel who talked with me. What are these? And he answered me. These are the horns or powers which have scattered Judah, Israel, and Jerusalem. Then the Lord showed me four smiths or workmen [one for each enemy horn, to beat it down]. Then said I, What are these [horns and smiths] coming to do? And he said, These are the horns or powers that scattered Judah so that no man lifted up his head. But these smiths or workmen have come to terrorize them and cause them to be panic-stricken, to cast out the horns or powers of the nations who lifted up their horn against the land of Judah to scatter it. (Zechariah 1:18–21 AMP)

And it was different from all the beasts that came before it, and it had ten horns [symbolizing ten kings]. (Daniel 7:7 AMP)

A horn in Bible prophecy represents kingdoms. When attached to a prophetic beast, the horn gives aid and power to the beast, as in Revelation 13 and 17. Alternatively, they represent subsequent powers or kingdoms that arise and come to power from a beast as it decays and falls away, as in Daniel 7. The term *horn* is also used as a symbol for strength and glory.

Heads represent rulers or leaders. We can see this from such texts as Micah 3:9, Exodus 18:25, and Ephesians 1:22. The number seven in the Bible is a symbol of completion or perfection. The heads or leaders of the beast will be blasphemous in character. As the dragon beast of chapter 12 was Satan, and secondarily pagan Rome through whom he worked, the beast of Revelation 13 is also a tool of Satan. Further, it is a continuation of Rome; thus, it is represented as also having ten horns with the addition of seven heads. We can readily see that the characteristics of the beast are not that of an individual antichrist, as is generally taught.

What does it mean that the heads or leaders are blasphemous? "Thou that makest thy boast of the law, through breaking the law dishonourest thou God? For the name of God is blasphemed among the Gentiles through you, as it is written" (Romans 2:23–24).

How is God's name blasphemed? By claiming to serve God and to live for Him when we don't really do so. This is blasphemy according to God. Now, this beast, this political power, is religious in nature. That is why its leaders are blasphemous. They claim to serve God, claim to be God's representatives on earth, but often do not really obey and follow Him.

Another definition of blasphemy is found in the gospel of John. "The Jews answered Him, saying, For a good work we stone thee not; but for blasphemy; and because that thou, being a man, makest thyself God. Say ye of Him, whom the Father hath sanctified, and sent into the world, Thou blasphemest; because I said, I am the Son of God?" (John 10:33, 36).

Jesus claimed to be the Son of God, and this is true. However, the religious leaders did not believe it. They said Jesus' claim was blasphemy. Blasphemy is to claim the prerogatives[2] of God when we are but created beings.

The book of Luke further defines the meaning of blasphemy. "And when He saw their faith, He said unto him, Man, thy sins are forgiven thee. And the scribes and the Pharisees began to reason, saying, Who is this which speaketh blasphemies? Who can forgive sins, but God alone" (Luke 5:20–21)?

The religious leaders did not recognize Jesus' divinity, even though Jesus was divine and had the right to forgive sins. "But when Jesus perceived their thoughts, He answering said unto them, What reason ye in your hearts? Whether is easier, to say, Thy sins be forgiven thee; or to say, Rise up and walk? But that ye may know that the Son of man hath power upon earth to forgive sins, (He said unto the sick of the palsy,) I say unto thee, Arise, and take up thy couch, and go into thine house" (Luke 5:22–24).

The heads or leaders of the beast are blasphemous in nature, believing that they can forgive sins and take the titles that belong to God alone. These political and religious leaders claim to serve God yet violate His law and Word. This is the spirit of blasphemy.

Prophetic Keys of Understanding

- The beast is a kingdom, not a person.
- The beast will come out of the sea; in other words, from a populated area.
- The beast has ten horns with crowns, representing political powers or kingdoms that supported it.
- The beast has leaders who are blasphemous in nature.

> And the beast which I saw was like unto a leopard, and his feet were as the feet of a bear, and his mouth as the mouth of a lion: and the dragon gave him his power, and his seat, and great authority. (Revelation 13:2)

The above description of the beast is not of some literal creature that the world will worship and follow. The book of Revelation uses symbols, and the Bible explains the meanings of those symbols. Once you understand the code, you can know the meaning of what is written.

In chapters 2, 7, 8, and 11 of the book of Daniel, he reveals prophetic powers or kingdoms under different symbols. These kingdoms are Babylon, Medo-Persia, Greece, Rome, and a little horn or kingdom that came out of the Roman Empire.

In chapter 7 Daniel sees these four prophetic powers as beasts coming up out of the sea, just like we see a beast coming out of the sea in John's vision. In Daniel's vision the sea is stirred by the winds, showing that these kingdoms came out of chaos, war, and social upheaval. In contrast, the beast of Revelation 13, while also coming out from the sea, has its power given to it.

> **The Lion**—The first was like a lion, and had eagle's wings: I beheld till the wings thereof were plucked, and it was lifted up from the earth, and made stand upon the feet as a man, and a man's heart was given to it. (Daniel 7:4; this lion with an eagle's wings was the kingdom of Babylon.)

The Bear—And behold another beast, a second, like to a bear, and it raised up itself on one side, and it had three ribs in the mouth of it between the teeth of it: and they said thus unto it, Arise, devour much flesh. (Daniel 7:5; this bear was Medo-Persia.)

The Leopard—After this I beheld, and lo another, like a leopard, which had upon the back of it four wings of a fowl; the beast had also four heads; and dominion was given to it. (Daniel 7:6; this leopard represents the Grecian kingdom).

The description of the beast in Revelation 13 reveals it has characteristics similar to the beasts of Daniel 7. The beast of Revelation is not an individual; it too is a kingdom, and it has absorbed characteristics of these previous kingdoms into itself.

The beast will come up in time after Babylon, Medo-Persia, Greece, and Rome. This reveals that the beast kingdom has been in existence since the fall of Rome, as it is a continuation of Rome under a different form.

The beast of Revelation 13 has the body of a leopard, so we should expect elements of Grecian thought and philosophy to be in this system. Its mouth is lion-like, so its words and teachings have elements of Babylon in it, "for out of the abundance of the heart the mouth speaketh" (Matthew 12:34).

The feet of the bear, which moves the beast, represents the twofold power of the Medes and Persians. This is similar to Daniel 2, where the feet were the combination of iron and clay, representing government and church. The horns of the Roman Empire are also part of the beast.

Daniel saw these powers in the order of lion, bear, leopard, and the fourth beast, then the little horn. When John wrote, Babylon was gone, as was Greece and Medo-Persia. He lived under the rule of the fourth beast. That is why he describes the nature of this beast in the opposite order of Daniel 7.

The little horn of Daniel 7 comes after Rome, and the beast out of the sea comes after Rome. The little horn and the beast are the same power.

	Daniel 7	Revelation 13
Babylon	Lion-like beast (verse 4)	Mouth of a lion (verse 2)
Medo-Persia	Bear-like beast (verse 5)	Feet of a bear (verse 2)
Greece	Leopard-like beast (verse 6)	Like a leopard (verse 2)
Rome	Ten-horned beast (verse 7)	Has ten horns (verse 1)
Church & State	Little horn (verses 8, 24)	The beast (verse 1–8)

The dragon gave the beast of Revelation 13 power and great authority. That dragon is Satan, and secondarily it represents the kingdom of Rome. It had dominion and a throne and authority, which would be passed to the beast of Revelation 13. Further, elements of paganism can be found in the beast of Revelation 13 since the dragon (Satan) is behind it. "And to him the dragon gave his [own] might and power and his [own] throne and great dominion" (Revelation 13:2 AMP).

Prophetic Keys of Understanding

- The beast of Revelation has the characteristics of the beasts of Daniel 7.

- The beast of Revelation comes up in time after the beasts of Daniel 7.

- The beast of Revelation receives his kingdom from pagan Rome.

- The beast of Revelation has elements of paganism in it, for the dragon, or the devil, is behind it.

And I saw one of his heads as it were wounded to death; and his deadly wound was healed: and all the world wondered after the beast. (Revelation 13:3)

The heads of the beast represent its rulers or leaders. This indicates the beast is a kingdom rather than an individual. One of the leaders of the system is wounded, apparently endangering the whole beast. But there is a recovery, for we read, "His deadly wound was healed."

"He shall judge among the heathen, he shall fill the place with dead bodies, he shall wound the heads over many countries" (Psalm 110:6). This expression, "I saw one of his heads as it were wounded to death," means an attack upon the head or leader and the heart of the beast's kingdom.

God foretells the wound to the beast so that all might know that He is God and that all might believe. Jesus said, "Now I tell you before it come, that, when it is come to pass, ye may believe that I am He" (John 13:19). It is not enough to go through these clues simply to identify the beast. We need to learn that God is in control; He is the sovereign Lord of this universe and has foretold these things before they take place.

The expression "all the world wondered after the beast" indicates awe. The reverence and worship of this beast comes most notably after its deadly wound is healed. After its recovery, the beast will, over time, regain strength. In the process, he will gain worldwide admiration and power. All the world will wonder after the beast. Then the power and influence exercised in the past will be repeated.

Prophetic Keys of Understanding

- One of the heads or leaders of the beast appears to be mortally wounded, thus endangering the beast itself. But the wound is healed.

- What appeared to be sure death is in fact only apparent, for the head of the beast system recovers. This system will go on to be admired by the whole world and will gain global influence.

And they worshipped the dragon which gave power unto the beast: and they worshipped the beast, saying, Who is like unto the beast? who is able to make war with him? (Revelation 13:4)

The word *worship* means "to kiss like a dog licking his master's hand; to fawn or to crouch to. Literally or figuratively, prostrate oneself in homage, (do reverence to, adore.)"[3] "Treated with divine honors; treated with civil respect."[4]

When people give worship or honor to the beast system, knowingly or unknowingly, they are worshiping the dragon, or Satan. Why? Because this beast is blasphemous in nature. Thus, in worshiping and giving civil respect to the beast, the people of this world are actually giving service to the devil. This should not be a surprise, for if we do not obey the gospel of Jesus Christ and submit to God's authority in love, allowing Jesus to transform our lives and to renew us, we are actually serving the devil. Therefore, those who follow this system, who give respect to this system, will do so in contrast to the worship of the true God and following His Word.

Worshiping the Dragon

They sacrificed unto devils, not to God; to gods whom they knew not, to new gods that came newly up, whom your fathers feared not. Of the Rock that begat thee thou art unmindful, and hast forgotten God that formed thee. And when the Lord saw it, he abhorred them, because of the provoking of his sons, and of his daughters. And he said, I will hide my face from them, I will see what their end shall be: for they are a very froward generation, children in whom is no faith. (Deuteronomy 32:17–20)

The Bible reveals that the children of Israel were sacrificing unto devils. Did they understand what they were doing? Often they did not. What led them to this? They didn't have faith in God, they did not believe His word, and they seemingly forgot the many miracles He did on their behalf. They became ungrateful, and thus their "foolish heart was darkened" (Romans 1:21).

To worship devils or the dragon means to live a life without faith. And true "faith cometh by hearing, and hearing by the word of God" (Romans 10:17). While most of the world makes a profession of belief in a god or even the true God, and will do so when worshiping or respecting the beast, such a religious faith does not lead to obedience to God, following Him in spirit and in truth.

As Israel forgot God, engaging in false worship, so too does the world have many lords and gods. There is faith in human institutions, the doctrines and commandments of men, and this prepares the world to worship this beast. The beast will be followed and respected and honored because people do not have saving faith.

> And I saw three unclean spirits like frogs come out of the mouth of the dragon, and out of the mouth of the beast, and out of the mouth of the false prophet. For they are the spirits of devils, working miracles, which go forth unto the kings of the earth and of the whole world, to gather them to the battle of that great day of God Almighty. (Revelation 16:13–14)

Who is guiding these powers? It is unclean spirits, not the spirit of God. The dragon, beast, and false prophet are all instruments through which the unclean spirits work to draw the leaders and the people of this planet into deception, to stand against God. Sadly, this is often done in the name of God. That is why the world worships the dragon and will follow his vicar, the beast.

> Ye are of your father the devil, and the lusts of your father ye will do. He was a murderer from the beginning, and abode not in the truth, because there is no truth in him. When he speaketh a lie, he speaketh of his own: for he is a liar, and the father of it. (John 8:44)

Jesus was addressing the religious leaders of His day, who claimed to serve God. The Jews had many privileges, for "unto them were committed the oracles of God" (Romans 3:2). Further, unto them were given "the covenants, and the giving of the law, and the service of God, and the promises" (Romans 9:4). Yet Jesus addressed this class of religious leaders as worshipers of the devil. They claimed to have the true religion, they claimed to believe in the true God. But in their hearts they were not converted. They were still sinful. When we have sinful, unconverted hearts, regardless of our religion, we worship the devil. Because of man's unconverted carnal nature, most of the world will worship the devil's representative, his political religious system on this earth, the beast power. The Jews in Jesus' day thought they were serving God but did not really do so. This will also be the experience of many who follow the beast.

The Bible reveals that the world will be deceived. This prepares them to accept the devil's representative, the beast, as a power for good. "He that committeth sin is of the devil; for the devil sinneth from the beginning. For this purpose the Son of God was manifested, that He might destroy the works of the devil" (1 John 3:8).

"In this the children of God are manifest, and the children of the devil: whosoever doeth not righteousness is not of God, neither he that loveth not his brother" (1 John 3:10). John shows us the determining factor as to who is on God's side and who is on the devil's side. It is righteousness by faith, made evident by love and obedience to God and loving others with heaven-born love.

The righteousness of Christ is ours by faith. "For I am not ashamed of the gospel of Christ: for it is the power of God unto salvation to every one that believeth" (Romans 1:16). Only the blood of Jesus Christ, and His cleansing power experienced in our lives day by day, washes us from our sins and keeps us from being found on the side of the evil one. Those who worship the beast have not been cleansed and washed by the blood of Jesus. They will worship the beast, give reverence to it, assist it, and go along with it. Why? Because they worship the dragon.

Now, very few people in this world outwardly and knowingly worship Satan. However, "to whom you yield yourselves servants to obey, his servants you are to whom you obey; whether of sin unto death, or of obedience unto righteousness" (Romans 6:16).

A life lived in sin, or a life of seeking righteousness: this determines whom you really obey and follow, God or the devil. The texts we have been studying reveal the characteristics of what it means to worship the dragon (Satan). This is what most of mankind does; therefore, it will be easy for the entire world to wonder after the beast.

For thousands of years, Satan has been developing his systems of counterfeit worship and has been manipulating the hearts and minds of men. He is an expert at this. Through his deceptive and subtle workings over the ages, and now especially, at the end of time, he is linking the human mind with his own. And man unknowingly follows his thoughts.

The great deceiver is confusing man's thinking so that only his voice is being heard. This is in contrast to what Jesus said, "My sheep hear My voice and follow Me; the voice of a stranger they will not follow." (See John 10.) All who do not truly follow Jesus hear another voice. They worship the dragon and will, in the end, worship and give allegiance to the beast.

Who Is Like Unto the Beast?

Revelation 13:4 says the world will declare, "Who is like unto the beast?" What can we learn about the condition of the world and the character of the beast from this expression?

Who is like unto the Lord our God, who dwelleth on high, who humbleth himself to behold the things that are in heaven, and in the earth! (Psalm 113:5–6)

Who is like unto thee, O Lord, among the gods? who is like thee, glorious in holiness, fearful in praises, doing wonders? (Exodus 15:11)

To the world at large, the beast is likened to God, or at least is His representative and stands in the place of God. Thus the world asks the question, "Who is like the beast?"

Happy art thou, O Israel: who is like unto thee, O people saved by the Lord, the shield of thy help, and who is the sword of thy excellency! and thine enemies shall be found liars unto thee; and thou shalt tread upon their high places. (Deuteronomy 33:29)

This term "who is like" is applied to God. And who is like God's people? When the world says, "Who is like unto the beast?" they are recognizing the beast as exercising God's authority, His representative on earth. By allegiance with this beast, we also will be considered God's people. This is why most people will receive the beast's mark.

Who Is Able to Make War with Him?

Wrath is cruel, and anger is outrageous; but who is able to stand before envy? (Proverbs 27:4)

And the men of Bethshemesh said, Who is able to stand before this holy Lord God? and to whom shall he go up from us? (1 Samuel 6:20)

The expression "who is able" indicates the utter inability and even unwillingness to fight against this beast. Why? Because to fight against this power is perceived to be fighting against God. "And his power shall be mighty, but not by his own power: and he shall destroy wonderfully, and shall prosper, and practice" (Daniel 8:24).

Prophetic Keys of Understanding

- The beast has influence and power because the world is in reality under the influence of the dragon, or Satan.

- Because of this, the world is readily deceived into accepting the beast as an instrument of God, to whom respect or worship should be given.

- The beast will command such respect that people dare not stand against it, for to do so is thought to be standing against God and His kingdom.

The warning is clear: "If any man worship the beast and his image, and receive his mark in his forehead, or in his hand, the same shall drink of the wine of the wrath of God" (Revelation 14:9–10). We must make an effort to know who the beast is. Though the beast appears to the world in a favorable and positive light, and will do many charitable and good things to recommend itself to the world, it is a counterfeit to the kingdom of God and to the gospel of Christ. It is God's enemy, and God declares, "Come out her, My beloved; come and follow Me." (See Revelation 18:4.)

My friend, unless we have a relationship with Jesus, we are going to be deceived into following the beast and receiving its mark. There are only two conclusions: we will ether worship the beast or we will worship Christ. May God give you the desire to serve Him and to follow Him in love. This is my hope and prayer, in Jesus' name, amen.

Endnotes

1. *The Antichrist 666,* by William Josiah Sutton (ISBN 1-57258-015-1). *The Illuminati 666,* by William Josiah Sutton (ISBN 1-57258-014-3). *The Dragon, The Beast, and The False Prophet,* by William Josiah Sutton. *Let Daniel and Revelation Speak,* by David Wilson (ISBN 978-0-9786002-6-6) also available as a free e-book at www.inspirationspeaks.com.
2. Prerogative —1. An exclusive privilege or right enjoyed by a person or group occupying a particular rank or position. 2. A privilege or right that allows a particular person or group to give orders or make decisions or judgments. 3. The right conferred by a natural advantage that places someone in a position of superiority. 4. The power or right of a monarch or government to do something or be exempt from something. 5. Superiority in rank or nature. *Encarta® World English*

Dictionary © 1999 Microsoft Corporation. All rights reserved. Developed for Microsoft by Bloomsbury Publishing Plc.

3. James Strong LL.D., S.T.D., *Strong's Exhaustive Concordance* (Grand Rapids, Michigan: Baker Book House, 1987).

4. Noah Webster, *American Dictionary of the English Language* (San Francisco, California: Foundation for American Christian Education, 1967).

Chapter Fourteen

If Any Man Worships the Beast—
The Beast Identified • Part Two

A nd the third angel followed them, saying with a loud voice, If any man worship the beast and his image, and receive his mark in his forehead, or in his hand, The same shall drink of the wine of the wrath of God, which is poured out without mixture into the cup of his indignation; and he shall be tormented with fire and brimstone in the presence of the holy angels, and in the presence of the Lamb. (Revelation 14:9–10)

In this chapter we will continue to look at the characteristics of the beast found in Revelation 13. In verses 5–7 the historical activities of the beast are described.

And there was given unto him a mouth speaking great things and blasphemies; and power was given unto him to continue forty and two months. (Revelation 13:5)

There are three characteristics in verse 5 that deal with the beast. He had a mouth; in other words, his teachings and pronouncements were great. *Great things* means "persons, eminent for ability, virtue, authority, power. Things esteemed highly for their importance: of great moment, of great weight, importance."[1] The beast speaks with authority on issues of global concern and importance. But the speech does not end there, for the beast is also a religious force, and some of his doctrines, decrees, and words are blasphemy in God's sight. The third identifying characteristic of the beast is that power is given him to continue for forty-two months.

It is typically thought that this three and a half years is sometime in the future. However, this time spoken of in Daniel 7 and again in Revelation 11 and 12 refers to the casting down of the truth and the oppression of God's people. In Daniel and Revelation this time is referred to as "time, times, and the dividing of time," as forty-two months or 1,260 days. It refers to prophetic time, or a day equaling a year. (See Numbers 14:34; Ezekiel 4:6.)

This simple code of a day for a year is one of the keys of understanding who the powers of the prophecy are in the symbolic prophecies of Daniel and Revelation. This "time" is not three and a half literal years either in the past or at some point in the future. It is a period of 1,260 years during which the beast power of Revelation (called the little horn in Daniel) was to develop into a dominant power.

> I considered the horns, and, behold, there came up among them another little horn, before whom there were three of the first horns plucked up by the roots: and, behold, in this horn were eyes like the eyes of man, and a mouth speaking great things. (Daniel 7:8)

The little horn here has the same characteristics as the beast of Revelation 13, including the same great words. As the little horn came from the fourth beast of Daniel 7, which is the Roman Empire, the beast also received power and influence from pagan Rome.

> And he shall speak great words against the most High, and shall wear out the saints of the most High, and think to change times and laws: and they shall be given into his hand until a time and times and the dividing of time. (Daniel 7:25)

The great things that are spoken by the little horn attract the world's attention, and at times may be good and necessary. At other times the great words are meant to lessen the truth and glory of God, to obscure or change His word, the holy Bible and His law and the gospel. Therefore, the great words are tantamount to blasphemy, for the character and truth of God is masked and substituted for the words and teachings and traditions of men.

The antichrist that many are looking for in the future is with us now, and has been in existence since the fall of Rome. Its influence and power was foretold in prophecy as lasting 1,260 years. This time would come to an end after he receives a deadly wound, which will be healed. After that it will have increasing global influence. This took place at the end of the 1,260 years, which lasted from A.D. 538 to A.D. 1798. And indeed, a leader of a religious political system that had great influence was wounded in 1798, apparently endangering the life of the beast.

Daniel reveals another characteristic of the little horn, which is also found with the beast in Revelation 13:7. The little horn "shall wear out the saints of the most High" (Daniel 7:25). Governments or kingdoms, for political and ethnic reasons, or for being considered enemies of the state, have killed people the world over, past and present.

Tens of millions perished at the hands of Communist governments in Russia and China. Saddam Hussein killed hundreds of thousands of his own countrymen. And in the twenty-first century hundreds of thousands have been killed in Darfur at the hands of the Sudanese government. Sadly, this has been and remains the state of affairs in our sin-cursed world. However, the beast, or the little horn, is noted not for the slaughter of its citizens but for persecution against the people of God, those who had the faith of Jesus and who loved His law and word. This reveals that the beast or little horn is a religious as well as a political power.

Revelation 11 and 12 also reveal the persecution of God's people and the casting down of His truth for a period of forty-two months, 1,260 days, "a time, times, and half a time," all referring to 1,260 years.

The little horn, or the beast, would "think to change times and laws" (Daniel 7:25).

The beast has been involved in propaganda warfare to change the times of the prophecies, just as Daniel predicted. The forty-two months, 1,260 days, and "time, times, and half a time," representing 1,260 years of the beast's dominance, has been reinterpreted to mean that the Antichrist was Nero or some other historical figure. What is more commonly believed today is that the 1,260 days is a literal period of three and a half years, during which time some charismatic and evil individual called the antichrist will rule the world.

Not only will the little horn change the meaning of the prophecies dealing with time, he will think in his heart that he can change the time in regard to God's law. However, God's moral law is unchanging.

There is only one commandment in the moral law dealing with time, and that is the seventh-day Sabbath. Considering the popular practice of hundreds of millions of sincere Christians, and even billions of non-Christians, the little horn's attempt to change time and law has been successful here as well.

The first angel's message to the world is to "worship Him that made heaven, and earth, and the sea, and the fountains of waters" (Revelation 14:7). This is a call to the worship of Jehovah as Creator and Savior every day and with all our heart, mind, and strength. It is also a call to recognize the Lord's day, the seventh day. The beast and the world largely refuse this, choosing rather to follow tradition and convenience.

Prophetic Keys of Understanding

- The beast will speak great words of importance that address the issues of the day.

- The beast, by its teaching and decrees, is guilty of blasphemy, speaking against God, His truth and word and law.

- The beast will reign for a prophetic period of 1,260 years, a time in which it will be noted for its persecution of the saints of God.

- The beast called the little horn in Daniel will change the time prophecies, putting them in the past or the future, so that people will not identify it as the antichrist.

- The beast called the little horn in Daniel will think, and sincerely so, that it can change God's law regarding the time of worship found in the fourth commandment.

And he opened his mouth in blasphemy against God, to blaspheme his name, and his tabernacle, and them that dwell in heaven. (Revelation 13:6)

He Opened His Mouth in Blasphemy

Verse six reiterates the spiritually harmful effects of the words of the beast in regard to the truth and glory of God. Lamentations gives us insight as to the meaning of the words "He opened his mouth against God."

"All thine enemies have opened their mouth against thee: they hiss and gnash the teeth: they say, We have swallowed her up: certainly this is the day that we looked for; we have found, we have seen it" (Lamentations 2:16).

The enemies of God were ridiculing Israel and Jerusalem because of the judgments of God; however, they were really ridiculing God. When they opened their mouths, they spoke against God. The opening of the beast's mouth is simply the pouring forth of its speech, which is notable for its blasphemous nature against God's truth and the plan of salvation.

The word *blasphemy* means "vilification against God." To *blaspheme* means to "speak impiously"[2] against God. The beast, being both a kingdom and a religious power, recognized and accepted by the world as largely a force for good, does not openly speak against God. Rather, it appears to be God's voice on earth. In what way, then, does it speak blasphemy?

"Blasphemy is an injury offered to God, by denying that which is due and belonging to him, or attributing to him that which is not agreeable to his nature." It means "that which derogates from the prerogatives of God."[3] *Derogate* means "to repeal, annul or destroy the force and effect of some part of law or established rule; to lessen the extent of a law. To take away; to detract; to lessen by taking away a part."[4]

The beast speaks great things that gain the world's confidence and respect, while at the same time it blasphemes God. This blasphemy is not in challenging or mocking God openly, but rather by appearing to speak for God while at the same time promoting the doctrines and traditions of men rather than God's Word. This has the effect of lessening the force of the everlasting gospel, the Bible and God's law, in the minds of the people, as substitutes and counterfeits are given to the world. This is blasphemy of a most serious nature, yet most people do not see it. Most of the world will be found with the beast, fighting against God and doing so in His name.

Blaspheme His Name

The beast is noted for blaspheming God's name. The word *name* means "authority, character."[5] The beast would blaspheme the authority of God and His character. How would this take place?

> And the Lord descended in the cloud, and stood with him there, and proclaimed the name of the Lord. And the Lord passed by before him, and proclaimed, The Lord, The Lord God, merciful and gracious, longsuffering, and abundant in goodness and truth. (Exodus 34:5–6)

When Moses asked God to show him His glory, God revealed Himself not in fire and thunder, as He did upon Sinai, but in declaring His character. The beast, by many of its decrees, traditions, teachings, and influence, ascribes to God's character that which is not true. It lessens, annuls, or substitutes something in the place of God's truth, and in this also blasphemes His name.

> I am the Lord: that is my name: and my glory will I not give to another, neither my praise to graven images. (Isaiah 42:8)

The beast works to undermine God's name, authority, and character by the veneration of images, icons, statues, and relics. God is not honored in this, regardless of the piety and sincerity demonstrated. Sadly, the world seems not to understand this. It readily goes along with the beast and honors it. Why? Because most people worship the idols of human reasoning and opinion above God's Word. Others make idols of material possessions. When we are idolaters, in whatever form, it is easy to accept the idolatry and falsehood of the beast. Idolaters do not have a love for the truth and therefore are ready to believe a lie.

> My doctrine shall drop as the rain, my speech shall distil as the dew, as the small rain upon the tender herb, and as the showers upon the grass: Because I will publish the name of the Lord: ascribe ye greatness unto our God. He is the Rock, his work is perfect: for all his ways are judgment: a God of truth and without iniquity, just and right is he. (Deuteronomy 32:2–4)

The truth and knowledge of God's mercy, goodness, and loving character fall like rain to refresh and enliven our sin-scorched, dry souls. Because of this, Moses said, "I will publish or make known the name, character, and authority of Jehovah." God is the rock, the sure foundation, but the beast seeks to place man's attention on substitutes and half-truths and outright distortions, creating a god that is false. In this way the beast and all who follow it, and those who are influenced by its teachings, blaspheme the name of God while, in many cases, professing to honor Him. This strange infatuation with error and falsehood is why God must speak so plainly through the message of Revelation, so that the world will be warned.

> If we have forgotten the name of our God, or stretched out our hands to a strange god; Shall not God search this out? for he knoweth the secrets of the heart. (Psalm 44:20–21)

The beast, as well as many of the religions of this world, work to cause people to forget the name of God while professing to serve Him. This is done as God's authority and His word and moral law is substituted, or its influence lessened, by the ideas of men.

Yet God, knowing our hearts, sees the sincerity of many. That is why He calls us out of Babylon, out of the spiritual error and confusion of this modern world. Now is the hour of judgment, when mankind must choose between the ways of God and the falsehood propagated by the beast, the dragon, and the false prophet.

The result of the blasphemy of the beast is that people do not have a clear concept of the nature of God, His truth, and His law. We learn further this power will blaspheme God's tabernacle.

Blaspheme His Tabernacle

Seeing then that we have a great high priest, that is passed into the heavens, Jesus the Son of God, let us hold fast our profession. For we have not an high priest which cannot be touched with the feeling of our infirmities; but was in all points tempted like as we are, yet without sin. Let us therefore come boldly unto the throne of grace, that we may obtain mercy, and find grace to help in time of need. (Hebrews 4:14–16)

Now of the things which we have spoken this is the sum: We have such an high priest, who is set on the right hand of the throne of the Majesty in the heavens; A minister of the sanctuary, and of the true tabernacle, which the Lord pitched, and not man. (Hebrews 8:1–2)

The beast, in its religious capacity and by its teachings and creeds, will be noted for blaspheming God's tabernacle. This is not speaking of defiling a rebuilt temple in Jerusalem. The beast undermines the ministry of Christ in the temple in heaven. How can men on earth affect the work of Christ as our High Priest? It is true that no man or power on earth can affect things in heaven, but it can mislead people on earth to misunderstand the work of Christ. The leaders and priesthood of the beast do this by their traditions and false practices and teachings.

So Christ was once offered to bare the sins of many, and unto them that look for him shall he appear a second time without sin unto salvation. (Hebrews 9:28)

The beast, in blaspheming the tabernacle in heaven, is undermining the ministry of Christ as man's only intercessor and redeemer. Christ's sacrifice was sufficient for every man's salvation and took place only once. However, the beast continually adds to Christ's sacrifice, making His sacrifice on Calvary of non-effect by adding to it mere human ritual.

For there is one God, and one mediator between God and men, the man Christ Jesus. (1 Timothy 2:5)

In blaspheming God's tabernacle the beast does not defile a physical structure, but undermines the ministry of Christ for the salvation of men, typified in the sanctuary service. For Jesus is the "minister of … the true tabernacle, which the Lord pitched, and not man" (Hebrews 8:2.) The beast, as well as all false religions, set before the people substitutions, or an additional mediator besides Christ, which lessens in the minds of people the true work of Christ. This has the effect of leading people away from salvation and eternal life. Saints, relics, statues, churches, holy men or women, and religious leaders and organizations are but some of the substitute mediators of false religion. All substitutions for the intercession of Christ are blasphemy in God's sight. And God calls us to separate from all these practices.

Prophetic Keys of Understanding

- The beast opens his mouth and, through his teachings and doctrines, speaks blasphemy against God's authority and character.

- The beast, through his speaking, teachings, and doctrines, attempts to obscure the work of Christ as our High Priest in the heavenly tabernacle, substituting something in its place so as to set human ideas in the place of God's truth.

- The beast, through substitution of God's truth, works to undermine the great work of salvation undertaken by the godhead and the work of the holy angels, who are sent as ministering spirits. This is how the beast blasphemes those who dwell in heaven.

And it was given unto him to make war with the saints, and to overcome them: and power was given him over all kindreds, and tongues, and nations. (Revelation 13:7)

The beast is noted for warfare, but not against other nations. The beasts in Daniel 7 came out of the wind-tossed sea, representing the winds of strife and warfare. The beast of Revelation 13 makes war, not with other states, but against the saints, the true people of God. Daniel says the same thing. "And I beheld, and the same horn made war with the saints, and prevailed against them" (Daniel 7:21). The little horn and the beast are one and the same power.

Revelation 17 reveals a similar scenario. "And I saw the woman drunken with the blood of the saints, and with the blood of the martyrs of Jesus: and when I saw her, I wondered with great admiration" (Revelation 17:6).

The zeal to persecute the saints comes about because of the delusion of false worship. Jesus said, "Yea, the time cometh, that whosoever killeth you will think that he doeth God service" (John 16:2). We read in Revelation 13 that the beast was a persecuting power in the past, and it will be again in the future, when the kings of this earth and the powers of this earth assist it to rise to global dominance after a period of great chaos. Then the world will look to "religion," the woman who will control the beast, "the state," to bring some degree of order out of the chaos the world finds itself in. Then the beast of Revelation 13, a political and religious kingdom or power, will have its deadly wound fully healed. It will then have power "over all kindreds, and tongues, and nations" (Revelation 13:7).

The persecution at the end of time will be as deadly and unreasonable as any in the past, as "no man might buy or sell, save he that had the mark" (Revelation 13:17). Further, as "many as would not worship the image of the beast should be killed" (Revelation 13:15). This will be done in the name of world harmony and peace and solidarity, and in the name of religion. Yet Jesus has told us, "These things will they do unto you, because they have not known the Father, nor Me" (John 16:3).

When men and their institutions, governments, or religions claim that they are speaking for God and that they have the truth, and also have the reigns of political power, what will they do? Jesus said they will persecute you, and they will do it in the name of God. There is no more dangerous and deadly delusion than when religious people, who claim to speak in the name of God, deny religious liberty to others because they are convinced that they have the truth. We see this already in some countries in the twenty-first century that are controlled by religion.

The book of Revelation reveals that this history of persecution of the saints will be repeated. The beast with the kings of the earth and the religions of the earth will be at the forefront. The beast is a power that was in the past, is with us now, and will be with us in the future. It is both political and religious in nature, and it is noted in the prophecies for making war with the saints.

Prophetic Keys of Understanding

- The beast was a persecuting power in the past.

- The beast will have worldwide authority, which will come when its deadly wound is fully healed.

    And all that dwell upon the earth shall worship him, whose names are not written in the book of life of the Lamb slain from the foundation of the world. (Revelation 13:8)

The whole world will be taken in the snare of deception and will worship the beast, all except those in the Lamb's book of life. Those in the Lamb's book have been washed and cleansed from sin, having saving faith that is motivated by love. Why will most of the world be deceived? Because they have not received the love of the truth. In the place of God's truth they follow delusions, believing a lie, having pleasure in unrighteousness. (See 2 Thessalonians 2:10–12.)

A love of sin, and the rejection of the truth in preference for error, leads the world to worship the beast, thinking they are worshiping and following God. However, the wonder, admiration, and worship of the beast is false worship, which is actually at war with God. Jesus declared, "Many false prophets shall rise, and shall deceive many." This atmosphere of deception will be especially effective "because iniquity shall abound, [and] the love of many shall wax cold" (Matthew 24:11–12). In contrast, the saints of God shall remain true to Him and to His Word and law. Jesus has promised, "He that shall endure unto the end, the same shall be saved" (Matthew 24:13).

> If any man have an ear, let him hear. He that leadeth into captivity shall go into captivity: he that killeth with the sword must be killed with the sword. Here is the patience and the faith of the saints. (Revelation 13:9–10)

> If any one is able to hear, let him listen: Whoever leads into captivity will himself go into captivity; if anyone slays with the sword, with the sword must he be slain. Herein is [the call for] the patience and the faith and fidelity of the saints (God's people.) (Revelation 13:9–10 AMP)

The above verses tell us to hear and perceive with heaven's wisdom. The beast, and indeed all the world's powers that align themselves against God and His truth and who use force to compel the conscience, will in the end reap what they have sown. "And the third angel poured out his vial upon the rivers and fountains of waters; and they became blood. And I heard the angel of the waters say, Thou art righteous, O Lord, which art, and wast, and shalt be, because thou hast judged thus. For they have shed the blood of saints and prophets, and thou hast given them blood to drink; for they are worthy. And I heard another out of the altar say, Even so, Lord God Almighty, true and righteous are thy judgments" (Revelation 16:4–7).

God calls His people to exercise consistent endurance, to resist the beast and the mark of rebellion, to believe and wait on the Lord, even though their loyalty may lead to persecution and even death. God has counseled us "as much as lieth in you, live peaceably with all men. Dearly beloved, avenge not yourselves, ... for it is written, Vengeance is mine; I will repay, saith the Lord" (Romans 12:18–19).

What the powers of apostasy do to the children of God shall be requited. "Reward her even as she rewarded you, and double unto her double according to her works: in the cup which she hath filled fill to her double" (Revelation 18:6). Therefore let not any of the children of God take up the weapons of carnal warfare. "Seeing it is a righteous thing with God to recompense tribulation to them that trouble you; And to you who are troubled rest with us, when the Lord Jesus shall be revealed from heaven with His mighty angels, In flaming fire taking vengeance on them that know not God, and that obey not the gospel of our Lord Jesus Christ: Who shall be punished with everlasting destruction from the presence of the Lord, and from the glory of His power; When He shall come to be glorified in His saints, and to be admired in all them that believe (because our testimony among you was believed) in that day" (2 Thessalonians 1:6–10).

A Summary of the Prophetic Keys

1. The beast comes from a populated area ("out of the sea").

   - The Roman church arose in the populated area of western Europe, a sea of people.

2. The beast has ten horns with crowns, representing political powers or kingdoms that support it.

- The Roman church was helped by the kings of Europe to maintain and gain its secular and religious power. This was true from its earliest days. It is still supported in its work and influence by the kings of the earth.

3. The beast has leaders who are blasphemous in nature.

   - The popes claim to be the vicars of Christ and His representative on earth. However, the popes, along with the cardinals, bishops, and priests, teach and practice many unbiblical doctrines, rites, and ceremonies and exalt human tradition above God's Word. Despite the claim to be the true church of Christ, their teachings and practices are often blasphemous in nature.

4. The beast comes up in time after Babylon the lion, Medo-Persia the bear, and Greece the leopard, and after the fourth beast, Rome. The beast would also have characteristics of these beasts. This shows us that the beast is a kingdom, as were the beasts before it, and comes up in time after these beasts. Rome collapsed in 476, so we should look for the beast of Revelation 13 to be on the scene in the fifth and sixth centuries.

   - The Roman church came up in time after Babylon, Medo-Persia, Greece, and Rome. There are no more prophetic powers after the ancient pagan Roman Empire, for the beast is simply a continuation of the fourth beast in the form of church and state combined. Papal Rome, in its doctrines and traditions and character, has elements of these previous powers within it.

5. The beast receives his power, dominion or territory, and throne or seat of his kingdom from the pagan Roman Empire.

   - The Roman church, developed as the Roman Empire, was waning, and much of its authority was simply acquired due to the vacuum left by the lessening influence of the Roman Empire.

6. One of the heads or leaders of the beast appears to be mortally wounded, thus endangering the beast itself. But the wound is healed, and what appeared to be sure death is in fact only apparent, for the beast system recovers.

    - One of the popes of the Roman church was taken captive by the French general Berthier in 1798; 1,260 years after this power's prophetic ascendancy began. Pope Pious died the following year in exile.

7. The beast has influence and power because the world is under the influence of the dragon, or Satan. Because of this, the world is readily deceived into accepting the beast as an instrument of God, to whom respect or worship should be given.

    - The Roman church commands worldwide respect for its commendable charitable and religious work. It also does a great deal, both openly and behind the scenes, to influence legislation in many countries of the world and is involved in numerous international organizations. These include the United Nations, World Trade Organization, and World Council of Churches, and the Organization for Security and Cooperation in Europe, to name but a few. Because of this vast influence, few in the world see it as Satan's instrument. People have largely ignored the Word of God and its authority on religious and moral matters, and Satan's counterfeit is readily accepted as God's instrument and representative on earth, and the mother church.

8. As it was in the past, so it will be in the future. The beast is sustained by the dragon, or Satan, who uses the power of an apostate state that supports the beast.

- Papal Rome is both a church and a political entity. Through the Holy See in Vatican City it is recognized as a country, and as of November 2006, 174 states maintain diplomatic relations with the Vatican. In addition are the Sovereign Military Order of Malta, and mission of the Russian Federation, and the Office of the Palestine Liberation Organization. It is supported diplomatically, and in its church activities, by most of the states of the world. In the last days it will be supported in its worldwide rule by the leaders of the world, with special help from the two-horned beast of Revelation 13:11.

9. The beast will command such awe and respect that people dare not stand against it, for to do so is thought to be standing against God's kingdom.

- The Roman church today is able to a large degree to modify and blunt negative publicity in the media, and is generally seen as an instrument of peace and morality in the world. This is why to identify the Catholic system as being the beast and antichrist of Revelation is looked down upon by most churches and political leaders of the world. In short, the world is already deceived as to the nature and purpose of the papal system, as most people reject God's Word and accept the papacy.

10. The beast will speak great words that attract the attention and admiration of the world, while at the same time speaking things that are blasphemous.

- By its doctrines, rites, ceremonies, and traditions, the Catholic system speaks blasphemies against God and His truth. And yet it attracts the admiration of many by its fair speeches, good words and deeds, and its pleas for social justice and human solidarity.

11. The beast power will occupy a position of prominence in the world for a period of 1,260 years. The wound one of its heads or rulers receives marks the end of the 1,260 years of dominance.

   • The Roman church is the mystery of iniquity, and it developed over time. By 538 AD it had established itself as the first of all churches, with increasing political power as the kings of the earth assisted it. It was in 538 that, for the first time since the fall of the Roman Emperors, the city of Rome was freed from the domination of Arian kingdoms. In 538 the Ostrogoths under pressure from the armies of Justinian, Emperor of the eastern Roman Empire, abandoned Rome. Now the decrees of the Emperor Justinian first proclaimed in 533, that confirmed the bishop of Rome as the "head of all the holy churches" and "head of all the holy priests of God" could be implemented. Thus 538 marks the start of the 1260 year prophecy during which time the papacy would grow in influence and power. This period terminated in 1798, at that time the pope was taken captive by the French army, and died in exile the following year. The papal power received its deadly wound, and the prophecy was fulfilled, "he that leadeth into captivity shall go into captivity."

   From 538 to 1798 is the 1,260-year prophecy marked out as the time of papal rule. This is a prophetic marker to help identify the beast, which was in the past and is presently with us, and in the future will gain global influence.

12. The beast opens his mouth, and through his teachings and doctrines speaks blasphemy against God's authority and character.

   • The papal system, though claiming to be Christian, teaches many things that are contrary to God's Word. These teachings come from paganism and exalt traditions above the

Word of God, thereby undermining God's name and His authority. They distort His character by virtue of the falsehood being propagated.

13. The beast, through his speaking and teachings, obscures the work of Christ as our High Priest in the heavenly tabernacle, substituting something in its place. This blasphemes God's tabernacle by placing human ideas in the place of God's truth.

    • The Roman church undermines the work of Christ in the minds of the people through substituting or adding to God's Word. Saints and Mary become our intercessors and helpers. Through the idolatry of the mass, where Jesus is worshiped in the form of the Eucharistic wafer and through a human priesthood to whom the adherents are told to confess to, Jesus is in reality deemphasized and obscured.

14. The beast was a persecuting power in its past and will be again in the future after the wound is fully healed.

    • Revelation 13 and 17 reveal that the beast's authority in the future will be sustained by the kings of the world. Though watered down, the Vatican admits to persecutions in the past. Prophecy reveals it will happen again in the future by economic boycotts, and death will be the ultimate penalty for not following the beast and receiving his mark.

15. The beast influenced much of western Europe's kindred tongues and peoples, and it will accomplish the same throughout the world before the end of time. As in the past, his power or authority will be given to it by others.

    • Revelation 13 reveals that another beast, called the two-horned beast, will exercise all the power of the first beast. Further, it will initiate a global system of worship called the mark of the beast. As in its past so in its future, the papacy will be helped to power. Revelation 17 reveals that the woman, the papal head of Mystery Babylon, will ride the beast or the state will carry her.

16. The beast will, in the future, receive the homage and admiration of the world's inhabitants. It is only the true children of God who will not worship the beast or his image.

The beast is with us now; it is the Roman Catholic Church. It is a church and a state system. The beast or antichrist popularly taught as a future charismatic individual does not fit the prophetic characteristics given to us in Daniel 7 and Revelation 13, for the little horn and the beast are the same power, and it is a political and religious kingdom.

We need God's wisdom in this age of religious deception, "that we henceforth be no more children, tossed to and fro, and carried about with every wind of doctrine, by the sleight of men, and cunning craftiness, whereby they lie in wait to deceive" (Ephesians 4:14).

"The fear of the Lord is the beginning of wisdom: and the knowledge of the holy is understanding" (Proverbs 9:10). I pray that you will have the wisdom of heaven, my friend, to understand the times in which we live, and to clearly understand who is on God's side and who is not; to truly understand who speaks for God, and who is a counterfeit.

I pray that this day you would "behold the Lamb of God, which taketh away the sin of the world," your sins and mine (John 1:29). Further, that in beholding the Lamb, you would follow Him and not the voice of strangers. (See John 10:1–10.) May God help you and me. That is my hope and prayer, amen.

Endnotes

1. Greek lexicon based on Thayer's Lexicon and Smith's Bible Dictionary plus others; keyed to the large Kittel and the *Theological Dictionary of the New Testament.* Online Bible CD 2.5.3, 1996

2. James Strong LL.D., S.T.D., *Strong's Exhaustive Concordance* (Grand Rapids, Michigan: Baker Book House, 1987).

3. Noah Webster, *American Dictionary of the English Language* (San Francisco, California: Foundation for American Christian Education, 1967).

4. Ibid.

5. *Strong's Exhaustive Concordance*, op cit.

Chapter Fifteen

If Any Man Worships the Beast— Sealed or Marked

And the third angel followed them, saying with a loud voice, If any man worship the beast and his image, and receive his mark in his forehead, or in his hand. The same shall drink of the wine of the wrath of God, which is poured out without mixture into the cup of his indignation; and he shall be tormented with fire and brimstone in the presence of the holy angels, and in the presence of the Lamb. (Revelation 14:9–10)

The Seal or the Mark

Many people have heard of the mark of the beast, though few really understand the issues at stake concerning this mark of apostasy. Even fewer give consideration to another sign or mark that Revelation calls the seal of God.

At the end of time the powers of apostasy will enforce a religious mark that indicates some degree of willingness to accept the authority of the beast. Revelation 13 repeatedly uses the term *worship* when referring to the recognition and acceptance of the beast and his mark. This may be wholehearted acceptance or a begrudging recognition merely to carry on with normal life.

The beast with the kings of the earth will bring forth a new global order of some kind. It will largely be the result of global disorder, with religion playing a leading role to bring order out of the chaos. Massive disease outbreaks, global terrorism, climate change, economic collapse, and increasing natural disasters are but a few of the current problems already seeking to rend the fabric of society as we know it.

The final crisis of the ages before Jesus comes will be spiritual in nature. It will be a religion that seeks to secure global harmony and peace in cooperation with the kings of the earth. Such movements have already begun, apparently seeking solutions to mankind's many problems.[1]

In the midst of the chaos, the development of a religious world order, and the implementation of the mark of the beast, the book of Revelation focuses attention on a remnant, the people of God. The Bible says they will not receive the mark. They will be empowered by God's Spirit, as on the day of Pentecost, to give a warning against the beast, his mark, and false religion. The remnant will be sealed, in contrast to earths teeming multitudes who receive the mark of the beast.

Many have looked at various advancements in technology and commerce as the possible instruments to be used as the mark.

Some people already have microchips implanted on their persons, and in some countries this has been used in animals for identification and tracking. No doubt such technologies will be implemented at some point to control the buying and selling of the world's inhabitants.

The mark involves not just a physical component but also the mind. It reveals who has your heart's allegiance; thus, it is religious in nature. Only when there is a quick and simple test to determine who is on God's side and who is on the side of the forces of apostasy will the physical mark be issued. No one will be constrained to receive the mark and therefore be doomed by God.

The beast will use flattery, rewards and inducements, threats, and loss of life and liberty to persuade the hesitant and doubting. However, in order to receive the mark, even under negative consequences, we must choose to reject God's message and warning and go along with the beast and the global order.

The Seal of God

What is the seal of God? The word *seal* means "to stamp with a signet or private mark for security or preservation."[2]

The seal of God is His sign showing we belong to Him. We use a seal or stamp on official documents to mark them as authentic and genuine. Similarly, God's seal is an outward sign that shows the validity and authority of God's Word, the Bible, and His law in our lives. This is in contrast to those who receive the mark, for they follow the authority of human laws in place of God's law and man's religion in the place of the Bible.

Revelation chapter 6 closes with a description of the fearful events accompanying the second coming and the despair, fear, and punishment of the wicked. The last verse closes with this question: "For the great day of His wrath is come; and who shall be able to stand?" (Revelation 6:17).

In response to that question Revelation chapter 7 describes those who will be sealed and alive at Christ's coming, ready and eager to receive their king and deliverer. The prophet Isaiah describes it this way: "And it shall be said in that day, Lo, this is our God; we have waited for Him, and He will save us: this is the Lord; we have waited for Him, we will be glad and rejoice in His salvation" (Isaiah 25:9).

And after these things I saw four angels standing on the four corners of the earth, holding the four winds of the earth, that the wind should not blow on the earth, nor on the sea, nor on any tree. And I saw another angel ascending from the east, having the seal of the living God: and he cried with a loud voice to the four angels, to whom it was given to hurt the earth and the sea. Saying, Hurt not the earth, neither the sea, nor the trees, till we have sealed the servants of our God in their foreheads. (Revelation 7:1–3)

A seal is placed upon God's people just prior to the letting loose of the four winds of the seven last plagues. The seal of God is placed upon the forehead, the moral seat and conscience of man. The seal is not something physical seen by men; rather, it is a sign of God's authority and a sign of the genuineness of our experience. The seal will show we have given our will and life totally to God, to be guided by Him. Obedience to God's Word, the Bible, and His holy law will be the outward sign of those who are sealed.

An inward heart experience will determine whether we are marked by the beast or sealed by God, for both the mark and the seal demonstrate our allegiance to the power that we recognize as the final authority in our life.

> And they shall see his face; and his name shall be in their foreheads. (Revelation 22:4)

That which is written upon the forehead is the name or character of God. Those who are sealed have given their hearts, minds, and strength to God. He is the final authority in the lives of the remnant, not the beast or the kings of the earth. Further, in accepting the everlasting gospel, those who are sealed fear God and give glory to Him, worshiping God alone as Creator and redeemer. The life of Christ has become theirs through faith in Him.

> And thou shalt make a plate of pure gold, and grave upon it, like the engravings of a signet, holiness to the Lord. And thou shalt put it on a blue lace, that it may be upon the mitre; upon the forefront of the mitre it shall be. And it shall be upon Aaron's forehead, that Aaron may bear the iniquity of the holy things, which the children of Israel shall hallow in all their holy gifts; and it shall be always upon his forehead, that they may be accepted before the Lord. (Exodus 28:36–38)

> But ye are a chosen generation, a royal priesthood, an holy nation, a peculiar people; that ye should shew forth the praises of him who hath called you out of darkness into his marvelous light. (1 Peter 2:9)

As children of God and followers of Christ, we are called to be a royal priesthood, a holy nation. As with Aaron and the high priests of old, upon our forehead is to be written "holiness to the Lord." This is to be an experience of dedication to God of heart and mind rather than simply a physical inscription upon a mitre. Holiness to the Lord comes as a result of "being made free from sin" and becoming "servants to God." In this experience we have "fruit unto holiness, and the end everlasting life" (Romans 6:22).

To be sealed comes as the result of accepting the first angel's message of the everlasting gospel, leading us to increasingly fear God and give glory to Him. In contrast, those who will eventually receive the mark increasingly give their service and lives to following man's commandments and principles and giving glory to manmade ideas and institutions. In the end, those who will worship the beast and receive his mark will have "changed the truth of God into a lie, and worshipped and served the creature more than the Creator" (Romans 1:25).

> Nevertheless the foundation of God standeth sure, having this seal, The Lord knoweth them that are his. And, Let every one that nameth the name of Christ depart from iniquity. (2 Timothy 2:19)

Departing from iniquity is a sign of the genuineness of our experience. For only he who does righteousness has been made righteous by the blood of the Lamb. (See 1 John 3:7, 10.) While many worshipers of the beast may be sincere in their belief, in rejecting truth and rejecting God's call in Revelation 14, they have chosen to believe a lie. They choose the commandments of men over the law and Word of God. When lawlessness is enforced by the religions of man and the kings of the earth, even though done in sincerity, it will be the mark of iniquity, the mark of the beast.

> Bind up the testimony; seal the law among my disciples. (Isaiah 8:16)

God, through the prophet Isaiah, warned Israel and Jerusalem not to trust in their confederacies or alliances, for they would come to nothing. (See Isaiah 8:11–12.) The book of Revelation warns us of the confederacy of Babylon and the kings and merchants of the earth, that they too will be cast down. (See Revelation 18.) The Lord, through Isaiah, invited the people to make Jehovah their refuge and safety instead of trusting in the plans and alliances of men. Isaiah further warned the people to fear God instead of honoring man and thereby despising God. (See Isaiah 8:13–14.)

God instructed Isaiah to take His message, His word, and His law and bind them up and preserve them. This may refer to the custom of binding up a document and affixing a seal to it, thereby showing its authority. But more than that, God's law and His word are to be bound upon heart and mind and lived out. Only in this way can it be kept and preserved.

The people of God who will be sealed do not merely have the Bible; they have made the Bible their counselor and guide. They have lived out the prayer of Jesus, "Thy kingdom come. Thy will be done in earth, as it is in heaven" (Matthew 6:10). In living by God's Word and obeying His law, they have lived the will of God in their own lives, and they will be sealed in that experience, set apart as God's own.

In contrast, the worshipers of the beast have followed the laws of man and his religions and thus will be marked as adherents to the authority of the powers of apostasy.

God's Sign and Seal of an Inward Heart Experience

But the seventh day is the sabbath of the Lord thy God: in it thou shalt not do any work, thou, nor thy son, nor thy daughter, thy manservant, nor thy maidservant, nor thy cattle, nor thy stranger that is within thy gates: For in six days the Lord made heaven and earth, the sea, and all that in them is, and rested the seventh day: wherefore the Lord blessed the Sabbath day, and hallowed it. (Exodus 20:10–11)

The seventh-day Sabbath is the seal of God. In a legal seal we find the author, his title, and his dominion. In the Sabbath we find God's name (Creator), His dominion (heaven and earth), and His title (Lord).

> Speak thou also unto the children of Israel, saying, Verily my sabbaths ye shall keep: for it is a sign between me and you throughout your generations; that ye may know that I am the Lord that doth sanctify you. (Exodus 31:13)

> Moreover also I gave them my sabbaths, to be a sign between me and them, that they might know that I am the Lord that sanctify them. And hallow my sabbaths; and they shall be a sign between me and you, that ye may know that I am the Lord your God. (Ezekiel 20:12, 20)

The Sabbath is called a sign. The word *sign* means "a signal (literal or figurative), as a flag, beacon, monument, evidence."[3]

The Sabbath is a sign of God's power to sanctify. Redemption is creation, and the Sabbath is a monument, the evidence or sign of God's power as Creator. Further, He is the re-creator of the estranged heart of man when he yields to God's drawing love and accepts Him as Savior and Lord.

> And the third angel followed them, saying with a loud voice, If any man worship the beast and his image, and receive his mark in his forehead, or in his hand, The same shall drink of the wine of the wrath of God, which is poured out without mixture into the cup of his indignation; and he shall be tormented with fire and brimstone in the presence of the holy angels, and in the presence of the Lamb: And the smoke of their torment ascendeth up for ever and ever: and they have no rest day nor night, who worship the beast and his image, and whosoever receiveth the mark of his name. Here is the patience of the saints: here are they that keep the commandments of God, and the faith of Jesus. (Revelation 14:9–12)

In the first angel's message (Revelation 14:7), there is a call to worship God because He is the Creator. The Sabbath is God's great memorial of this work. The Sabbath commandment in the last days will be God's seal and sign that distinguish the patient, faithful commandment-keepers from the worshipers of the beast. It is a sign of an experience of holiness unto the Lord, of obedience. It is a sign of God's re-creative power, of His authority, and of our acceptance of Him as Lord of lords and King of kings.

Whatever the beast's mark of religious authority is, it is in contrast to God's people, who are sealed. God's people are noted for patiently and consistently following the right and being obedient to God's word and His law, the Ten Commandments. They have not only a profession of Jesus but also the enabling "faith of Jesus" (Revelation 14:12). Therefore, in spite of threats and inducements to give up the truth of God and follow the ways of man, they remain firm. Just like the believers in Smyrna who lived in the time of the Roman Empire, so God's people who live in a time of a global confederacy involving religion, politics, and finance will gain comfort from these words of Jesus:

> I know thy works, and tribulation, and poverty, (but thou art rich) and I know the blasphemy of them which say they are Jews, and are not, but are the synagogue of Satan. Fear none of those things which thou shalt suffer: behold, the devil shall cast some of you into prison, that ye may be tried; and ye shall have tribulation ten days: be thou faithful unto death, and I will give thee a crown of life. (Revelation 2:9–10)

The mark will be accepted despite God's warning in the book of Revelation and the Spirit empowering God's messengers and coming upon the inhabitants of the world to reprove and convince, as it was on the day of Pentecost. The time of the mark of the beast will be as it was in the days of Elijah the prophet. God's people, the Elijah of the last days, will give a message of separation and a call to choose between truth and error as he did. "And Elijah came unto all the people, and said, How long halt ye between two opinions? if the Lord be God, follow Him: but if Baal, then follow him. And the people answered him not a word" (1 Kings 18:21).

The powers of apostasy will be working along with Satan and demon spirits. There will be "power and signs and lying wonders." This work will go forward "with all deceivableness of unrighteousness in them that perish; because they received not the love of the truth, that they might be saved. And for this cause God shall send them [this is by God's allowance because they have rejected truth] strong delusion, that they should believe a lie: that they all might be damned who believed not the truth, but had pleasure in unrighteousness" (2 Thessalonians 2:9–12).

Most of mankind will think this apostasy is actually following God. They will be deceived into believing that obedience to the beast is God's will for man.

Technology will no doubt be involved. However, the technology is not the beast's mark. That is determined because we have rejected the law of God for the laws of men; man's word is accepted instead of God's Word. In this rebellion against God, which is obedience to man, people will be allowed to buy and sell and carry on with life, having been granted the privilege of receiving the technology necessary to do so.

A Lesson from the Past

> Then he brought me to the door of the gate of the Lord's house which was toward the north; and, behold, there sat women weeping for Tammuz. And he brought me into the inner court of the Lord's house, and, behold, at the door of the temple of the Lord, between the porch and the altar, were about five and twenty men, with their backs toward the temple of the Lord, and their faces toward the east; and they worshipped the sun toward the east. And the Lord said unto him, Go through the midst of the city, through the midst of Jerusalem, and set a mark upon the foreheads of the men that sigh and that cry for all the abominations that be done in the midst thereof. (Ezekiel 8:14, 16; 9:4)

In Ezekiel's vision God showed him example after example of the terrible apostasy that was transpiring among His professed people in Jerusalem. The women were weeping for Tammuz, a false god, who, according to legend, was the child of Semiramis, wife of Nimrod, who was impregnated by the sun god. Tammuz was worshiped variously as the son or lover of the goddess Ishtar. Remnants of these pagan beliefs are still with us today in some of the traditions and practices that surround Easter.

Ezekiel was further shown the false worship taking place in the temple of God, as abomination after abomination was revealed to him. God reveals to us as well, through His prophet John, the woman (religion) that is responsible for the abominations on the earth in our day. (See Revelation 17:5.)

Ezekiel saw that it was the ancients of the house of Israel, the religious leaders, who were at the forefront of the apostasy from God. Twenty-five of them were seen turning their backs from the temple to worship the sun. History is being repeated as abominations are practiced today in the name of God, in the temples and churches and hearts and lives of professed worshipers.

God revealed to the prophet another class of people, who were not partaking in these sins but who were sighing and crying for the abominations being done and the dishonor of God and His truth. A special sealing work was done for the faithful and true, while judgment was to fall upon the disobedient. This vision finds its parallel in the book of Revelation, where God's true commandment-keeping people are sealed before the four winds of strife are let loose. As in Ezekiel's day, the worshipers of the beast will go further and further into religious apostasy. The seal of God shows the distinction between the true and faithful and those involved in false worship, ceremonies, and teachings.

The distinction between the true and the false in Ezekiel's day was manifested by obedience or disobedience to God's word and law. This same distinction will be seen between the worshipers of the beast, who receive a mark of rebellion, obeying man rather than God, and those who have the faith of Jesus, who keep His commandments and are thus sealed with the seal of God.

A Spiritual Parallel

And it shall be for a sign unto thee upon thine hand, and for a memorial between thine eyes, that the Lord's law may be in thy mouth: for with a strong hand hath the Lord brought thee out of Egypt. (Exodus 13:9)

And it shall be for a token upon thine hand, and for frontlets between thine eyes: for by strength of hand the Lord brought us forth out of Egypt. (Exodus 13:16)

And thou shalt bind them for a sign upon thine hand, and they shall be as frontlets between thine eyes. (Deuteronomy 6:8)

Therefore shall ye lay up these my words in your heart and in your soul, and bind them for a sign upon your hand, that they may be as frontlets between your eyes. (Deuteronomy 11:18)

As we can see from these texts in Exodus and Deuteronomy, there was to be a token, mark, or sign on the hand and the area between the eyes, meaning the forehead, which is the seat of the will and where we exercise our power of choice. And what was to be on the hand and between the eyes? It was God's word and law.

Our minds and hands, our thoughts and works, are to be in obedience to God's word and law. The Jews took these words in the literal, physical sense as they wore the Scriptures on their persons. Jesus condemned this practice, as He did with all meaningless outward forms. (See Matthew 23:5.)

God was teaching Israel of their need to be converted and receive His Spirit, which would lead to His word and law guiding their daily acts and filling their thoughts. The people were to know and experience that "man doth not live by bread only, but by every word that proceedeth out of the mouth of the Lord doth man live" (Deuteronomy 8:3; see also Matthew 4:4). Living such a life is what is meant by having God's word and law upon the hand and as frontlets between the eyes.

In the above Scripture examples, God is calling for a surrendered mind and life to do His will, to follow His word and commandments. Such a life is only possible when we have "faith which worketh by love (Galatians 5:6). Revelation 14 calls it "the faith of Jesus." Therefore, the seal of God is a heart and mind fully surrendered to Him so that in life and thought we follow His word and law.

To receive the mark of the beast is to surrender the will to the word and commandments of the beast, willingly from the heart, for we have the same mind as the beast. This is a mind or attitude in opposition to God; thus, we are marked in the forehead, as shown by our willing compliance to the beast system. To be marked in the hand shows by our works that we accept the beast, regardless of our mental assent.

God's seal is only in the forehead, for with God a heart surrendered in love is the only acceptable service. The issue of the mark of the beast is over worship and authority, allegiance to God or to the church-state system of the revived beast. Indeed the whole issue at the end of time boils down to this: Shall I obey man and his religion and ideas, or shall I follow the Bible and the religion of Christ?

What Is the Seal of God?

1. It is a sign of genuineness placed upon the forehead, representing the moral seat of man. This seal is spiritual, not literal; it is, however, manifested by obedience to God's word and law.

2. The seal represents holiness to the Lord in thought and life.

3. It is placed on God's people before the seven last plagues.

4. The name or character of God is written upon the forehead. This means He has our full allegiance and we fully recognize His authority in our lives.

5. Those who are being sealed depart from sin.

6. Those who are sealed maintain their allegiance and fidelity to God in the midst of false worship and wickedness, grieved in their hearts when they see the word and character of God being dishonored.

What Is the Mark of the Beast?

1. It is a mark of disobedience to the commandments of God.

2. It is a sign of manmade religion in opposition to God's will and word.

3. It is based on the commandments of men.

4. It is a sign of allegiance to the god of this world.

5. It is a disposition of the mind to neglect or reject the will of God for our lives.

6. It is man's attempt to usurp the authority of God, who alone is to be worshiped and obeyed. It is the symbol of man's attempt to build a religion or society apart from God. It is a religion that passes as a way of honoring God but actually rejects Him, for it is in vain that we worship God when we are "teaching for doctrines the commandments of men" (Mark 7:7).

Let us ask the beast power of Scripture, a political and religious system identified as the Roman church, what its mark of authority is. A mark that is yet *future*, when it will be enforced by law. This mark will be a sign that distinguishes the beast's religious authority that exalts the word and commandments of men above the word and law of God.

Is not every Christian obliged to sanctify Sunday, and to abstain on that day from unnecessary servile work? Is not the observance of this law among the most prominent of our sacred duties? But you may search the Bible from Genesis to Revelation, and you will not find a single line authorizing the sanctification of Sunday. The Scriptures enforce the religious observance of Saturday, a day which we never sanctify.[4]

It is well to remind the Presbyterians, Baptists, Methodists, and all other Christians, that the Bible does not support them anywhere in their observance of Sunday. Sunday is an institution of the Roman Catholic Church, and those who observe the day observe a commandment of the Catholic Church.[5]

The church using the power of binding and loosing which Christ gave to the Pope, changed the Lord's Day to Sunday.[6]

Protestants...accept Sunday rather than Saturday as the day for public worship after the Catholic Church made the change ... But the Protestant mind does not seem to realize that in accepting the Bible, in observing the Sunday, they are accepting the authority of the spokesman for the church, the Pope.[7]

He [Pope Leo XIII] affirms the need for Sunday rest so that people may turn their thoughts to heavenly things and to the worship which they owe to Almighty God. No one can take away this human right, which is based on a commandment. ...The state must guarantee to the worker the exercise of this freedom.[8]

All Americans would do well to petition the President and the Congress to make a Federal law—an amendment to the Constitution if need be—to reestablish the Sabbath (Sunday) as a national Day of Rest.[9]

Sunday is a Catholic institution, and its claims to observance can be defended only on Catholic principles... From beginning to end of Scripture there is not a single passage that warrants the transfer of weekly public worship from the last day of the week to the first.[10]

It was the Catholic Church which, by the authority of Jesus Christ, has transferred this rest from the Bible Sabbath to the Sunday.... Thus the observance of Sunday by the Protestants is an homage they pay, in spite of themselves, to the authority of the Catholic Church.[11]

Therefore, also in the particular circumstances of our own time, Christians will naturally strive to ensure that civil legislation respects their duty to keep Sunday holy.[12]

Address on the Value of Sunday "The Symbol Par Excellence of All That Christianity Has Stood For"

CASTEL GANDOLFO, Italy, AUG. 18, 2003 (Zenit.org) Here is the address John Paul II delivered Aug. 3 when praying the Angelus with pilgrims gathered in the courtyard of the papal summer residence.

Dear Brothers and Sisters,

... 2. Special attention should be paid to safeguarding the value of Sunday, "Dies Domini." This day is the symbol par excellence of all that Christianity has stood for and still stands for, in Europe and throughout the world: the perennial proclamation of the Good News of the Resurrection of Jesus, the celebration of his victory over sin and death, the commitment to the human being's full liberation.

By preserving the Christian meaning of Sunday a notable contribution is made to Europe for the preservation of an essential part of its own particular spiritual and cultural heritage.[13]

While the above statement sounds biblical and is accepted as true by millions, it sadly cannot be upheld by the word of truth, the Bible. This is why *when* Sunday is enforced by law it will *then* become a mark of allegiance to the global religious and political system of the last days. This outward allegiance given willingly from the heart or begrudgingly simply going along to get along, will at that time allow access to the technology that enables you to continue to buy and sell.

The Sabbath comes from God. It is God's idea of worship. Therefore true Sabbath-keeping will lead to God. Sunday sacredness was man's idea of honoring the resurrection of Christ, and as reasonable as that sounds, there is no biblical basis or commandment for such a belief. Irrespective of man's intention, there can be no blessing in the Sunday sabbath. It is like the offering of Cain, based as it is on the religion and tradition of men.

Sunday sacredness is the image of a man. It comes from the heart of a man. The eyes of man's understanding formed it. Man's word has declared it sacred. The number of a man is written all over it. This is why God has singled out the mark of the beast for such stern condemnation. As with Cain, the religion that comes from man will in the last days lead to force, to murder, and to the mark of separation from God.

Endnotes

1. Organizations such as the World Parliament of Religions, www.cpwr.org. United Religions Initiative, www.uri.org. World Assembly of Religions for Peace, www.religionsfor-peace-2006-kyoto.net/index.html
2. James Strong LL.D., S.T.D., *Strong's Exhaustive Concordance* (Grand Rapids, Michigan: Baker Book House, 1987).
3. Ibid.
4. Cardinal Gibbons, *The Faith of our Fathers*, pp. 111–112
5. Father Brady, reported in the Elizabeth, N. J. News of March 18, 1903

6. Instructions in the Catholic Faith, 1985 Catechism by Killgallen and Weber, p. 243

7. Our Sunday Visitor, February 5, 1950

8. John Paul II, Encyclical, Centemus Annus, May 1991

9. Catholic Twin Circle, August 25, 1985, "Sacking Sunday."

10. Catholic Press, Sydney Australia, August 1900

11. Monsignor Louis Segur, *Plain Talk about the Protestantism of Today*, p. 213, 1868

12. John Paul II, Dies Domini, p. 23, section 67, May 31, 1998,

13. Zenit News, Castel Gandolfo, Italy August 18, 2003.

Chapter Sixteen

The Same Shall Drink of the Wine of the Wrath of God

And the third angel followed them, saying with a loud voice, If any man worship the beast and his image, and receive his mark in his forehead, or in his hand, The same shall drink of the wine of the wrath of God, which is poured out without mixture into the cup of his indignation; and he shall be tormented with fire and brimstone in the presence of the holy angels, and in the presence of the Lamb. (Revelation 14:9–10)

In this chapter we will seek to understand the wrath of God, the nature of His wrath, and why it comes. As we do, we will gain insight into why God has given such a dire warning in Revelation regarding the worshipers of the beast, and why they will receive the seven last plagues. Though many will not perceive that they are in rebellion against God, ignorance will not save them from His wrath. He has given clear warning in the Scriptures. Further, He will send His Spirit in latter-rain measure upon His people to empower them to give the final warning, as the Spirit brings His truth home to every individual's conscience.

Babylon the great is fallen, is fallen, and is become the habitation of devils, and the hold of every foul spirit, and a cage of every unclean and hateful bird. For all nations have drunk of the wine of the wrath of her fornication, and the kings of the earth have committed fornication with her, and the merchants of the earth are waxed rich through the abundance of her delicacies. And I heard another voice from heaven, saying, Come out of her, my people, that ye be not partakers of her sins, and that ye receive not of her plagues. (Revelation 18:2–4)

During the final crisis of the ages, and before the plagues are poured out, there will be judgments mixed with mercy as the separation message goes forth. Then there will be judgments un-mixed with mercy at the pouring out of the seven last plagues. (See Revelation 16.) The final demonstration of God's wrath will come at the judgment and destruction of the wicked at the end of the millennium. (See Revelation 20:11–14.)

The word *wrath* means "the just punishment of an offense or crime. God's wrath, in Scripture, is His holy and just indignation against sin."[1] The word *indignation* means "extreme anger; particularly, the wrath of God against sinful men for their ingratitude and rebellion."[2]

How could a God of love ever be angry or wrathful? First of all, God is not like man, even though the Bible uses human language. Second, God has had to endure the sinful ways of man and all the pain and heartache it brings for every second, minute, and hour of every day for thousands of years. Truly God's mercy is abundantly greater than His wrath. When mankind has filled the cup of iniquity and spurned His last call of mercy, and the plagues begin to fall, the inhabitants of heaven, who know God best, declare, "He is righteous and just in all that He does." (See Revelation 16:5–7.)

Drinking the Wine

Thou hast shewed thy people hard things: thou hast made us to drink the wine of astonishment. (Psalm 60:3)

For in the hand of the Lord there is a cup, and the wine is red; it is full of mixture; and he poureth out of the same: but the dregs thereof, all the wicked of the earth shall wring them out, and drink them. (Psalm 75:8)

For thus saith the Lord God of Israel unto me; Take the wine cup of this fury at my hand, and cause all the nations, to whom I send thee, to drink it. (Jeremiah 25:15)

The wine that the worshipers of the beast will drink is not literal. It represents an experience that is passed through. Further, as wine that causes drunkenness, the wine of wrath will negatively affect heart and soul, leading to despair and anguish.

Wrath without Mixture

He too shall [have to] drink of the wine of God's indignation and wrath, poured undiluted into the cup of His anger. (Revelation 14:10 AMP)

God's wrath being poured out without mixture means it is poured out without mercy. This comes after thousands of years of His patience and grace, after the rejection of heaven's light and truth. "And after these things I saw another angel come down from heaven, having great power; and the earth was lightened with His glory" (Revelation 18:1).

God will not bring this world's history to a close and shut the door of mercy until all have heard His last message: "Come out of her, My people, that ye be not partakers of her sins, and that ye receive not of her plagues" (Revelation 18:4). Those who, like Lot's family and wife, prefer not to listen to heaven's messengers will be left to reap what they have sown. (See Genesis 19:12–14, 24–26.)

The Two Ways: Wrath or Life

He that believeth on the Son hath everlasting life: and he that believeth not the Son shall not see life; but the wrath of God abideth on him. (John 3:36)

Whether man experiences the wrath of God or His mercy, and whether the worshipers of the beast receive the plagues, is really the choice of man. Christ endured the wrath of God for your sin and mine. It was not fair that He "who is holy, harmless, undefiled, separate from sinners, and made higher than the heavens" (Hebrews 7:26) should have to die in man's place. But it is wonderfully true, for He who knew no sin became sin for us. (See 2 Corinthians 5:21.) This is the most important event of all time, for it demonstrated God's great love and provided for man's salvation if he accepts God's free gift. On the cross God demonstrated "His righteousness for the remission of sins" (Romans 3:25). He has made it plain that He is "just, and the justifier of him which believeth in Jesus" (Romans 3:26).

Man may declare that God is unfair in pouring out the plagues or bringing men to accountability and executing the sentence of eternal death, yet truly God has been more than fair. Revelation reveals just how merciful God is, for at the beginning of the book we read that Jesus Christ "loved us, and washed us from our sins in His own blood" (Revelation 1:5). The kindness, mercy, and love of God extend to the edge of time, until just before the door of mercy shuts, for we read, "And the Spirit and the bride say, Come. And let him that heareth say, Come. And let him that is athirst come. And whosoever will, let him take the water of life freely" (Revelation 22:17). Further, He has told us in advance what is to happen and invites us through the everlasting gospel to receive His gift of salvation. Jesus' words in John 3:36 are clear. We have one of two paths to choose: eternal life by the grace of God or wrath and indignation, which comes because of our own choice and the rejection or neglect of God's mercy.

Rebellion Leads to Wrath

Remember, and forget not, how thou provokedst the Lord thy God to wrath in the wilderness: from the day that thou didst depart out of the land of Egypt, until ye came unto this place, ye have been rebellious against the

Lord. Also in Horeb ye provoked the Lord to wrath, so that the Lord was angry with you to have destroyed you. (Deuteronomy 9:7–8)

But they mocked the messengers of God, and despised his words, and misused his prophets, until the wrath of the Lord arose against his people, till there was no remedy. (2 Chronicles 36:16)

Despising God's word, ignoring and ridiculing His prophets, and having a rebellious attitude brought God's wrath upon Israel. In the end of this world's history, the same actions will bring the same results, only it will be wrath without mercy.

Some might say, "God is being petty by getting angry and punishing people because they do not do as He says." But "God is not a man" (Numbers 23:19). The Bible says, "My thoughts are not your thoughts, neither are your ways My ways, saith the Lord. For as the heavens are higher than the earth, so are My ways higher than your ways, and My thoughts than your thoughts" (Isaiah 55:8–9).

The rebellious attitude of ancient Israel was exhibited despite numerous miracles God performed on their behalf, including their deliverance from Egypt. Their sin was in the face of great light. Such sin, if left unpunished, grows into a settled rebellion that spreads and becomes entrenched. For God to not deal with Israel's rebellion would not only be a mockery of His goodness but would lead to the loss of many other souls. You see, God's judgments come not only to punish for wrong but also to correct and redeem. And severity upon a few may in fact be mercy for the many.

Even now God's judgments are allowed to come upon nations and individuals as correction. They come mainly when we separate from Him. God's wrath is, for the most part, the result of our choices rather than arbitrary acts of divine power. In the last days God's wrath will be poured out upon those who choose to reject Him, and the plagues they receive will reflect their choices.[3]

Wrath Is Stored Up

> But the hypocrites in heart heap up wrath: they cry not when he bindeth them. (Job 36:13)

> But after thy hardness and impenitent heart treasurest up unto thyself wrath against the day of wrath and revelation of the righteous judgment of God. (Romans 2:5)

> But by your callous stubbornness and impenitence of heart you are storing up wrath and indignation for yourself on the day of wrath and indignation, when God's righteous judgment (just doom) will be revealed. (Romans 2:5 AMP)

> But you have a hard and stubborn heart, and so you are making your own punishment even greater on the Day when God's anger and righteous judgments will be revealed. (Romans 2:5 TEV)

Previous to the worldwide deluge in the days of Noah, and after the flood to our time, God's wrath has always been mingled with mercy. "It is of the Lord's mercies that we are not consumed, because His compassions fail not" (Lamentations 3:22). God has also held in check the wrath of man. Despite the atrocities of men and nations over the centuries, our merciful God has kept man from complete self-destruction. Enlightened self-interest and bold diplomacy has not saved this planet from total chaos. No, the real reason has been God's mercy.

In Revelation we read in symbolic language how God holds in check the winds of strife. "I saw four angels standing on the four corners of the earth, holding the four winds of the earth, that the wind should not blow on the earth, nor on the sea, nor on any tree" (Revelation 7:1). God is holding in check the evil passions of mankind and the destructive malignity of the devil and his angles.

But God's mercy does not do away with His justice. "Sentence against an evil work is not executed speedily, [and] therefore the heart of the sons of men is fully set in them to do evil. [And even]

though a sinner do evil an hundred times, and his days be pro-
longed, … it shall not be well with the wicked, neither shall he
prolong his days, which are as a shadow; because he feareth not
before God" (Ecclesiastes 8:11–13).

God intends that His mercy and kindness will lead us to repentance. (See Romans 2:4.) Sadly, unconverted man is storing up
guilt continually. Man's sin and guilt could be forgiven in a moment by the blood of Christ and because of His merciful kindness.
However, the worshipers of the beast will reject, ignore, or put a
counterfeit in the place of the gospel, setting the religion and commandments of man in its place.

Christ Took the Wrath of God for Us

Thy wrath lieth hard upon me, and thou hast afflicted me
with all thy waves. Selah. Thou hast put away mine ac-
quaintance far from me; thou hast made me an abomination unto them: I am shut up, and I cannot come forth.
Thy fierce wrath goeth over me; thy terrors have cut me
off. (Psalm 88:7–8, 16)

For he hath made him to be sin for us, who knew no sin;
that we might be made the righteousness of God in him.
(2 Corinthians 5:21)

But we see Jesus, who was made a little lower than the
angels for the suffering of death, crowned with glory and
honour; that he by the grace of God should taste death for
every man. (Hebrews 2:9)

God is abundantly gracious to mankind in allowing Christ to
take our place and to endure our punishment. There is coming a
day when we will understand that more clearly, and I pray that the
day of revelation will be one of joy and not shame for you. We can
experience an unimaginably wonderful eternity or the horror of
standing before a holy God to answer for our own sins. Before us is

the joy of seeing our Lord, and eternity will bring a greater understanding of what He has done for us. Alternatively if we are lost we will know the darkness and wrath that Christ bore on our behalf. The wrath of God will become ours to bear alone if we reject the everlasting gospel.

The worshipers of the beast, as with the inhabitants before the flood, will have willingly chosen darkness instead of light. Truly it can be said of the final generation, who experience the seven last plagues, "He that sinneth against me wrongeth his own soul: all they that hate me love death" (Proverbs 8:36). The worshipers of the beast will hate God's word and His law and therefore, God Himself. (See Romans 8:6–8.)

Wrath Comes upon the Children of Disobedience

But fornication, and all uncleanness, or covetousness, let it not be once named among you, as becometh saints; Neither filthiness, nor foolish talking, nor jesting, which are not convenient: but rather giving of thanks. For this ye know, that no whoremonger, nor unclean person, nor covetous man, who is an idolater, hath any inheritance in the kingdom of Christ and of God. Let no man deceive you with vain words: for because of these things cometh the wrath of God upon the children of disobedience. Be not ye therefore partakers with them. (Ephesians 5:3–7)

Mortify therefore your members, which are upon the earth; fornication, uncleanness, inordinate affection, evil concupiscence, and covetousness, which is idolatry: For which things' sake the wrath of God cometh on the children of disobedience. (Colossians 3:5–6)

Many of those who yield to the beast willingly, or who follow it under pressure to get along, will be religious people. However, the worshipers of the beast are "children of disobedience," in obstinate opposition to the divine will, exercising a spirit of unbelief.

The religion that comes from God is the only religion that can lead to God, transforming the heart and making us His children. The religion of the followers of the beast is the result of the eyes of human understanding. The number of man is upon all such religion. Therefore, men follow Satan's bidding and do his work. In the sight of God they are children of disobedience and rightfully deserving of wrath.

No One Can Hide from God's Wrath

> And said to the mountains and rocks, Fall on us, and hide us from the face of him that sitteth on the throne, and from the wrath of the Lamb. (Revelation 6:16)

> But the Lord is the true God, he is the living God, and an everlasting king: at his wrath the earth shall tremble, and the nations shall not be able to abide his indignation. (Jeremiah 10:10)

> Therefore wait ye upon me, saith the Lord, until the day that I rise up to the prey: for my determination is to gather the nations, that I may assemble the kingdoms, to pour upon them mine indignation, even all my fierce anger: for all the earth shall be devoured with the fire of my jealousy. (Zephaniah 3:8)

The nature of sin is to deceive the heart and mind of man. And the worshipers of the beast, in ignoring or neglecting or substituting human ideas for the everlasting gospel, receive strong delusion. By accepting the falsehood that comes from the unclean spirits working through the beast, the dragon, and the false prophet, the world is at war against God. In rejecting God's warnings, His Spirit, and His truth, the final system of apostasy will have opted to stand against God, believing it is the right thing to do.

Will such a belief save them from God's wrath and the punishment that is their due? As with ancient Israel in apostasy, who sinned against great light, love, and mercy, the worshipers of the beast may think they too have "made a covenant with death" (Isaiah 28:15).

The worshipers of the beast, like men long ago, will reject God's warnings and comfort themselves with the thought that "when the overflowing scourge shall pass through, it shall not come unto us: for we have made lies our refuge, and under falsehood have we hid ourselves" (Isaiah 28:15). Though men may hold on to such a delusive hope, we cannot hide from the wrath of God that we have chosen and deserve. The prophet of God declares, "The hail shall sweep away the refuge of lies, and the waters shall overflow the hiding place. And your covenant with death shall be disannulled, and your agreement with hell shall not stand; when the overflowing scourge shall pass through, then ye shall be trodden down by it" (Isaiah 28:17–18).

In Past and Current Judgments, Wrath Is Mixed with Mercy

In a little wrath I hid my face from thee for a moment; but with everlasting kindness will I have mercy on thee, saith the Lord thy Redeemer. (Isaiah 54:8)

And the sons of strangers shall build up thy walls, and their kings shall minister unto thee: for in my wrath I smote thee, but in my favour have I had mercy on thee. (Isaiah 60:10)

The wrath of God in the seven last plagues and the execution of judgment upon the children of disobedience, at the white throne judgment, is the end result of sin. Before that time, God's wrath has been mixed with mercy. Wrath comes as the result of separating from God. This leaves us open to Satan's cruel rule and to the results of our rebellious course. Because we have chosen to go against God, His hand of protection and blessing is to some degree withdrawn, and we are subject to reap that which we have sown, subjecting ourselves to the onslaughts of wicked men and demons and even to the forces of unrestrained nature.

Why would a God of love allow this? And is there any good that can come from God's wrath, which results from our sins? It is not God's desire that we separate from Him in rebellion and sin. But when we do, His wrath is intended to bring about a change of heart to lead us to repentance.

With my soul have I desired thee in the night; yea, with my spirit within me will I seek thee early: for when thy judgments are in the earth, the inhabitants of the world will learn righteousness. (Isaiah 26:9)

I said, Surely thou wilt fear me, thou wilt receive instruction; so their dwelling should not be cut off, howsoever I punished them: but they rose early, and corrupted all their doings. (Zephaniah 3:7)

I said, Only let her [reverently and worshipfully] fear Me, receive correction and instruction, and [Jerusalem's] dwelling shall not be cut off. However, I had punished her [according to all that I have appointed concerning her in the way of punishment], but all the more they are eager to make all their doings corrupt and infamous. (Zephaniah 3:7 AMP)

Run ye to and fro through the streets of Jerusalem, and see now, and know, and seek in the broad places thereof, if ye can find a man, if there be any that executeth judgment, that seeketh the truth; and I will pardon it. And though they say, The Lord liveth; surely they swear falsely. O Lord, are not thine eyes upon the truth? thou hast stricken them, but they have not grieved; thou hast consumed them, but they have refused to receive correction: they have made their faces harder than a rock; they have refused to return. Therefore I said, Surely these are poor; they are foolish: for they know not the way of the Lord, nor the judgment of their God. (Jeremiah 5:1–4)

God's wrath, afflictions, and judgments are intended as corrective, remedial measures to awaken us to the folly of sin and rebellion. Sadly, few respond to God's love and grace, speaking to their hearts of His goodness, and thereby repent. For many it is only in the midst of affliction, disappointment, and difficulty that they begin to consider their ways. In times of helplessness many cry unto the Lord and allow God into their lives. Tragically, as it was with ancient Israel, in many cases, men and nations again turn from God after affliction and difficulty is past.

However, God is gracious. He will hear our plea, even as He did with David, who declared, "I waited patiently for the Lord; and He inclined unto me, and heard my cry. He brought me up also out of an horrible pit, out of the miry clay, and set my feet upon a rock, and established my goings. And He hath put a new song in my mouth, even praise unto our God: many shall see it, and fear, and shall trust in the Lord" (Psalm 40:1–3). David's experience in crying unto God, and his subsequent change of heart, is what God desires for all who have tasted the bitterness of sin and its subsequent sorrows and difficulties.

God brings wrath and judgment so that we might be led to cry unto Him and to experience His deliverance and change by His grace. However, as Jeremiah said, all who refuse to return to God are foolish because they open themselves to further judgments and afflictions. This can lead to individuals and nations and eventually a whole planet reeling under the wrath of God, with no thought of repentance.

The pressures upon men and nations will be one of the causative factors for the woman riding the beast at the end of time, as religion and the kings of the earth join forces seeking to bring order out of chaos. Sadly, however, people will think that apostasy is the means to appease God and remove His judgments and thereby gain His favor. Mankind, in his delusion, will believe that the substitution of God's Word and His law for the mark of the beast will enable him to return to God and gain His blessings.

This is why the people who follow the religion of Mystery Babylon and who receive the mark of the beast are singled out for wrath without mercy.

By Sin and Rebellion We Experience God's Wrath, for We Have Separated from Him

> Therefore have I poured out mine indignation upon them; I have consumed them with the fire of my wrath: their own way have I recompensed upon their heads, saith the Lord God. (Ezekiel 22:31)

> O Israel, thou hast destroyed thyself; but in me is thine help. (Hosea 13:9)

Much of the wrath of God and the judgments man experiences are the direct result of our separation from Him. It is a case of cause and effect, for sin and rebellion do not bring peace and joy but sorrow and loss. Most often God's wrath and judgments are not initiated by Him; He is simply standing back and allowing things to run their natural course. We can only reap what we sow. This is true in the natural world and in the spiritual world. This is why the prophet Hosea said, "Thou hast destroyed thyself." We see this principle with many individuals today and with nations and empires of the past. We are often our own worst enemies because of the self-destructive nature of our sin and rebellion.

> Behold, the Lord's hand is not shortened, that it cannot save; neither his ear heavy, that it cannot hear: But your iniquities have separated between you and your God, and your sins have hid his face from you, that he will not hear. For your hands are defiled with blood, and your fingers with iniquity; your lips have spoken lies, your tongue hath muttered perverseness. None calleth for justice, nor any pleadeth for truth: they trust in vanity, and speak lies; they conceive mischief, and bring forth iniquity. Their feet run to evil, and they make haste to shed innocent blood: their thoughts are thoughts of iniquity; wasting and destruction are in their paths. The way of peace they know not; and there is no judgment in their goings: they have made them crooked paths: whosoever goeth therein shall not know

peace. Therefore is judgment far from us, neither doth justice overtake us: we wait for light, but behold obscurity; for brightness, but we walk in darkness. We grope for the wall like the blind, and we grope as if we had no eyes: we stumble at noonday as in the night; we are in desolate places as dead men. According to their deeds, accordingly he will repay, fury to his adversaries, recompence to his enemies; to the islands he will repay recompence. (Isaiah 59:1–4, 7–10, 18)

Hear now this, O foolish people, and without understanding; which have eyes, and see not; which have ears, and hear not: Fear ye not me? saith the Lord: will ye not tremble at my presence, which have placed the sand for the bound of the sea by a perpetual decree, that it cannot pass it: and though the waves thereof toss themselves, yet can they not prevail; though they roar, yet can they not pass over it? But this people hath a revolting and a rebellious heart; they are revolted and gone. Neither say they in their heart, Let us now fear the Lord our God, that giveth rain, both the former and the latter, in his season: he reserveth unto us the appointed weeks of the harvest. Your iniquities have turned away these things, and your sins have withholden good things from you. (Jeremiah 5:21–25)

It is often difficult for us to determine, in the lives of individuals and nations and even a planet, when our difficulties are the result of our separation from God and when God directly intervenes with judgments. But in either case, the Bible attributes wrath and judgments to Him. Because of this many blame Him, or doubt His existence or goodness, because of the many problems all around us. They would do well to consider the words of the prophet Jeremiah, who, with Israel, was experiencing the results of God's wrath. "Thou hast removed my soul far off from peace: I forgat prosperity. And I said, My strength and my hope is perished from the Lord: This I recall to my mind, therefore have I hope. It is of the Lord's mercies that we are not consumed, because His compassions fail not. They are new every morning: great is thy faithfulness" (Lamentations 3:17–18, 21–23).

God, even in wrath, remembers mercy. (See Habakkuk 3:2.) If it were not for His protective hand, we as individuals and a world would surely perish at our own hands.

The Bible reveals that the long-suffering mercy of God will one day come to an end, as man will have sinned away heaven's light and grace so that only darkness remains and justice without mercy must fall.

The Seven Last Plagues: the Wrath of God without Mercy

> And I heard a great voice out of the temple saying to the seven angels, Go your ways, and pour out the vials of the wrath of God upon the earth. And I heard the angel of the waters say, Thou art righteous, O Lord, which art, and wast, and shalt be, because thou hast judged thus. For they have shed the blood of saints and prophets, and thou hast given them blood to drink; for they are worthy. And I heard another out of the altar say, Even so, Lord God Almighty, true and righteous are thy judgments. (Revelation 16:1, 5–7)

For thousands of years, as the result of sin and rebellion, mankind has treasured up wrath against the day of wrath. When the time comes, and the cup of iniquity is full, the God of love and mercy will do His strange work. The angels of heaven that dwell in the presence of God and know Him best declare at the time of the seven last plagues, "True and righteous are thy judgments."

All the judgments that have come upon men and nations prior to the close of the door of salvation have been mingled with degrees of mercy. This is due to God's long-suffering heart of love. "As I live, saith the Lord God, I have no pleasure in the death of the wicked; but that the wicked turn from his way and live: turn ye, turn ye from your evil ways; for why will ye die, O house of Israel?"

(Ezekiel 33:11). What was true of God's dealings with Israel is true for our whole planet.

The immensity of God's long-suffering mercy, extended moment by moment, day by day, for thousands of years, to a planet in rebellion, will be nearly equaled in His justice, as mercy has been spurned and wrath is poured out.

When God begins to punish the worshipers of the beast and the powers of apostasy, there will be no respite. The storm of God's approaching wrath is gathering, and the only ones who will escape are those who, in the love of Christ, are sanctified through the truth. God, through the prophet Isaiah, speaks of that day when He says, "Come, My people, enter thou into thy chambers, and shut thy doors about thee: hide thyself as it were for a little moment, until the indignation be overpast. For, behold, the Lord cometh out of His place to punish the inhabitants of the earth for their iniquity: the earth also shall disclose her blood, and shall no more cover her slain" (Isaiah 26:20–21).

What about you? Do you love a lie or God's truth? Are you being washed and cleansed by the blood of Christ, or are you trusting in your own righteousness and the religion of men? We are preparing day by day for our eternal destiny. Even now we are being marked or sealed into an experience that will determine whether we shall know God's mercy, love, grace, and eternal life, or wrath and eternal death. Who has your heart and allegiance today? This is the most vital of all questions. May God send His Spirit upon us to open our understanding so that we might examine where we stand.

I close this chapter with the promise of God given for His children during the time of wrath.

He that dwelleth in the secret place of the most High shall abide under the shadow of the Almighty. I will say of the Lord, He is my refuge and my fortress: my God; in him will I trust. Surely he shall deliver thee from the snare of the fowler, and from the noisome pestilence. He shall cover thee with his feathers, and under his wings shalt thou trust: his truth shall be thy shield and buckler. Thou shalt not be afraid for the terror by night; nor for the arrow that flieth by day; nor for the pestilence that walketh in darkness; nor for the destruction that wasteth at noonday. A thousand shall fall at thy side, and ten thousand at thy right hand; but it shall not come nigh thee. Only with thine eyes shalt thou behold and see the reward of the wicked. Because thou hast made the Lord, which is my refuge, even the most High, thy habitation; He shall call upon me, and I will answer him: I will be with him in trouble; I will deliver him, and honour him. (Psalm 91:1–9, 15)

Endnotes

1. Noah Webster, *American Dictionary of the English Language* (San Francisco, California: Foundation for American Christian Education, 1967).
2. Ibid.
3. The reader is encouraged to read the author's book *Let Daniel and Revelation Speak*. The chapter on Revelation 16 examines the wrath of God and the seven last plagues. A free PDF e-book, as well as information on how to purchase the printed copy, can be found at www.inspirationspeaks.com.

Chapter Seventeen

The Smoke of Their Torment Ascendeth Up for Ever and Ever

The same shall drink of the wine of the wrath of God, which is poured out without mixture into the cup of his indignation; and he shall be tormented with fire and brimstone in the presence of the holy angels, and in the presence of the Lamb: And the smoke of their torment ascendeth up for ever and ever: and they have no rest day nor night, who worship the beast and his image, and whosoever receiveth the mark of his name. (Revelation 14:10–11)

The warning regarding the fate of the worshipers of the beast points forward to the punishment that all those who have rejected God will face. The specific punishment the worshipers of the beast will endure is the seven last plagues. Why, then, does the prophet John point to a future punishment that is not only the fate of the worshipers of the beast but also the fate of all who reject God and the salvation He offers?

Scripture tells us the world will "worship the beast, saying, Who is like unto the beast? who is able to make war with him?" (Revelation 13:4). The world at large will consider the new order implemented by the kings of the earth in conjunction with a revived Roman power a good thing. However, God clearly warns us of His hatred of it, for it is a counterfeit to the truth. Though the new order claims to lead people to God and offers order out of chaos, it actually leads people away from Him, preparing them to accept Satan as the god of this world. The prophet warns of the horrendous consequences that await all who worship the beast and receive his mark.

Will the worshipers of the beast and all the rebellious really burn and suffer for eternity?

An Example of Fire and Brimstone

> Then the Lord rained upon Sodom and upon Gomorrah brimstone and fire from the Lord out of heaven; And he overthrew those cities, and all the plain, and all the inhabitants of the cities, and that which grew upon the ground.... And Abraham gat up early in the morning to the place where he stood before the Lord: And he looked toward Sodom and Gomorrah, and toward all the land of the plain, and beheld, and, lo, the smoke of the country went up as the smoke of a furnace. (Genesis 19:24–25, 27–28)

> Even as Sodom and Gomorrha, and the cities about them in like manner, giving themselves over to fornication, and going after strange flesh, are set forth for an example, suffering the vengeance of eternal fire. (Jude 7)

> [The wicked are sentenced to suffer] just as Sodom and Gomorrah and the adjacent towns...as an exhibit of perpetual punishment [to warn] of everlasting fire. (Jude 7 AMP)

> And turning the cities of Sodom and Gomorrha into ashes condemned them with an overthrow, making them an ensample unto those that after should live ungodly. (2 Peter 2:6)

The destruction of Sodom and Gomorrah is not a myth. Many Bible writers refer to this event, and so did Jesus. (See Luke 17:29; Matthew 11:23–24.) What took place at Sodom is both a warning of the results of sin and an example of the nature of eternal fire and brimstone.

Sodom and Gomorrah were located near what is known today as the Dead Sea, which is located on the border between the West Bank, Israel, and Jordan, and lies in the Jordan Rift Valley. The Bible says these cities suffered the vengeance of eternal fire and were "an exhibit of perpetual punishment to warn of everlasting fire." Obviously this fire is not still burning. Therefore, eternal fire and perpetual fire is meant to teach us of the effects of such punishment rather than its duration.

The Consuming Smoke

There is a saying that wherever there is smoke there is fire. But if the fire goes out, how long does the smoke continue? Indeed, it soon ends once there is nothing left to burn. Note the examples of smoke and judgment in the verses below.

The anger of the Lord and his jealousy shall smoke against that man, and all the curses that are written in this book shall lie upon him, and the Lord shall blot out his name from under heaven. (Deuteronomy 29:20)

But the wicked shall perish, and the enemies of the Lord shall be as the fat of lambs: they shall consume; into smoke shall they consume away. (Psalm 37:20)

As smoke is driven away, so drive them away: as wax melteth before the fire, so let the wicked perish at the presence of God. (Psalm 68:20)

For, behold, the day cometh, that shall burn as an oven; and all the proud, yea, and all that do wickedly, shall be stubble: and the day that cometh shall burn them up, saith the Lord of hosts, that it shall leave them neither root nor branch. And ye shall tread down the wicked; for they shall be ashes under the soles of your feet in the day that I shall do this, saith the Lord of hosts. (Malachi 4:1, 3)

And I saw a great white throne, and him that sat on it, from whose face the earth and the heaven fled away; and there was found no place for them. And I saw the dead, small and great, stand before God; and the books were opened: and another book was opened, which is the book of life: and the dead were judged out of those things which were written in the books, according to their works. And the sea gave up the dead which were in it; and death and hell delivered up the dead which were in them: and they were judged every man according to their works. And death and hell were cast into the lake of fire. This is the second death. And whosoever was not found written in the book of life was cast into the lake of fire. (Revelation 20:11–15)

The destruction associated with smoke indicates how the name or character of a man—which is his thoughts and feelings, what we might refer to as his spirit—is blotted out, destroyed. The wicked are consumed even as the fat of an animal is consumed when placed on a fire. The wicked will perish as wax melts on the fire.

The prophet Malachi says the fate of the wicked is not to be eternally burning and in torment of soul and body; rather, they will be reduced to ashes. Jesus said, "Fear not them which kill the body, but are not able to kill the soul: but rather fear Him which is able to destroy both soul and body in hell" (Matthew 10:28). This indicates the utter annihilation and destruction of the wicked rather than the wicked being tormented for eternity.

The fate of the wicked after the great white throne judgment is the lake of fire, and it is referred to as the second death. In death there is no life, no feeling, nothing. Jesus said in Matthew 10:28, that "hellfire" means the destruction of the body and the soul.

We see in the above texts the final annihilation of the wicked; their lives are not sustained for an unending eternity as they suffer torment and continual burning. The consuming smoke rises up through the atmosphere into the infinite space above as a sign of perpetual desolation.

While popular theology teaches an eternal hell of punishment, the Bible refers to the eternal *effect* of hellfire. Eternal death and destruction cannot be mitigated or turned back.

The Ascending Smoke Forever

If the smoke of the wicked ascends forever and ever, does that not indicate that the fire and torment is ongoing and for eternity?

> It [the burning of Edom] shall not be quenched night nor day; the smoke thereof shall go up for ever: from generation to generation it shall lie waste; none shall pass through it for ever and ever. But the cormorant and the bittern shall possess it; the owl also and the raven shall dwell in it: and he shall stretch out upon it the line of confusion, and the stones of emptiness. They shall call the nobles thereof to the kingdom, but none shall be there, and all her princes shall be nothing. And thorns shall come up in her palaces, nettles and brambles in the fortresses thereof: and it shall be an habitation of dragons, and a court for owls. (Isaiah 34:10–12)

Edom was located between the Dead Sea and the Gulf of Aqaba. It contained, among other cities, the rock-hewn city known in Greek as Petra. It is a rugged region, traversed by fruitful valleys. The modern kingdom of Jordan is found in some of the territory known as the biblical Edom. We have read that the burning and judgment upon Edom was forever, meaning it was full and complete but the territory remained and the judgment ended. And what happened to the people? The Edomites existed as a people for nearly seventeen hundred years; however, they have totally disappeared and their language forgotten.

In Revelation 14:11, the punishment is short in duration but eternal in its consequences. "Yes," someone may say, "but doesn't the text say the burning is forever and ever? And doesn't that mean unending and for all eternity?" The term does mean unending when applied to God, as noted in the following verses:

And when those beasts give glory and honour and thanks to him that sat on the throne, who liveth for ever and ever, The four and twenty elders fall down before him that sat on the throne, and worship him that liveth for ever and ever, and cast their crowns before the throne, saying, Thou art worthy, O Lord, to receive glory and honour and power: for thou hast created all things, and for thy pleasure they are and were created. (Revelation 4:9–11)

And the four beasts said, Amen. And the four and twenty elders fell down and worshipped him that liveth for ever and ever. (Revelation 5:14)

The Lord shall reign for ever and ever. (Exodus 15:18)

Thy throne, O God, is for ever and ever: the sceptre of thy kingdom is a right sceptre. (Psalm 45:6)

Before the mountains were brought forth, or ever thou hadst formed the earth and the world, even from everlasting to everlasting, thou art God. (Psalm 90:2)

In contrast to God, who is timeless in His existence, when "forever" or "ever and ever" is applied to man's nature and duration, it means *to the end of his life*.

Then thou shalt take an aul, and thrust it through his ear unto the door, and he shall be thy servant for ever. And also unto thy maidservant thou shalt do likewise. (Deuteronomy 15:17)

When an indentured servant was granted his freedom at the end of six years of service, but chose to stay with his master, he would serve the master until his death, not forever into the afterlife. *Forever* here refers to the end of the servant's life on this earth.

> And the man Elkanah, and all his house, went up to offer unto the Lord the yearly sacrifice, and his vow. But Hannah went not up; for she said unto her husband, I will not go up until the child be weaned, and then I will bring him, that he may appear before the Lord, and there abide for ever. (1 Samuel 1:21–22)

When Hannah dedicated her son to the service of God, he was to be in the "house of the Lord in Shiloh" (1 Samuel 1:24) and abide there forever. Samuel served the Lord from childhood and was a prophet and teacher of the people, not only serving in the house of the Lord but to the nation at large. Samuel's ministry and service in the temple was for ever, meaning to the end of his life.

> Howbeit the Lord God of Israel chose me [king David] before all the house of my father to be king over Israel for ever: for he hath chosen Judah to be the ruler; and of the house of Judah, the house of my father; and among the sons of my father he liked me to make me king over all Israel. (1 Chronicles 28:4)

> He asked life of thee, and thou gavest it him, even length of days for ever and ever. (Psalm 21:4)

King David lived a long and eventful life, but Peter declares in Acts 2:29–34 that he is dead and buried and has not yet ascended to heaven. David was not a king in Israel forever, with a reign lasting for eternity. His length of days that lasted "forever and ever" meant to the end of his life on earth.

> The fire shall ever be burning upon the altar; it shall never go out. (Leviticus 6:13)

The term *forever* is applied to the Jewish ceremonial and temple services. Yet they came to an end when Christ instituted the new covenant by His death on the cross. The feast of first fruits and the Day of Atonement were also to last forever.

> And ye shall proclaim on the selfsame day, that it may be an holy convocation unto you: ye shall do no servile work therein: it shall be a statute for ever in all your dwellings throughout your generations. (Leviticus 23:21)

> Ye shall do no manner of work: it shall be a statute for ever throughout your generations in all your dwellings. (Leviticus 23:31)

Jesus ministry was the fulfillment of all the types and shadows of the Old Testament, for they were the gospel in symbols. These ceremonies did not last forever but only until the coming of Christ, to whom all the ceremonies pointed. So again we find the term *forever* is limited in its duration.

> The sons of Amram; Aaron and Moses: and Aaron was separated, that he should sanctify the most holy things, he and his sons for ever, to burn incense before the Lord, to minister unto him, and to bless in his name for ever. (1 Chronicles 23:13)

The Levitical priesthood came to an end with the more perfect priesthood of Christ. Further, Aaron and his sons did not remain in the office of priest forever but only until the end of their lives.

> The Lord hath sworn, and will not repent, Thou art a priest for ever after the order of Melchizedek. (Psalm 110:4)

The above verse is applied to Christ in Hebrews 8 and 9. Yet there is a time coming when Christ's priestly work as intercessor will come to an end; it shall not last forever or eternity. Likewise, for the lost and the worshipers of the beast, the smoke of their torment ascending forever, is of limited duration but eternal in its consequences.

What Happens to the Worshipers of the Beast at Christ's Second Coming?

> Seeing it is a righteous thing with God to recompense tribulation to them that trouble you; And to you who are troubled rest with us, when the Lord Jesus shall be revealed from heaven with his mighty angels, In flaming fire taking vengeance on them that know not God, and that obey not the gospel of our Lord Jesus Christ: Who shall be punished with everlasting destruction from the presence of the Lord, and from the glory of his power. (2 Thessalonians 1:6–9)

At Christ's coming there will be two classes of people on the earth: the faithful remnant who follow Christ and the worshipers of the beast. Though claiming to know God, the people of this planet will have spurned the everlasting gospel and the faith of Jesus and God's call to come out of all the falsehood of Babylon. The people will have refused to "fear God, and give glory to Him,… and worship Him that made heaven, and earth, and the sea, and the fountains of waters" (Revelation 14:7).

Therefore, when "the hour of His judgment is come" (Revelation 14:7), and all are called to make a decision for truth or error, the law of God or the traditions of men, the followers of the beast, like the inhabitants in Noah's day, will be found wanting.

Before Christ comes the second time, mankind will fully reject the faith of Jesus, choosing rather to believe a lie. In doing so, they will be "giving heed to seducing spirits, and doctrines of devils" as they reject the truth of God, "having their conscience seared with a hot iron" (1 Timothy 4:1–2). Those who are unprepared when Christ comes will be destroyed.

Therefore prophesy thou against them all these words, and say unto them, The Lord shall roar from on high, and utter his voice from his holy habitation; he shall mightily roar upon his habitation; he shall give a shout, as they that tread the grapes, against all the inhabitants of the earth. A noise shall come even to the ends of the earth; for the Lord hath a controversy with the nations, he will plead with all flesh; he will give them that are wicked to the sword, saith the Lord. Thus saith the Lord of hosts, Behold, evil shall go forth from nation to nation, and a great whirlwind shall be raised up from the coasts of the earth. And the slain of the Lord shall be at that day from one end of the earth even unto the other end of the earth: they shall not be lamented, neither gathered, nor buried; they shall be dung upon the ground. (Jeremiah 25:30–33)

And I saw heaven opened, and behold a white horse; and he that sat upon him was called Faithful and True, and in righteousness he doth judge and make war. And I saw an angel standing in the sun; and he cried with a loud voice, saying to all the fowls that fly in the midst of heaven, Come and gather yourselves together unto the supper of the great God; That ye may eat the flesh of kings, and the flesh of captains, and the flesh of mighty men, and the flesh of horses, and of them that sit on them, and the flesh of all men, both free and bond, both small and great.

And I saw the beast, and the kings of the earth, and their armies, gathered together to make war against him that sat on the horse, and against his army. And the beast was taken, and with him the false prophet that wrought miracles before him, with which he deceived them that had received the mark of the beast, and them that worshipped his image. These both were cast alive into a lake of fire burning with brimstone. And the remnant were slain with the sword of him that sat upon the horse, which sword proceeded out of his mouth: and all the fowls were filled with their flesh. (Revelation 19:11, 17–21)

The followers of the beast will all be destroyed at Christ's second coming. Their lives are not taken away while their souls or spirits suffer on somewhere. No, they are utterly destroyed, only to rise again at the second resurrection to receive eternal punishment: the second death.

At the second resurrection, the lost will be arraigned before the judgment seat of God. This will be a time of great anguish and horror. The guilt of a lifetime, no longer held in check by mercy, will overwhelm the lost. The shame of standing before God without the covering, redeeming grace of Christ cannot be imagined.

The lost will be "tormented with fire and brimstone in the presence of the holy angels, and in the presence of the Lamb" (Revelation 14:10). This torment will not be eternal in its duration but in its effect, even as Sodom and Gomorrah suffered the vengeance of eternal fire. As with the inhabitants of Sodom, so it will be with the lost of all ages and those who worshiped the beast, for after the great white throne judgment, "fire came down from God out of heaven, and devoured them" (Revelation 20:9).

The wicked of all ages will perish forever, totally annihilated. They are not punished for eternity, but the punishment will be eternal; the consequences will last forever. There will be no escape from the lake of fire, which is called the second death. All life will eventually end.

Thus the psalmist wrote as he foresaw the fate of the wicked: "When the wicked spring as the grass, and when all the workers of iniquity do flourish; it is that they shall be destroyed for ever" (Psalm 92:7).

Noah's Day Was a Type of the Final Destruction of the Wicked

And every living substance was destroyed which was upon the face of the ground, both man, and cattle, and the creeping things, and the fowl of the heaven; and they were destroyed from the earth: and Noah only remained alive, and they that were with him in the ark. (Genesis 7:23)

They did eat, they drank, they married wives, they were given in marriage, until the day that Noah entered into the ark, and the flood came, and destroyed them all. (Luke 17:27)

They purposely ignore the fact that long ago God gave a command, and the heavens and earth were created. The earth was formed out of water and by water, and it was also by water, the water of the flood, that the old world was destroyed. But the heavens and the earth that now exist are being preserved by the same command of God, in order to be destroyed by fire. They are being kept for the day when godless people will be judged and destroyed. (2 Peter 3:5–7 TEV)

God has reserved this world for judgment by fire, even as in the days of the flood. His word decreed then that the world and its inhabitants would be destroyed by water. By a similar example, the fires of the last days will destroy the wicked; they will cease to exist.

There Is a Choice before Every Man: Everlasting Life or Everlasting Destruction

And these shall go away into everlasting punishment: but the righteous into life eternal. (Matthew 25:46)

Verily, verily, I say unto you, He that heareth my word, and believeth on him that sent me, hath everlasting life, and shall not come into condemnation; but is passed from death unto life. (John 5:24)

Note Jesus' words carefully. There are two alternatives before every human being; eternal life filled with joy and happiness in the presence of God, or unending death.

> But now being made free from sin, and become servants to God, ye have your fruit unto holiness, and the end everlasting life. For the wages of sin is death; but the gift of God is eternal life through Jesus Christ our Lord. (Romans 6:22–23)

> Verily, verily, I say unto you, He that believeth on me hath everlasting life. (John 6:47)

Hellfire was never intended for the human family, but for Satan and his angels. (See Matthew 25:41; Jude 6.) However, if we cling to our rebellion, we will receive the just reward of our deeds. As the righteous receive their reward of unending life, so also the wicked will receive the punishment that is everlasting, from which there is no escape.

Notice that the Bible speaks of everlasting punishment, not punishing. When a convicted criminal is executed, his punishment is everlasting in the sense that there is no escaping it, no reversal of its effects. It is final; his life ends. He is not being punished continually, repeatedly—there is simply a one-time, irrevocable, unchanging punishment.

Even so is everlasting punishment in the fires of hell. After the great white throne judgment there will be a period of indescribable mental anguish, knowing the full force of guilt and shame, knowing that eternal life has been forever lost. This eternal destruction will be a torment and punishment beyond our comprehension.

In a short time the lake of fire will destroy soul and body for all eternity. The justice and finality of the lake of fire is real and frightening, but it is also fair and in keeping with the gracious compassion of our God, as sin and sinners shall be no more. Then love and righteousness and eternal peace shall reign in the universe, for sin and its affliction shall never again arise. Eternal death or eternal life, which will you choose?

Section Four

The Character of Those Who Overcome the Beast

Chapter Eighteen

Here Is the Patience of the Saints

Here is the patience of the saints: here are they that keep the commandments of God, and the faith of Jesus. (Revelation 14:12)

John beholds the loyal people of God in contrast to the worshipers of the beast. Of them he says, "Here are those with fortitude and who keep the commandments of God and have the faith of Jesus."

Mystery Babylon, is represented as holding a wine cup in her hand, from which all the nations drink. Under the influence of the wine of falsehood, the nations of the world commit spiritual fornication. They separate themselves from God and trample on His Word and His commandments. These will receive the mark of the beast, yet in their confused state they will believe they are entering an age of peace and development.

For the faithful saints of God, this is a trying time. They will refuse to give allegiance to the beast system and will subsequently bear all the consequences that come, including persecution and the wrath of man. Despite all the difficulties, the saints will maintain patience, manifested in consistent endurance and fidelity to God. They continue to be steadfast in the faith, even though this enduring faithfulness may cost them their liberty or their lives.

How Patience Begins

Therefore being justified by faith, we have peace with God through our Lord Jesus Christ. (Romans 5:1)

Patience is a desirable character attribute and saves us from many frustrations in life. Patience is commonly understood to mean "the ability to endure waiting or delay without becoming annoyed or upset, or to persevere calmly when faced with difficulties."[1] To a degree, people from all religions, even those without any religion, can develop patience. But the patience we will need to stand before God is a consistent endurance. True, godly patience can only come from being justified by faith.

> And not only so, but we glory in tribulations also: knowing that tribulation worketh patience. (Romans 5:3)

> Moreover [let us also be full of joy now!] let us exult and triumph in our troubles and rejoice in our sufferings, knowing that pressure and affliction and hardship produce patient and unswerving endurance. (Romans 5:3 AMP)

Patience is developed by God's grace and by faithfully enduring the troubles, afflictions, and persecution that come when living for God in a world of sin. Being patient, in the common sense of the term, is good. But we need the patience of the saints, which is steadfastness, constancy, endurance. "In the New Testament the characteristic of a man who is not swerved from his deliberate purpose and his loyalty to faith and piety by even the greatest trials and sufferings."[2]

Patience is not simply a good attribute to have, true patience is to live for God.

> And endurance (fortitude) develops maturity of character (approved faith and tried integrity). And character [of this sort] produces [the habit of] joyful and confident hope of eternal salvation. (Romans 5:4 AMP)

To be justified by faith is not only to have sins forgiven; it also involves the development of character. The patience of the saints is to develop endurance and a life of increasing spiritual maturity, a character that can stand the test. God wants us to "be blameless and harmless, the sons of God, without rebuke, in the midst of a crooked and perverse nation, among whom ye shine as lights in the world" (Philippians 2:15).

Such a life is the result of justification, learning to fear God and give glory to Him. Revelation reveals that the people of God will exhibit this character to the world at a time when most of mankind worships the beast. God's people have the endurance of the saints; thus they keep God's commandments. The true people of God will have the faith of Jesus rather than departing from the faith and giving heed to seducing spirits.

Endurance is the result of justification by faith and growing in grace. And yet sometimes we become more irritable the more trouble we have. However, tribulation and pressure do not develop patience and hope if we are not in the condition the apostle describes in Romans 5:4. Tribulation works godly patience only for those who are justified by faith. Nothing but faith in God can keep someone patient under all circumstances.

If you find the call to patience grows more intense when pressures and hardships and frustrations increase, remember that you are justified by faith. You have access to the grace of God, which can give you the endurance and strength you need. (See Hebrews 4:16.)

Remember the words of Christ: "He that endureth to the end shall be saved" (Matthew 10:22). Endurance builds character, and character is the only thing we can take from this life to the next.

The Word of God a Source of Patience

For whatsoever things were written aforetime were written for our learning, that we through patience and comfort of the scriptures might have hope. (Romans 15:4)

We cannot have the faith we need unless we get it from the Word of God. "For faith cometh by hearing, and hearing by the word of God" (Romans 10:17). We cannot have consistent endurance unless we appropriate the promises of God. To the children of God "are given … exceeding great and precious promises: that by these ye might be partakers of the divine nature, having escaped the corruption that is in the world through lust" (2 Peter 1:4).

All the promises, blessings, deliverances, and sustaining grace recorded in the Scriptures are ours to learn from. The God who sustained Moses, Elijah, and countless others is the same God who will sustain us. The patience of Job, Jeremiah, and many other apostles and prophets is the same patience we can receive by faith and God's grace.

Many of the worshipers of the beast will have patience in the common sense of the word, but only the children of God will have the patience of the saints as they live by the Word of God while the worshipers of the beast follow the words of man.

To trust God in sorrow and affliction both now and in the future, we must know "the God of patience and consolation" (Romans 15:5). This comes only as we make the Scriptures our own in faith and life practice.

Patience Is to Be Sought For

> But thou, O man of God, flee these things; and follow after righteousness, godliness, faith, love, patience, meekness. (1 Timothy 6:11)

To have patience is to endure hardship. And not just any hardship. The difficulties that come as a result of being children of light develop true godly patience. Sadly, many Christians know very little of such enduring faith.

Patience is something we are to seek or follow after. We do not create the difficulties and go looking for them; if we live for God in a world of darkness, trials and problems will come. When they do, rather than moaning and complaining or seeking for an accommodating, crossless religion, we take up our cross and follow Christ. (See Mark 8:34.)

How Patience Is Maintained

> Rest in the Lord, and wait patiently for him: fret not thyself because of him who prospereth in his way, because of the man who bringeth wicked devices to pass. (Psalm 37:7)

> Be still and rest in the Lord: wait for Him and patiently lean yourself upon Him; fret not yourself because of him who prospers in his way, because of the man who brings wicked devices to pass. Cease from anger and forsake wrath; fret not yourself—it tends only to evil doing. (Psalm 37:7–8 AMP)

Difficulties, trials, frustrations, and disappointments come to every person to one degree or another. For the saints of God, our patience comes from resting in God. Jesus taught us what this means. "Come unto Me, all ye that labour and are heavy laden, and I will give you rest. Take My yoke upon you, and learn of Me; for I am meek and lowly in heart: and ye shall find rest unto your souls. For My yoke is easy, and My burden is light" (Matthew 11:28–30).

Our rest—therefore, our patience or consistent endurance to live by faith—can only come as we yoke with Christ. This involves surrender. As we lean on Him, He takes our burdens, making them lighter. What may appear to be the easy path of the compromised Christian or the unbeliever cannot be our example, for it is an illusion. Resting in God brings true patience, which is a character of faith and love, and will carry us into eternity. In contrast, the easy path is the downward path, the broad road that leads so often to heartache in this life and the loss of eternal life.

> For this cause we also, since the day we heard it, do not cease to pray for you, and to desire that ye might be filled with the knowledge of his will in all wisdom and spiritual understanding; That ye might walk worthy of the Lord unto all pleasing, being fruitful in every good work, and increasing in the knowledge of God. Strengthened with all

might, according to his glorious power, unto all patience and longsuffering with joyfulness. (Colossians 1:9–11)

To live a life of patience is to be filled with the knowledge of God's will. This is not a mystery. To live "by every word that proceedeth out of the mouth of God" (Matthew 4:4) means to live by the counsel of Scripture. To maintain a life of endurance and consistency, we must walk in a way that is pleasing to God. When God's Spirit impresses upon us our need for Him, we will hunger and thirst after righteousness. (See Matthew 5:3, 6.) Then we can be strengthened by God's might, enabled to live a life of joy and patient endurance, living by faith in a world of unbelief.

The Work of Patience

For ye have need of patience, that, after ye have done the will of God, ye might receive the promise. (Hebrews 10:36)

For you have need of steadfast patience and endurance, so that you may perform and fully accomplish the will of God, and thus receive and carry away [and enjoy to the full] what is promised. (Hebrews 10:36 AMP)

The manifestation of true patience is seen in doing the will of God. Many unbelievers, and certainly the worshipers of the beast, can be patient in the sense of remaining calm in difficulties or in not getting annoyed when enduring delays. However, only believers have the patience manifested in following God through all the difficulties of life and living by His Word. We have the promise of grace to endure now as well as the promise of eternal life.

To them who by patient continuance in well doing seek for glory and honour and immortality, eternal life. (Romans 2:7)

The life of godly patience is not an on-and-off experience; it is to be continual. If we fall we must seek the Lord's grace and forgiveness and carry on, moving forward. "Forgetting those things which are behind, and reaching forth unto those things which are before, I press toward the mark for the prize of the high calling of God in Christ Jesus" (Philippians 3:13–14).

The life of patience moves toward the goal with a resolve and a hope that cannot be shaken. God provides the ability to obtain the prize, but it is ours only by faith and consistent endurance.

The Apostle Paul: an Example of Endurance

The experience of the apostle Paul provides us with an illustration of patience. At a time when the early church seemed to need the apostle's labors the most, his liberty was taken away: he was imprisoned. Nevertheless, this was the time for the Lord to work. Not only did Paul write much of the New Testament from prison, his example of patient endurance under affliction and trial encouraged many.

From prison, it seemed Paul could do very little for the cause of Christ. However, while he was incarcerated, the truth found an entrance into Caesar's court, which at that time was the highest realm of earthy power.

Paul's Spirit-inspired testimony before the great men of the Empire, while he was in bondage, attracted their attention. Throughout his captivity he was a conqueror for Christ. The meekness with which Paul submitted to his long and unjust confinement, caused many to be drawn to his testimony. Even the guards and soldiers set over Paul saw the Spirit of Christ that filled him and gave him hope. Paul's experience is to be ours: living for God even in the midst of trials. The saints at the end, like Paul, may lose liberty or their life. But a character of patient endurance means victory for this life and the next.

Trials Are to Develop Patience

> My brethren, count it all joy when ye fall into divers temptations; Knowing this, that the trying of your faith worketh patience. But let patience have her perfect work, that ye may be perfect and entire, wanting nothing. (James 1:2)

Patience must be allowed to work in our lives or we cannot be made perfect, wanting nothing. Troubles and afflictions are part of life, and by submission to Christ and His enabling grace we can bear them patiently or we can make life more difficult by complaining.

In mining, to gain that which is valuable, the ore must go through a process of smelting, so the impurities may be removed. Our character must undergo the purifying process as well. Therefore, we are to be patient amidst the afflictions and troubles allowed by God to refine and develop the gold of faith and love.

Trials borne patiently are meant to develop a character that trusts wholly in God. We must not allow ourselves to settle into a dissatisfied state of mind. Rather, by faith and God's enabling grace, we are to show calm trust in our heavenly Father, counting it all joy when we are permitted to endure trials for Christ's sake.

Like it or not, temptation will come upon all children of God. James does not say that we are to count it all joy when we fall *under* temptation, but when we fall *into* temptation. Falling under temptation means sin and failure and shame.

Temptation, trials, difficulties, and pressure come upon us for the testing of our faith. This testing is intended to develop patience, not failure and murmuring. If we put our trust in Jesus, He will keep us, and He will be our strength. God wants us to learn lessons of faith, trust, and hope in Him from the trials we experience.

The apostle Paul says, "We glory in tribulations also: knowing that tribulation worketh patience; And patience, experience; and experience, hope: And hope maketh not ashamed; because the love of God is shed abroad in our hearts by the Holy Ghost which is given unto us" (Romans 5:3–5).

It may seem at times that we have the greatest temptations when we seek God and earnestly desire to do right. Why? Satan is content with our condition when we are self-satisfied and do not realize our need of divine help and grace. However, when we see our great need for God's help, and begin to draw near to Him, the devil places hindrances in the way so that we will not come into close connection with the Source of our strength. Thus, we are to "count it all joy when ye fall into divers temptations; knowing this, that the trying of your faith worketh patience."

> Take, my brethren, the prophets, who have spoken in the name of the Lord, for an example of suffering affliction, and of patience. Behold, we count them happy which endure. Ye have heard of the patience of Job, and have seen the end of the Lord; that the Lord is very pitiful, and of tender mercy. (James 5:10–11)

The root meaning of the word *patience* means "suffering." This is where we get our word *patient,* meaning "one in a hospital or undergoing affliction or receiving treatment." When the mark of the beast is implemented, God's people will undergo much tribulation and persecution. Like the faithful prophets of old, they will be ridiculed and mocked. However, like God's faithful messengers of old, they will be preachers of righteousness, bearing a message of judgment and a call to separation. This will be a time that tries men's souls. But the admonition of God is, "Be thou faithful unto death, and I will give thee a crown of life" (Revelation 2:10).

There can be no growth of patience where there is no suffering. Trouble does not destroy patience, but develops it. We develop patience in daily annoyances and trials overcome in Christ.

The time of the beast system will fully develop patience. All earthly support will be stripped away, and our trust and hope will need to be centered upon God and His Word alone.

Temperance Is an Aid to Patience

> And beside this, giving all diligence, add to your faith virtue; and to virtue knowledge; And to knowledge temperance; and to temperance patience; and to patience godliness. (2 Peter 1:5–6)

The apostle says we need the grace of temperance, which is a fruit of the Spirit. (See Galatians 5:22–23.) Temperance, which is self-control, is necessary in order that we may add the grace of patience to our character. The Christian needs to be temperate in all things so that he can be patient, for the self-discipline of being temperate is the self-discipline required to be patient. To develop both patience and temperance in our character is a part of being "partakers of the divine nature, having escaped the corruption that is in the world through lust" (2 Peter 1:4).

Enduring Accusation Develops Patience

> For this is thankworthy, if a man for conscience toward God endure grief, suffering wrongfully. For what glory is it, if, when ye be buffeted for your faults, ye shall take it patiently? but if, when ye do well, and suffer for it, ye take it patiently, this is acceptable with God. For even hereunto were ye called: because Christ also suffered for us, leaving us an example, that ye should follow his steps: Who did no sin, neither was guile found in his mouth: Who, when he was reviled, reviled not again; when he suffered, he threatened not; but committed himself to him that judgeth righteously. (1 Peter 2:19–23)

In a world of sin and darkness, to live for God and by His Word will at times bring heartache and loss. Why? Because to live for God is out of harmony with the world and its practices. Our will aligned with the will of God comes into collision with the practices of this world. This is why Jesus suffered. However, like

Jesus, we must bear it all patiently. This is not a grim determination coming from our own efforts. Rather, when we surrender to the will of God, we are enabled to live for Him regardless of what happens. Our surrender to Christ in the midst of difficulties will develop patience, the consistency of a Christian experience that in love for God "beareth all things, believeth all things, hopeth all things, endureth all things" (1 Corinthians 13:7).

Patience in the Hour of Temptation

> Because thou hast kept the word of my patience, I also will keep thee from the hour of temptation, which shall come upon all the world, to try them that dwell upon the earth. (Revelation 3:10)

The "word of patience" is the example of Christ, our Master, who endured affliction and trial. The word of patience is the counsel of God lived out in the midst of trial and opposition and the character developed thereby. Those who have the patience of the saints will exercise steadfast endurance to live for Christ, to follow His Word and obey His law, even in the midst of worldwide apostasy. The word of patience, by grace through faith, enables the children of God to live for Him in times of difficulty.

The hour of trial and testing that will come upon the whole world is the mark of the beast, when all will have to make a decision: to obey God or to obey man. Only those who have the patience of the saints will endure and be sealed and saved. Living a life of surrender is not always a joy. However, we have God's promise that if we surrender heart and mind, "when it is all over we can see that it has quietly produced the fruit of real goodness in the characters of those who have accepted it in the right spirit" (Hebrews 12:11 Phillips).

Endnotes

1. *Encarta® World English Dictionary* (Microsoft Corporation, 1999). All rights reserved. Developed for Microsoft by Bloomsbury Publishing Plc.
2. Greek lexicon based on *Thayer's Lexicon* and *Smith's Bible Dictionary* plus others; keyed to the large Kittel and the *Theological Dictionary of the New Testament*. Online Bible, 1996.

Chapter Nineteen

Here Are They That Keep the Commandments of God

I have seen an end of all perfection: but thy command-ment is exceeding broad. (Psalm 119:96)

God's people will keep His commandments. This includes the whole counsel of Scripture and the moral law of God as He wrote it on the enduring tablets of stone. Obedience or disobedience is what separates those who truly serve God and those who do not.

It is one thing to talk about keeping the law, and another thing entirely to be doers of the law. Only the doers of the law will be justified before God. (See Romans 2:13.) Those who do the law are led by the Spirit and represent the character of God; they do not lie against the truth by false profession.

Whether the law should be kept or if it has been done away with is not the issue of the New Testament. Rather, it is what a man must do to be saved. We are saved by grace through faith rather than by anything we can do of ourselves apart from God's grace. (See Ephesians 2:8.) Obedience to God's law is the result of justifi-cation by faith, and a life of obedience is lived in the Spirit.

In this chapter we will look at the commandments of God that His people are noted for keeping. Further, we will explore what the psalmist called the broadness of the commandments. In the Sermon on the Mount, Jesus taught that the commandments of God must regulate not only our outward actions, but our thoughts and motives as well.

The First Commandment

And God spake all these words, saying, I am the Lord thy
God, which have brought thee out of the land of Egypt,
out of the house of bondage. Thou shalt have no other
gods before me. (Exodus 20:1–3)

Egypt and bondage can be synonymous terms. God declared
that His purpose was to deliver Israel from bondage. This deliverance was not for Israel alone but for all.

What is bondage?

Then said Jesus to those Jews which believed on him, If
ye continue in my word, then are ye my disciples indeed;
and ye shall know the truth, and the truth shall make you
free. They answered him, We be Abraham's seed, and were
never in bondage to any man: how sayest thou, Ye shall
be made free? Jesus answered them, Verily, verily, I say
unto you, Whosoever committeth sin is the servant of sin.
(John 8:31–34)

Many look to the religion of their fathers or the religion of
family or country and culture, even as the Jews looked to Abraham.
However, such religion cannot free anyone from the bondage of
sin. Israel was delivered from the bondage of Egyptian servitude
to serve the true God. Our deliverance from the bondage of sin
is likewise only in God. And with that deliverance comes the
command, "You shall have no other gods before or besides Me"
(Exodus 20:3 AMP). More than a command, it is a glorious privilege and benefit to serve the God of creation rather than the gods
man has created.

While they promise them liberty, they themselves are the
servants of corruption: for of whom a man is overcome, of
the same is he brought in bondage. For if after they have
escaped the pollutions of the world through the knowledge of the Lord and Saviour Jesus Christ, they are again

entangled therein, and overcome, the latter end is worse with them than the beginning. (2 Peter 2:19–20)

Know ye not, that to whom ye yield yourselves servants to obey, his servants ye are to whom ye obey; whether of sin unto death, or of obedience unto righteousness? (Romans 6:16)

The bondage of sin leads to death. But God desires to deliver us from the pain, sorrow, guilt, and condemnation of our sins. When He does we are brought into the glorious liberty of the sons of God. As children of God we are set free from the law of sin and death and are transformed. Therefore we seek to obey God in love, which leads to following His law, which James declares is the law of liberty. (See James 2:12.)

God brought the children of Israel into a relationship with Himself so they could be His witnesses. This deliverance included obedience to His law. Sadly, they failed, for they sought to keep God's law not by faith but by their own efforts.

Many in Babylon seek God, but they often seek Him by the things they can do and by human efforts rather than by faith and love. In contrast, the people of God live by a faith that is not theirs alone; it is the faith of Jesus. This is why and how they keep God's commandments, His moral law. This obedience by faith distinguishes the people of God from the worshipers of the beast.

The First Commandment Amplified

God is eternal, self-existent, and uncreated. He is the source and sustainer of all life. Thus He alone is entitled to reverence and worship. Man, as a created being, is forbidden from giving first place in his affections or his service to any other object. This command is not a prohibition only, but the result of a conscience enlightened. He who comes to know God will not desire to have any other gods before Him. Whatever we love and cherish in life that lessens our love for God or interferes with the service due Him becomes for us a god before the Lord.

> For great is the Lord, and greatly to be praised: he also is to be feared above all gods. For all the gods of the people are idols: but the Lord made the heavens. (1 Chronicles 16:25)

The age we live in, of ecumenicalism and increasing interfaith contacts and cooperation among religions, is leading many to assume that all of man's religions are just different pathways to God. It is increasingly believed God may be man or woman, Allah or Jehovah. Others assume the gods of the Hindu, or Buddhist concepts of eternity and deity, are all manifestations of the truth and reality of God.

However, God's Word is clear that there is one God, one truth, and one Savior of the world. The gods and lords of this world are not gods at all, but merely idols of human thought and imagination. They do not really exist. The false gods of man, regardless of the name or thought behind them, are merely Lucifer by another name. (See Isaiah 14:13–14.)

> Then saith Jesus unto him, Get thee hence, Satan: for it is written, Thou shalt worship the Lord thy God, and him only shalt thou serve. (Matthew 4:10)

Jesus was not one of a long line of holy men, leaving us the option to seek God as we see best. Satan appeared to Him as an angel of light, and Jesus' own example shows us that we cannot follow dreams or visions, angels or holy men. For only one is worthy of worship, and that is God alone. Not just any god, but the God of creation, the God revealed in the Bible.

In Christ God has given us the privilege of being His sons and daughters. (See John 1:12.) Apart from Him we are children of disobedience, at best estranged children who cannot know the salvation and promises of God. We are to serve God with undivided service.

We are violating the conditions of His covenant with us when we partake of the religion of Babylon, which does not truly fear God and give glory to Him. Those who choose to be Christians after the pattern of Babylon by following a way that suits them may be satisfied with this kind of service. But in God's eyes it is of no value; it is having other gods before the Lord, and this is a violation of the first commandment.

Men are to worship and serve the Lord God and Him only. Most of mankind does not do this. Therefore, the message of Revelation calls the world to "worship Him that made heaven, and earth, and the sea, and the fountains of waters" (Revelation 14:7).

For many in this world, selfish pride is served as a god. For others, money and possessions are made a god. For still others, uncontrolled sensuality and base passion have become their god. Anything that is made the subject of undue thought and admiration, taking up our time and thoughts and life, can be a god chosen before the Lord.

The Second Commandment

> Thou shalt not make unto thee any graven image, or any likeness of any thing that is in heaven above, or that is in the earth beneath, or that is in the water under the earth: Thou shalt not bow down thyself to them, nor serve them: for I the Lord thy God am a jealous God, visiting the iniquity of the fathers upon the children unto the third and fourth generation of them that hate me; and shewing mercy unto thousands of them that love me, and keep my commandments. (Exodus 20:4–6)

What is an idol? This is an important question, for many may be worshiping idols unknowingly. An idol is not simply something made by the hands of man and bowed down and prayed to. An idol is "anything on which we set our affections; that to which we indulge an excessive and sinful attachment. (1 John 5:21 quoted.)

An idol is anything which usurps the place of God in the hearts of his rational creatures."[1]

Those who will follow the beast system in the future, and those today who follow the religion of Babylon, worship the idols of their own ideas, philosophies, and religion. All these things counterfeit or deny the truth of God and obscure the way of salvation He has set forth as the only way to eternal life.

> They that make them are like unto them; so is every one that trusteth in them. (Psalm 115:8)

The danger of devotional aids such as statues, pictures, icons, and relics, though we say they are not idols, is that they obscure the glory of God. Those who offer incense and burn candles and pray to or venerate these things, regardless of their sincere belief, are becoming like that which they adore. Such worship leads people away from the true God.

Millions in the world today worship gods of gold and silver, gods represented in art and statues, claiming these are devotional tools or simple representations of deity. Buddhists, Hindus, Catholics, and Orthodox venerate literal idols. But all of this is condemned in the second commandment. Making any kind of representation of deity, or of a saint who we believe will intercede for us, is making God like ourselves.

The followers of the beast and its system of religion will also become like that which they follow. The commandments of men, the ideologies of men, and the idols of men can lead man to no higher religious experience than that which is manmade. However, God desires to have a people who worship and obey Him and are thus being "changed into the same image from glory to glory, even as by the Spirit of the Lord" (2 Corinthians 3:18).

> Thus says the Lord God: Every man of the house of Israel who takes his idols [of self-will and unsubmissiveness] into his heart and puts the stumbling block of his iniquity [idols of silver and gold] before his face, and yet comes to the prophet [to inquire of him], I the Lord

will answer him, according to the multitude of his idols.
(Ezekiel 14:4 AMP)

Mortify therefore your members which are upon the earth; fornication, uncleanness, inordinate affection, evil concupiscence, and
covetousness, which is idolatry. (Colossians 3:5)

So kill (deaden, deprive of power) the evil desire lurking
in your members [those animal impulses and all that is
earthy in you that is employed in sin]; sexual vice, impurity,
sensual appetites, unholy desires, and all greed and covetousness, for that is idolatry (the deifying of self and other
created things instead of God). (Colossians 3:5 AMP)

Therefore, my dearly beloved, shun (keep clear away
from, avoid by flight if need be) any sort of idolatry (of loving or venerating anything more than God).
(1 Corinthians 10:14 AMP)

Whatever divides our affections, or takes away from our love
for God, or prevents unlimited confidence and entire trust in Him
becomes an idol in our hearts, and this is a violation of the second
commandment. The first great commandment says, "Thou shalt
love the Lord thy God with all thy heart, and with all thy soul, and
with all thy mind" (Matthew 22:37; see also Deuteronomy 6:5).
Nothing is to come between our love for God or our confidence
in Him. Our will, wishes, plans, desires, and pleasures must all be
in subjection to God and His Word or we will make an idol of the
things of this life.

Christ declares, "Whosoever he be of you that forsaketh not
all that he hath, he cannot be My disciple" (Luke 14:33). Whatever
takes our hearts' affections away from God must be released.
Money and possessions, or the striving for them, are idols for
many. Others worship reputation and worldly honor above God. It
is not possible to be half the Lord's and half the world's. Anything
less than a full commitment to God is idolatry. This is why most of
the world will follow the beast, for they are idolaters at heart.

For many more some cherished idea, some idol of opinion, becomes their god. They refuse the truth of the gospel and the plan of salvation, which comes down from the Father of light. As in Jesus' day, so it is today. Many trust in themselves and depend upon their own wisdom. They do not realize their spiritual poverty.

Many desire to be saved by some act they perform, some important work for their salvation, believing they are gaining merit or acceptance with God. When they see that there is no way of weaving human works into God's grace, they reject the salvation He has provided, and in essence worship gods of their own minds. However, there will be a remnant who love and reverence God. "These are they which were not defiled with women" (Revelation 14:4). The people of God will separate from the defiling influences of human religion and works, and the doctrines and commandments of men. Only the remnant will truly worship God and keep His commandments.

The Third Commandment

> Thou shalt not take the name of the Lord thy God in vain; for the Lord will not hold him guiltless that taketh his name in vain. (Exodus 20:7)

Taking God's name in vain includes linking the sacred with the common in such a way as to lessen the sacred nature of God's word or His character. Some Christian entertainers make light of the Bible or God thinking they are creating a light-hearted laugh. Some T-shirts, coffee mugs, games, and other common items take the name of God in vain by trying to make a connection between commercial marketing campaigns and spiritual truths.

The careless manner in which politicians use God's name to gain sympathy or votes, while their lives indicate they are not dedicated servants of God, is another common way God's name is taken in vain.

By the thoughtless mention of God in common conversation, and by the frequent and thoughtless repetition of His name, we dishonor Him. "Holy and reverend is His name" (Psalm 111:9).

The Third Commandment Amplified

You shall not use or repeat the name of the Lord your God in vain [that is, lightly or frivolously, in false affirmations or profanely]; for the Lord will not hold him guiltless who takes His name in vain. (Exodus 20:7 AMP)

The third commandment not only prohibits false oaths and common swearing, it forbids us to use the name of God in a light or careless manner. Repetitious prayers that use the name of God or Jesus over and over again are a violation of the third commandment. Would it not be offensive if we addressed men in the same way?

Even careless expressions such as "God bless you" or "God bless our country," when used by those whose hearts are not really surrendered to God, is a vain expression of the name of God. Men violate the third commandment in many ways without realizing what they are doing.

For the wrath of God is revealed from heaven against all ungodliness and unrighteousness of men, who hold the truth in unrighteousness. (Romans 1:18)

For God's [holy] wrath and indignation are revealed from heaven against all ungodliness and unrighteousness of men, who in their wickedness repress and hinder the truth and make it inoperative. (Romans 1:18 AMP)

The beast system claims to follow the truth, but what truth they do have is made to serve a lie because the commandments of men usurp the commandments of God. Therefore, all who follow the beast and receive his mark will worship God in vain, profaning His name by substituting the religion of men for the truth of God.

Many people today know about the way of salvation. They may even be able to prove their doctrines to be scripturally sound. But the way in which they live denies the Savior. They have violated the third commandment by taking His name in vain. Unless God opens their eyes and they repent, their experience will lead them into worshiping the beast.

O ye sons of men, how long will ye turn my glory into shame? How long will ye love vanity, and seek after leasing? (Psalm 4:2)

The word *vanity* means "emptiness, figurative, a worthless thing."[2] The word *leasing* means "falsehood, literally untruth, figurative idol."[3]

God's message calls us to "fear God and give glory to Him" (Revelation 14:7). But man distorts God's glory by following religions that are to no purpose; they have no saving virtue. We fill our lives with entertainment and frivolity. That which is light and fruitless does not improve our character; on the contrary, it often debases it. Thus while many of the worlds inhabitants are very religious, their religion is, in essence, idolatry.

But to the wicked, God says: What right have you to recite My statutes or take My covenant or pledge on your lips? Seeing that you hate instruction and correction and cast My words behind you [discarding them]? (Psalm 50:16–17 AMP)

God calls it wickedness when we profess to believe in Him, pray to Him, and claim to worship Him, yet we neglect or ignore His word and counsel. This is what many do, despite their religious profession. Even Christians take God's name in vain, for many "will not endure sound doctrine; but after their own lusts shall they heap to themselves teachers, having itching ears; and they shall turn away their ears from the truth, and shall be turned unto fables" (2 Timothy 4:3–4).

> And they come unto thee as the people cometh, and they sit before thee as my people, and they hear thy words, but they will not do them: for with their mouth they shew much love, but their heart goeth after their covetousness. (Ezekiel 33:31)

Our religion is vain if we hear God's words but do not follow them. For many people, religion is simply a cultural practice. Jesus warned us of the nature of vain religion. He said to the people of His day, "This people draweth nigh unto Me with their mouth, and honoureth Me with their lips, but their heart is far from Me. But in vain they do worship Me, teaching for doctrines the commandments of men" (Matthew 15:8–9). This principle applies to our day as well.

The Fourth Commandment

> Remember the sabbath day, to keep it holy. Six days shalt thou labour, and do all thy work: But the seventh day is the sabbath of the Lord thy God: in it thou shalt not do any work, thou, nor thy son, nor thy daughter, thy manservant, nor thy maidservant, nor thy cattle, nor thy stranger that is within thy gates: For in six days the Lord made heaven and earth, the sea, and all that in them is, and rested the seventh day: wherefore the Lord blessed the sabbath day, and hallowed it. (Exodus 20:8–10)

The Sabbath was instituted in the Garden of Eden at the foundation of creation. It is the most ancient and sacred of institutions, and it was given for mankind's benefit. In Exodus God urges the children of Israel to remember the Sabbath, as if to say, "Do not forget that when I finished My creation I instituted the Sabbath, and remember why I did so and for what purpose." In sanctifying and blessing the seventh day, God desires to sanctify and bless the man who keeps it.

If we consider the Sabbath as a type for the Jews alone, we should understand that types remain in full force until the thing signified by them takes place. That which is signified by the Sabbath is the rest in glory that remains for the people of God. Therefore, the moral obligation of the Sabbath will continue until time is swallowed up in eternity.

The Lord is God, and there is no other besides Him. This is the lesson of the Sabbath. Both holiness and re-creation are to be experienced by faith; therefore, the Sabbath is a sign of righteousness by faith and an acknowledgement of the sovereignty and power of the Creator God.

God has given the Sabbath to man as a day in which he may rest from labor of body and mind, and to devote himself to worship and the improvement of his spiritual condition. The seventh-day Sabbath is to be a day of blessing to us—a day when we can lay aside all the burdens and business of secular matters and center our thoughts upon God and heaven.

Is Sunday the Same as the Seventh-Day Sabbath?

Since the fourth commandment is not specifically referred to in the New Testament as a moral precept, many believe that there is no Sabbath under the Christian dispensation, or that it has been replaced by Sunday. However, Jesus taught by His example how to keep the Sabbath, in contrast to the traditions of men that had been heaped upon it, thereby making it a burden rather than the delight God intended it to be.

There are numerous examples of Sabbathkeeping after Jesus ascended to heaven. (See Acts 17:2; 18:4; 13:14, 42–44.) The New Testament contains fifty-nine references to the Sabbath. The book of Acts records eighty-four Sabbaths on which the apostle Paul and his associates held religious services.

In addition, no New Testament Scripture passage commands that the Sabbath be changed or replaced. For more than 150 years after Christ and the apostles completed their work, the majority in the early church kept the Sabbath. Gradually over hundreds of years Sunday took the place of the seventh-day Sabbath.

Though the Sabbath is found in the heart of the moral law, people often claim it was ceremonial and therefore done away with.

Unlike other moral laws, conscience does not figure in Sabbathkeeping as it does with killing, stealing, committing adultery, or bearing false witness. This is why God says, "Remember." It is an act of faith, love, and obedience to follow what God commands, even if our conscience is not pierced.

Many wholeheartedly believe that Sunday is the Sabbath of the New Covenant. But that places the traditions of men above God's Word and law. God declares of His people, "Here are they that keep the commandments of God, and the faith of Jesus" (Revelation 14:12.) By keeping God's commandments, they "worship Him that made heaven, and earth, and the sea, and the fountains of waters." In this worship, they keep God's seventh-day Sabbath, the true Lord's day. This is a sign of God's authority in their lives.

The Fifth Commandment

Honor thy father and thy mother: that thy days may be long upon the land which the Lord thy God giveth thee. (Exodus 20:12)

Parents are entitled to a degree of love and respect that is due to no other person. Such honor is not to be simply outward and formal. God's plan for man is that such love would be natural. However, sin and selfishness often affect the natural bond between child and parent and the mutual love that should be there.

The fifth commandment requires children, whether young or old, to respect and obey their parents, to give them love, and to lighten their cares. Children are to help and comfort their parents in old age. Paul the apostle said this "is the first commandment with promise" (Ephesians 6:2).

When God gave the moral law on Mount Sinai, the people of Israel expected to soon enter Canaan. The fifth commandment was a pledge to the obedient that they would live long in the Promised Land. However, we should not assume that this promise is limited to Israel alone, for it includes all the children of God. Paul taught by the unction of the Spirit, "Honour thy father and mother; (which is the first commandment with promise;) that it may be well with thee, and thou mayest live long on the earth" (Ephesians 6:2–3). This is a promise of eternal life upon the new earth, when it will be freed from the curse of sin. This promise only applies to the overcomer who, by faith, keeps the commandments of God.

The Fifth Commandment Amplified

Hearken unto thy father that begat thee, and despise not thy mother when she is old. (Proverbs 23:22)

The Bible teaches, "Children, obey your parents in the Lord: for this is right" (Ephesians 6:1). This is not a blind and unquestioning obedience. When children have unbelieving parents, and their rules or commands contradict the requirements of Christ and His Word, they must obey God and trust Him.

The fifth commandment confers a duty upon parents as well. With God's help, they are to exercise their authority with wisdom. "And, ye fathers, provoke not your children to wrath: but bring them up in the nurture and admonition of the Lord" (Ephesians 6:4). Paul further declared, "Fathers, provoke not your children to anger, lest they be discouraged" (Colossians 3:21).

The failure of parents and children to seek God and obey Him causes strife and turmoil in many homes. Satan is actively at work in such families. By accepting his influence and ignoring God's principles, men do not love and respect one another. However, children are not excused for disobedience because of their parent's unsanctified ways.

The Sixth Commandment

Thou shalt not kill. (Exodus 20:13)

Whosoever hateth his brother is a murderer: and ye know that no murderer hath eternal life abiding in him. (1 John 3:15)

But I say to you that everyone who continues to be angry with his brother or harbors malice (enmity of heart) against him shall be liable to and unable to escape the punishment imposed by the court; and whoever speaks contemptuously and insultingly to his brother shall be liable to and unable to escape the punishment. (Matthew 5:22 AMP)

You are jealous and covet [what others have] and your desires go unfulfilled; [so] you become murderers. [To hate is to murder as far as your hearts are concerned]. You burn with envy and anger and are not able to obtain [the gratification, the contentment, and the happiness that you seek], so you fight and war. You do not have, because you do not ask. (James 4:2 AMP)

The spirit of hatred and revenge originated with Satan, for "he was a murderer from the beginning" (John 8:44). Therefore, when we exhibit malice, unkindness, bitterness, or anger toward a fellow human being, we are violating God's law. With a revengeful and bitter spirit, the sin of murder stirs in our hearts. Thus guilt is incurred, not only by our actions but also by our thoughts and emotions. Even if such emotions and thoughts do not find expression in outward action, they are sin in God's sight, a violation of the sixth commandment. We will be brought to account for such things in the day when "God shall bring every work into judgment, with every secret thing" (Ecclesiastes 12:14).

Even taking pleasure in watching murder and killing in the form of entertainment—video games, television programs, movies, etc.—is also a violation of the sixth commandment. The violation of Gods law is not alone in actions committed but in the thoughts and emotions of the heart and what the mind dwells upon and takes pleasure in.

The Seventh Commandment

Thou shalt not commit adultery. (Exodus 20:14)

I have seen also in the prophets of Jerusalem an horrible thing: they commit adultery, and walk in lies: they strengthen also the hands of evildoers, that none doth return from his wickedness: they are all them unto me as Sodom, and the inhabitants thereof as Gomorrah. (Jeremiah 23:14)

Ye adulterers and adulteresses, know ye not that the friendship of the world is enmity with God? whosoever therefore will be a friend of the world is the enemy of God. (James 4:4)

You [are like] unfaithful wives having illicit love affairs with the world and breaking your marriage vow to God! Do you not know that being the world's friend is being God's enemy? So whoever chooses to be a friend of the world takes his stand as an enemy of God. (James 4:4 AMP)

The nature of spiritual adultery is to claim to serve God, but in reality to follow our own way, preferring falsehoods to God's truth. Worshipers of the beast will be guilty of this sin.

But I say unto you, That whosoever shall put away his wife, saving for the cause of fornication, causeth her to commit adultery: and whosoever shall marry her that is divorced committeth adultery. (Matthew 5:32)

In the Sermon on the Mount, Jesus declared that there could be no dissolution of marriage except for unfaithfulness to the marriage vow. Though a man or woman may be legally divorced, and though the divorce may be accepted by friends, family, and religious organizations, a married couple cannot be divorced in the sight of God. According to the teachings of Christ, only one sin can free a husband or wife from the marriage vow in the sight of God, and that is adultery.

This may sound restrictive or unreasonable in today's world. However, God's unchanging standard is for all ages, cultures, and societies. And it is for our own good. We are not free to adjust the moral law of God and the principles of His word to our human preferences.

If an unbeliever opposes the Christian faith of his or her spouse, in light of the law of God, divorce on this ground alone is not according to the commandment. "But if the unbelieving depart, let him depart. A brother or a sister is not under bondage in such cases: but God hath called us to peace" (1 Corinthians 7:15).

The Seventh Commandment Amplified

Moral purity is demanded not only in the outward life but also in the secret intents and emotions of the heart. Christ taught the far-reaching obligation of the law of God when He said, "Whosoever looketh on a woman to lust after her hath committed adultery with her already in his heart" (Matthew 5:28).

The seventh commandment forbids acts of impurity. Though many may believe that sexual fantasies and sexually explicit videos or photos are innocent fun that harms no one, yet even here the seventh commandment is violated.

"Like the sparrow in her wandering, like the swallow in her flying, so the causeless curse does not alight" (Proverbs 26:2 AMP). The wise man's words give us an insight as to why the violation of the seventh commandment and the disease and sorrow that often follow cannot be fixed solely by a vaccine or investments of billions of dollars.

The wise man further stated, "For as he thinketh in his heart, so is he" (Proverbs 23:7). It is as man becomes sensual rather than principled with a conscience enlightened that he often sinks so low in moral debasement, calling it fun, entertainment, or freedom. The law of God still speaks in our time, "Thou shalt not commit adultery.

The Eighth Commandment

Thou shalt not steal. (Exodus 20:15)

The eighth commandment condemns misrepresentation or overcharging in trade. Further, it requires the payment of our debts and the prompt payment of wages due to workers. This command condemns any attempt on our part to take advantage of another person's ignorance, weakness, or misfortune to gain advantage.

The Eighth Commandment Amplified

The wicked borroweth, and payeth not again: but the righteous sheweth mercy, and giveth. (Psalm 37:21)

To keep what we have borrowed, from the bank or from our neighbor or friend, is stealing. So is asking to borrow something when we know in our hearts we cannot or will not repay or return what we have borrowed. Declaring bankruptcy, though legal according to men, can be theft. Counterfeiting and piracy of goods, even when encouraged or overlooked by government, is stealing. A great deal of advertising is deceptive, even though companies often go to great lengths to technically avoid deception according to the law.

Verily, verily, I say unto you, He that entereth not by the door into the sheepfold, but climbeth up some other way, the same is a thief and a robber. (John 10:1)

Christ is the door to salvation. As shown in types, symbols, and the writings of the prophets, as well as during His life on earth, Jesus was "the Lamb of God, which taketh away the sin of the world" (John 1:29).

Throughout the ages, many have presented to the world false religions, philosophies, ceremonies, and rituals in order to gain acceptance with God and thus find entrance to heaven. But the only door is Christ. All who have introduced something to take the place of Christ are thieves and robbers.

The book of Revelation reveals Babylon and the beast system are robbers of men's souls and eternal life. This is why God gives such a stern warning regarding the need for us to separate from Babylon and avoid the mark of the beast.

The world's philosophies, standards, and religions will demand our lives and our attention. However, our hearts and lives belong to the One who redeemed us. If we give our hearts, minds, and strength to the world, we are stealing from God and ourselves. Our true purpose and happiness can be found only in serving Him.

The Ninth Commandment

Thou shalt not bear false witness against thy neighbor. (Exodus 20:16)

You shall not go up and down as a dispenser of gossip and scandal among your people, nor shall you [secure yourself by false testimony or by silence and] endanger the life of your neighbor. I am the Lord. (Leviticus 19:16 AMP)

Where no wood is, there the fire goeth out: so where there is no talebearer, the strife ceaseth. (Proverbs 26:20)

The ninth commandment says, basically, "Thou shall not lie." False speaking in any matter, from intentional overstatements to exaggerated impressions, is included in the prohibition. Even a statement of facts can be presented in a misleading way. The ninth commandment also condemns harming an individual's reputation by misrepresentation, evil surmising, or slander.

Falsehood is part of our daily life, in politics, culture, and commerce. But most tragic of all is the falsehood of religions that lead mankind away from the true God and His salvation.

It is not a sin to believe a lie; however, when we reject God's truth, we learn to accept lies and are thereby led away from saving truth.

Truth finds its source in God, "for all His ways are judgment: a God of truth and without iniquity, just and right is He" (Deuteronomy 32:4). In contrast, falsehood, deception, and lies are of Satan. "Because there is no truth in him. When he speaketh a lie, he speaketh of his own: for he is a liar, and the father of it" (John 8:44). Unless we repent, breaking the ninth commandment puts us on Satan's side.

The Tenth Commandment

> Thou shalt not covet thy neighbor's house, thou shalt not covet thy neighbor's wife, nor his manservant, nor his maidservant, nor his ox, nor his ass, nor any thing that is thy neighbor's. (Exodus 20:17)

Covetousness is the strong desire to posses what belongs to someone else. It is also the desire to possess things for the benefit of self. The spirit of Satan is greed for selfish aims, but the spirit of Christ is to give.

> Perverse disputings of men of corrupt minds, and destitute of the truth, supposing that gain is godliness: from such withdraw thyself. But godliness with contentment is great gain. For we brought nothing into this world, and it is certain we can carry nothing out. And having food and raiment let us be therewith content. But they that will be rich fall into temptation and a snare, and into many fool-

ish and hurtful lusts, which drown men in destruction and perdition. (1 Timothy 6:5–9)

The above verses from Timothy make it plain that the prosperity gospel is false. The tenth commandment condemns this modern doctrine, which is gaining popularity in Christian circles the world over. All who subscribe to the prosperity gospel are preparing themselves to worship the beast, for they have come to believe that gain is godliness. Being faithful to God and keeping His commandments instead of following the beast will endanger their prosperity; therefore they will receive the mark in order to continue buying and selling.

Let your conversation be without covetousness; and be content with such things as ye have: for he hath said, I will never leave thee, nor forsake thee. (Hebrews 13:5)

Let your character or moral disposition be free from love of money [including greed, avarice, lust, and craving for earthly possessions] and be satisfied with your present [circumstances and with what you have]; for He [God] Himself has said, I will not in any way fail you nor give you up nor leave you without support. (Hebrews 13:5 AMP)

And He said to them, Guard yourselves and keep free from all covetousness (the immoderate desire for wealth, the greedy longing to have more); for a man's life does not consist in and is not derived from possessing overflowing abundance or that which is over and above his needs. (Luke 12:15 AMP)

Devotion to securing money and possessions runs the economy of the modern world. However, the selfishness that a desire for possessions and money creates removes the favor of God from our hearts and deadens our spirituality. This is why, to a great degree, Christianity in the developed world is so weak. We are covetous, "and covetousness … is idolatry" (Colossians 3:5).

When our thoughts and daily pursuits are occupied with working for the accumulation of possessions and things, the claims of God and humanity are forgotten. The possessions God has given us, or allowed us to secure, are not for our benefit alone. Nothing should take our time and attention away from Him. The Giver is greater than the gift. And we are not our own; we have been bought with a price. Therefore, we should glorify God instead of seeking the glory of possessions.

"And this is the record, that God hath given to us eternal life, and this life is in His Son" (1 John 5:11). If we are partakers of eternal life, our hearts' affections and our time and effort will be to serve God, not self. Our desire for possessions will be in subjection to the will and Word of God. We are to conduct our affairs with an enlightened conscience, realizing that "a man's life consisteth not in the abundance of the things which he possesseth" (Luke 12:15).

> Let us hear the conclusion of the whole matter: Fear God, and keep his commandments: for this is the whole duty of man. (Ecclesiastes 12:13)

Obeying God's law from a heart that is in love with the Creator is the essence of fearing God and giving Him glory. Revelation distinguishes this experience as being a sign of God's true people. Those who drink of the wine of false religion and spiritual experiences exalt the commandments and religion of men. This will lead them to fear men and give deference to manmade systems of religion more than God. One way ends in life, the other in death.

My friend, may you know today the joy of salvation and the delight of living in harmony with God's will, His Word, and His law. For only those who can say from the heart with the psalmist, "I delight to do thy will, O my God: yea, thy law is within my heart" (Psalm 40:8), can truly be the children of God and inheritors of eternal life.

Endnotes

1. Noah Webster, *American Dictionary of the English Language* (San Francisco, California: Foundation for American Christian Education, 1967).
2. James Strong LL.D., S.T.D., *Strong's Exhaustive Concordance* (Grand Rapids, Michigan: Baker Book House, 1987).
3. Ibid.

Chapter Twenty

The Faith of Jesus—
Justifying Faith

Centuries before the coming of Christ, the prophet Isaiah penned the following words, which describe the ministry of the Messiah and His purpose for Israel and mankind.

The Spirit of the Lord God is upon me; because the Lord hath anointed me to preach good tidings unto the meek; he hath sent me to bind up the brokenhearted, to proclaim liberty to the captives, and the opening of the prison to them that are bound. (Isaiah 61:1)

Luke in his gospel narrative gives us the setting in which Jesus announces His mission and purpose as the Lord's anointed, in fulfillment of Isaiah's prophecy.

And he came to Nazareth, where he had been brought up: and, as his custom was, he went into the synagogue on the sabbath day, and stood up for to read. And there was delivered unto him the book of the prophet Esaias. And when he had opened the book, he found the place where it was written, The Spirit of the Lord is upon me, because he hath anointed me to preach the gospel to the poor; he hath sent me to heal the brokenhearted, to preach deliverance to the captives, and recovering of sight to the blind, to set at liberty them that are bruised, To preach the acceptable year of the Lord. And he closed the book, and he gave it again to the minister, and sat down. And the eyes of all them that were in the synagogue were fastened on him.

And he began to say unto them, This day is this scripture fulfilled in your ears. (Luke 4:16–21)

Christ came to set the captives free, and His deliverance is for the whole human family. Every man, regardless of race or religion, is bound by sin. Therefore, every man faces eternal condemnation.

The deliverance Christ brought was the good news of the gospel, which is salvation from guilt and sin, made available by His grace when we accept it by faith. The gospel is not limited to any one class. It is for all: high and low, rich and poor, educated and uneducated.

The poverty Jesus speaks of in this verse is the result of His Spirit humbling us so that we might set aside our pride, our unbelief, and our cultural or religious views and understand our great need of salvation. God's Spirit works sorrow and humility in us so that we might recognize that Christ can do for us what no amount of good works or religion can ever do.

Christ's ministry of grace, to those who understand their need and become poor enough to desire help, is to heal the brokenness of spirit, emotions, and body that results from the destructive nature of sin.

The adherents of Babylon's religion may, to some degree, recognize their need or have a desire for eternal life. However, they cannot be healed, for they seek salvation by the things they do, substituting their way for God's way. All such religion is doomed to failure.

The words of Christ are the words of life and brings deliverance to those in the prison of sin. "It is the Spirit Who gives life [He is the Life-giver]; the flesh conveys no benefit whatever [there is no profit in it]. The words (truths) that I have been speaking to you are spirit and life" (John 6:63 AMP).

While Jesus walked this earth, He ministered to the physical needs of man. However, His miracles were not only to heal the body, but also that people might believe that He was the Messiah and Savior of mankind. His work of healing the blind was mostly to heal spiritual blindness.

Jesus said to the religious leaders and teachers of His day, "Woe unto you, ye blind guides" (Matthew 23:16). That woe is upon all who are spiritually blind yet claim to see. Jesus said, "Can the blind lead the blind? shall they not both fall into the ditch?" (Luke 6:39).

The purpose of Revelation 14 is to open the eyes of our understanding, which have been blinded by our own sinfulness. Mankind, in rejecting in one form or another the everlasting gospel, often remains religious; thus we readily accept the wine of Babylon's falsehood, which benumbs our spiritual faculties.

The pervasive influence of the three unclean spirits coming from the dragon, the beast, and the false prophet have been used by "the god of this world," who has "blinded the minds of them which believe not, lest the light of the glorious gospel of Christ, who is the image of God, should shine unto them (2 Corinthians 4:4). Yet Scripture reveals that God will have a people who have been delivered and set free. They have the faith of Jesus, which is justification by faith.

How Are We Set Free?

> For what saith the scripture? Abraham believed God, and it was counted unto him for righteousness. (Romans 4:3)

We are saved by reliance on God, not ourselves. Those who believe that meritorious good works will recommend them to God seek salvation in vain. Salvation is not found in pilgrimages to Mecca or Lourdes or the river Ganges or any supposed holy site or shrine. Our religious works, our long prayers or appeasement of the deity, can never save us. Salvation is not gained in anything man can do.

Salvation's source is in God alone. It is received by man when, through faith and submission, he accepts God's free gift.

The religions of Babylon and the kings of the earth will unite under the beast, the revived Roman power. This will be the climax of the long ages of apostasy. The faith that saves will be set aside for faith in falsehood. The people of this planet will give themselves over to following "seducing spirits, and doctrines of devils" (1 Timothy 4:1). This deception is even now gaining strength and influence.

Only those with the faith of Jesus, who have been pardoned and set free, will avoid the great deception of the last days.

What Is Man's Condition in God's Sight?

> As it is written, There is none righteous, no, not one: There is none that understandeth, there is none that seeketh after God. They are all gone out of the way, they are together become unprofitable; there is none that doeth good, no, not one. Their throat is an open sepulcher; with their tongues they have used deceit; the poison of asps is under their lips: Whose mouth is full of cursing and bitterness: Their feet are swift to shed blood: Destruction and misery are in their ways: And the way of peace have they not known: there is no fear of God before their eyes. (Romans 3:10–18)

These verses describe the state of man in his condition apart from God. We do not naturally seek God. It is only because of God's mercy and love, constantly exercised toward men, that some respond to His grace. Since the fall of man God has offered mankind salvation by grace through faith. Yet ever since Cain, mankind has sought God in his own way and on his own terms. Satan has blinded man into accepting false paths of spirituality and religion. This is Satan's way of usurping God in the hearts of man so that he might be a god to the people of this planet.

> Now we know that what things soever the law saith, it saith to them who are under the law: that every mouth may be stopped, and all the world may become guilty before God. (Romans 3:19)

The law speaks to all men, for the whole world has sinned and is under the burden of guilt and condemnation. It condemns us as sinners—subject to the judgment of God. It speaks condemnation so that we might seek a Savior. The Spirit of God brings the knowledge of sin to the heart so the righteous standard of God and our accountability to Him will be known.

Those with the faith of Jesus keep the law, not as a means of salvation but as the result of faith and love. For the love of Christ known in the forgiveness of sin becomes love for Christ expressed in willing service and obedience to His law and word. Such a transformation is day by day as we "put on the new man, which after God is created in righteousness and true holiness" (Ephesians 4:24).

All men "have sinned, and come short of the glory of God" (Romans 3:23). Those who worship the beast may sense their sinfulness and need of God. Sadly, however, they will seek salvation in human works, ceremonies and rituals, and the doctrines and commandments of men.

Can Keeping the Law Save?

Therefore by the deeds of the law there shall no flesh be justified [made righteous, acquitted, and judged acceptable] in his sight: for by the law is the knowledge of sin. (Romans 3:20)

Adherence to any religious ritual or work is insufficient to gain pardon and acceptance with God. The religion of Babylon does not accept this. The worshipers of the beast will not know the justifying love of God, which comes by faith alone, apart from anything man can do.

How Then Are We Saved?

But now the righteousness of God without the law is manifested, being witnessed by the law and the prophets; Even the righteousness of God which is by faith of Jesus Christ unto all and upon all them that believe: for there is no difference. (Romans 3:21–22)

Righteousness comes through Christ alone. His unmerited grace and favor is freely offered to all. However, righteousness by faith is effectual only for "them that believe."

God, in His great love and kindness, has encircled the world with an atmosphere of grace. He not only speaks to man through the law and the prophets and by His Spirit, but even the heavens declare His glory. (See Psalm 19:1–3.) There is no place where the voice of God's heart of love is not heard. His Spirit speaks to the heart of every man.

Mankind can resist this love, refusing to be drawn to Christ by the Holy Spirit. However, if he does not resist, he will be pardoned and set free from condemnation and sin.

As He extends grace to mankind, the Lord also brings us sorrow for sin as well as the desire to turn to Him for pardon. He presents His righteousness to our minds, and He has placed in every man's heart a measure of faith. (See Romans 12:3.)

If it were possible to take everything that is good and noble in man, and present this to God in an effort to gain merit for even one soul, the idea would be rejected. Yet this is what much of mankind does through his religious practices. It makes God obligated to man because of what he does. However, righteousness is only obtained by grace through faith because of what God has done for man.

How Is Man to Be Justified and Pardoned?

How then can man be justified with God? or how can he be clean that is born of a woman. (Job 25:4)

Being justified freely by his grace through the redemption that is in Christ Jesus. (Romans 3:24)

Through faith in Christ we receive His love and are counted righteous in God's sight. Since pardon is freely bestowed upon us as a gift, there is nothing we can do to purchase it. No one pays for a gift bestowed in love. To seek to pay for such a gift would be considered an offense to the giver. We simply accept the gift with appreciation.

When a gift is given unexpectedly, even undeservedly, the gift awakens in us thoughts of gratitude and love. So it is with Christ's free gift of justification, pardon, and salvation. We do not deserve it; neither can we work for it. We can only accept it by faith.

And even this faith is not our own. It too is a gift of God, as is the heart's desire to turn to Him in recognition of our need. We must choose to surrender; otherwise, we cannot be saved. Yet the promptings of God's Spirit helps us, "for it is God which worketh in you both to will and to do of His good pleasure" (Philippians 2:13). Therefore, in Christ, God can "be just, and the justifier of him which believeth in Jesus" (Romans 3:26). Truly, "If God be for us, who can be against us?" (Romans 8:31). For by His grace, through faith, we are no longer "guilty before God." We have passed from death unto life.

Justification is wholly of God's mercy and love, not obtainable by any works that fallen man can do. However, the religious system of the beast will be largely based on man's work and man's religious beliefs. The beast will use both force and reward to induce all to follow its way. The remnant who have experienced pardon and justification by faith know that there is no way to save themselves. Their surrender to Christ is by faith. This faith will enable the saints to endure the onslaughts of the lying religions of men, even if it means the loss of economic privileges, liberty, or even life.

For by grace are ye saved through faith; and that not of yourselves: it is the gift of God. (Ephesians 2:8)

For it is by free grace (God's unmerited favor) that you are saved (delivered from judgment and made partakers of Christ's salvation) through [your] faith. And this [salvation] is not of yourselves [of your own doing, it came not through your own striving], but it is the gift of God. (Ephesians 2:8 AMP)

When a man's conscience is made tender by the Holy Spirit, and he discerns Christ's sacrifice on his behalf, he accepts this atonement as his only hope for acceptance with God and eternal life. His sins are pardoned. This is justification by faith.

There is no merit in faith. The ability for a soul to turn to God is the work of God in the man.

Such a work not only pardons; it also changes and enables. This is why God's people in Revelation are represented as over-comers, rather than being overcome by the prevailing iniquity, deception, and false religion.

Is There a Place for Man's Boasting?

Where is boasting then? It is excluded. By what law? of works? Nay; but by the law of faith. (Romans 3:27)

Is there any place for boasting of our merits of goodness? Is there any place for us to add to our salvation or gain more merit with God? No. It is by grace through faith that we are saved, which eliminates any place for boasting.

Not because of works [not the fulfillment of the Law's demands], lest any man should boast. [It is not the result of what anyone can possibly do, so no one can pride himself in it or take glory to himself.] (Ephesians 2:9 AMP)

The idea that we can do anything to make ourselves deserving of the grace and pardon of God is false. So is the idea that once we are pardoned and set right we can do additional things to gain more favor or grace. Further, it is the love of Christ responded to and allowed to grow in our hearts that develops faith, which works by love.

The result of a life of love and faith is that we shall "[live] as children of obedience [to God]; do not conform yourselves to the evil desires [that governed you] in your former ignorance [when you did not know the requirements of the Gospel]. But as the One Who called you is holy, you yourselves also be holy in all your conduct and manner of living" (1 Peter 1:14–15 AMP).

Therefore we conclude that a man is justified by faith without the deeds of the law. (Romans 3:28)

Faith is the means to justification, not the end. Faith surrenders the will to what God has said. Our standing before God is based on what He has done for us and our acceptance of that gift, not what we can do for ourselves.

The worshipers of the beast also have faith in their system of religion. But saving faith comes only when we believe in the everlasting gospel, the good news that salvation is in Christ alone. True saving faith is centered on Jesus and surrendered to His love.

Many worshipers of the beast will claim to believe in Jesus. However, Jesus taught that despite their claims to do things in His name, they would be lost because they were workers of iniquity and did not do His Father's will. (See Matthew 7:21–23.)

Now to him that worketh is the reward not reckoned of grace, but of debt. (Romans 4:4)

Man often thinks that when he makes an offering to the Lord, he has merited the favor of God; therefore, the Lord is under obligation to him. The attitude that God will regard us with special favor because of our gifts is not limited to the rich or to any one religion. Many consider their works, their giving of time and money, their membership in a religious organization, and various other things as sufficient to merit God's favor and grace. Such ideas will lead the world away from the everlasting gospel and prepare people to follow or worship the beast.

No one can give God anything that is not already His. "All things come of Thee, and of thine own have we given Thee" (1

Chronicles 29:14). We have nothing of value to offer, be it our works, religious zeal, or possessions, which we have not first received of God.

The only faith that will benefit us is that which takes Christ as our personal Savior and which appropriates His merits to ourselves. Many hold faith as merely an opinion on religious matters; however, saving faith is a transaction. Those who receive Christ join themselves in covenant relation with God.

Genuine faith is life, which is why the saints will be sealed as God's own, accepting no authority in religious matters other than God's Word. The worshipers of the beast will have faith, but it is not a faith that surrenders totally to Jesus and His word. The followers of the beast will accept the word of men instead of God's word; thus they are marked as Satan's followers, for their faith is really the faith of devils. (See James 2:18–20.)

> What shall we say then that Abraham our father, as pertaining to the flesh, hath found? For if Abraham were justified by works, he hath whereof to glory; but not before God. (Romans 4:1–2)

It is impossible to affect our standing before God through our own merits. If faith and good works could purchase the gift of salvation, the Creator would be under obligation to the creature. If a man could merit salvation by something he could do, salvation would be like a debt that can be eliminated by our payment. However, man cannot merit salvation by any of his good works or religious zeal. Acceptance with God is wholly of grace, received by a sinner because he believes in Jesus.

Some of those who have grasped this glorious truth become misled or mistaken, believing that obedience to God's law or following biblical standards are opposed to grace by faith. But this idea is an error that leads some astray.

> Do we then by [this] faith make the law of no effect, overthrow it or make it a dead letter? Certainly not! On the

contrary, we confirm and establish and uphold the Law. (Romans 3:31 AMP)

We are to exercise a faith that is motivated and awakened by love. The apostle Paul admonishes believers to "try to learn [in your experience] what is pleasing to the Lord [let your lives be constant proofs of what is most acceptable to Him]" (Ephesians 5:10 AMP).

No work of man can merit the pardoning love of God, but the love of God filling the heart and captivating the mind will lead us to do those things that are required by God. The love of Christ in our hearts leads us to follow the Lord and His law and Word with pleasure. In denying our way for God's way, we are enabled to walk by faith.

God lays the glory of man in the dust so that He can do for us that which we cannot do for ourselves. This enables the saints to live lives of consistent endurance, to do right before the Lord in love. Justification by faith enables the saints to keep God's commandments rather than following the commandments and religion of men.

Justification by faith seals the saints in their experience so that they cannot be moved by the beast's offers of reward or threats of punishment. They endure "as seeing Him who is invisible" (Hebrews 11:27), for the saints live by faith. This is the victory that overcomes the world, the beast, and his mark: the faith of Jesus, the joy of knowing the forgiveness of sin, and the pardoning love of God.

Chapter Twenty-one

The Faith of Jesus—
The Substance of Faith

H ere is the patience of the saints: here are they that keep the commandments of God, and the faith of Jesus. (Revelation 14:12)

Today, we refer to people of faith as individuals or groups that worship a higher power. Such faith, though sincere, may not be of any saving virtue.

In one of Jesus' parables, He said, "When the Son of man cometh, shall He find faith on the earth?" (Luke 18:8). Jesus did not ask if He would find religion when He comes the second time, but if would He find faith. Despite the great prevalence of religion today, most are "giving heed to seducing spirits, and doctrines of devils" (1 Timothy 4:1). The book of Revelation describes those who are truly people of faith as those with consistent endurance to serve and follow the principles of heaven and obedient to God's law through the faith of Jesus.

In this chapter we will pursue the theme of faith, studying what is it and how it manifests itself in the true child of God. Let us start by defining *faith*:

Moral conviction (of religious truth, or the truthfulness of God.) Especially reliance upon Christ for salvation, constancy in such profession.[1]

In theology, the assent of the mind or understanding to the truth of what God has revealed. Simple belief in the scriptures, of the being and perfections of God, and the existence, character and doctrines of Christ, founded on the testimony of the sacred writers. This is called historical or speculative faith; a faith little distinguished from the belief of the existence and achievements of Alexander or of Caesar.

Evangelical, justifying or saving faith, is the assent of the mind to the truth of Divine revelation, on the authority of God's testimony, accompanied with a cordial assent of the will or approbation of the heart; an entire confidence or trust in God's character and declarations, and in the character and doctrines of Christ, with an unreserved surrender of the will to his guidance, and dependence on his merits for salvation. That firm belief in God's testimony, and of the truth of the gospel, which influences the will, and leads to an entire reliance on Christ for salvation.[2]

Saving faith is centered on God's Word. Faith is awakened in our hearts by God's Spirit and grows through exercise and the motivation of love.

God has placed in the heart of man the ability to have and exercise faith. Indeed, all could believe and be saved. However, many do not believe, or they place their faith in the doctrines and religions of men. A great battle is taking place between truth and error, between the religion of men and the salvation God offers.

What Is the Source of Faith?

So then faith cometh by hearing, and hearing by the word of God. (Romans 10:17)

Now faith is the substance of things hoped for, the evidence of things not seen. [For example.] Through faith we understand that the worlds were framed by the word of God, so that things which are seen were not made of things which do appear. (Hebrews 11:1, 3)

Faith perceives as real what is not revealed to the senses, "for we walk [live] by faith, not by sight" (2 Corinthians 5:7). This is not a mystical, make-believe life, for to live by faith is to live by the Word of God. To live by God's Word is faith; to be religious and neglect God's Word is presumption. True faith leads to salvation, while presumption causes us to be fallen from God.

> For I say, through the grace given unto me, to every man that is among you, not to think of himself more highly than he ought to think; but to think soberly, according as God hath dealt to every man the measure of faith. (Romans 12:3)

The worshipers of the beast will have taken the portion of faith placed in their hearts by God and distorted it. Rather than fearing God and giving Him glory, they will fear man. And "they are proud of what they should be ashamed of, and they think only of things that belong to this world" (Philippians 3:19 TEV).

The enemy of God and man has "blinded the minds of them which believe not, lest the light of the glorious gospel of Christ, who is the image of God, should shine unto them" (2 Corinthians 4:4). This blindness is not sin; however, when God's light and love and grace come to an individual, and that person refuses the truth, the words of Jesus are fulfilled: "If ye were blind, ye should have no sin: but now ye say, We see; therefore your sin remaineth" (John 9:41).

The Work of Faith

> For therein is the righteousness of God revealed from faith to faith: as it is written, The just shall live by faith. (Romans 1:17)

> But that no man is justified by the law in the sight of God, it is evident: for, The just shall live by faith. (Galatians 3:11)

Now the just shall live by faith: but if any man draw back,
my soul shall have no pleasure in him. (Hebrews 10:38)

The just are those who have been justified and pardoned by
God. By faith they have accepted His grace and the salvation purchased for them by Christ. To live by faith is to live by the Word of
God. Every plan and purpose of our lives should be influenced by
the faith and love we have toward God. The object of our constant
contemplation is the goodness of God and how we might please
Him. Every activity of life, including our entertainment and leisure time, our buying and selling, the raising of our children, and
the way we use our time and resources should all be conducted by
faith. To live such a life means we live by the light God has given
us in His Word.

Do we then make void the law through faith? God forbid:
yea, we establish the law. (Romans 3:31)

Saving faith, which is the faith of Jesus lived out in the life,
will uphold the law of God, not merely outwardly but as a heart
experience as well. With true faith there will be what the prophet
Ezekiel spoke of as a new heart, and a new spirit. The law is written
in the mind and lived out in the life. (See Ezekiel 36:26–27; also
Hebrews 10:15–16.)

Those who have the faith of Jesus will keep God's ten commandments in love. This is not done by human effort or for hope
of reward or fear of punishment. The faith of Jesus is the life of
Christ worked out in the life of the believer. This is sanctification
by faith. Just as Jesus obeyed His Father's law out of love, so too
will the children of God obey Him from a heart touched and transformed by love.

By whom also we have access by faith into this grace
wherein we stand, and rejoice in hope of the glory of God.
(Romans 5:2, see also Hebrews 4:15–16.)

Faith gives us access to grace, which is God's unmerited favor, and the divine influence, which keeps us from sin. But unless we accept God's grace, it will have no saving effect on our lives. Faith merits nothing, but we must believe and exercise faith in accepting God's grace so that we might be pardoned, justified, and strengthened.

> Therefore being justified by faith, we have peace with God through our Lord Jesus Christ. (Romans 5:1)

To be *justified* means to be "acquitted, declared righteous and given a right standing with God" (Romans 5:1 AMP). Those with the faith of Jesus are at peace with God, seeking to be conformed to His will and living to please Him. The worshipers of the beast will consider this peace to be at war with their system of religion. For the religion of the world substitutes peace with men and obedience to his religions for being at peace with God.

> I am crucified with Christ: nevertheless I live; yet not I, but Christ liveth in me: and the life which I now live in the flesh I live by the faith of the Son of God, who loved me, and gave himself for me. (Galatians 2:20)

> The life I now life in the body I live by faith in (by adherence to and reliance on and complete trust in) the Son of God, Who loved me and gave Himself up for me. (Galatians 2:20 AMP)

Wherever the principle of saving faith is at work, there is death. Jesus said we must take up our cross, representing self-denial, and follow Him. (See Mark 8:34.) Paul said, "Our old man is crucified with Him, that the body of sin might be destroyed, that henceforth we should not serve sin" (Romans 6:6). To be crucified is to respond to the Spirit of God and to yield heart and life to Christ. For the sinful, wayward heart, this requires surrender. However, what appears at first to be bitterness is actually a delight. The more we surrender, the more Christ is revealed in our lives.

Many who follow the religions of Babylon are also involved in self-denial, but it is not of faith. Rather, it is done in the hope of gaining merit and acceptance with God. Crossless religions follow their own way rather than the way of light and truth as found in the Bible.

> And I pray that Christ will be more and more at home in your hearts, living within you as you trust in him. May your roots go down deep into the soil of God's marvelous love. (Ephesians 3:17 TLB)

True faith that brings salvation is not faith in an idea or philosophy or religious practices. True faith brings a relationship with Christ, the Creator and Savior. This relationship is based on His love, not ours. We love God because "He loved us, and sent His Son to be the propitiation for our sins" (1 John 4:10).

In the plant kingdom, vegetation from the smallest plant to the towering tree draws nutrients and water to sustain life and growth by its roots. So it is with us. We are to have an experience that is deepening and taps into the source of strength, which is God. This experience of faith grounds us, giving us stability so that we can live by faith, hope, and love.

> ... and be found in him, not having mine own righteousness, which is of the law, but that which is through the faith of Christ, the righteousness which is of God by faith. (Philippians 3:9)

A right standing with God can never come from the law or any outward religious works.

Many in the world believe certain types of prayers, done at certain places or at certain times, gains merit with God. Others believe going to certain declared holy sights is required to please Him. Celebrating certain holidays or festivals are considered a means of gaining His favor. Religious ritual is a chain that binds people as they seek acceptance with God, but in vain.

In countless ways man seeks to fill the void that only a relationship with God can fill. Sensing his need for God, man seeks to cover his sin and guilt, not by God's grace through faith in the death of Christ, but in what he can do.

The apostle Paul once practiced many religious observances to gain God's favor. However, when faith came and grace was made known to his heart, he said of his past religious practices, "I have put aside all else, counting it worth less than nothing, in order that I can have Christ, and become one with Him, no longer counting on being saved by being good enough or by obeying God's laws, but by trusting Christ to save me; for God's way of making us right with Himself depends on faith—counting on Christ alone" (Philippians 3:8–9 TLB).

> What doth it profit, my brethren, though a man say he hath faith, and have not works? Can faith save him? If a brother or sister be naked, and destitute of daily food, and one of you say unto them, depart in peace, be ye warmed and filled; notwithstanding ye give them not those things which are needful to the body; what doth it profit? Even so faith, if it hath not works, is dead, being alone. Yea, a man may say, thou hast faith, and I have works: shew me thy faith without thy works, and I will shew thee my faith by my works. Thou believest that there is one God; thou doest well: the devils also believe, and tremble. But wilt thou know, O vain man, that faith without works is dead? For as the body without the spirit is dead, so faith without works is dead also. (James 2:14–20, 26)

> So also faith, if it does not have works (deeds and actions of obedience to back it up), by itself is destitute of power (inoperative, dead). (James 2:17 AMP)

With true faith there is also work. This work is not the source of faith; neither is the work saving in itself. Rather, works are the evidence of true faith. The life of one having true saving faith is to live by the counsel of God as found in the Bible, with a conscience captive to the will of God and directed by His Spirit.

The religions represented by the beast, the dragon, and the false prophet will be filled with zealous adherents who seem to have great faith and do wonderful charitable works. Most of the people on this planet will accept the beast (see Revelation 13:8) because of the apparently good works He does. But there is one standard by which all things must be judged: God's truth. The way of salvation is not through a plurality of ideas, no matter how good they may seem. All religious faith, both genuine and false, and the works they bring forth, are to be judged according "to the law and to the testimony: if they speak not according to this word, it is because there is no light in them" (Isaiah 8:20).

> For whatsoever is born of God overcometh the world: and this is the victory that overcometh the world, even our faith. (1 John 5:4)

Genuine faith overcomes "the lust of the flesh, and the lust of the eyes, and the pride of life" (1 John 2:16). Jesus "gave Himself for our sins, that He might deliver us from this present evil world, according to the will of God and our Father" (Galatians 1:4).

To overcome the world by faith is to live for God in a world of darkness. It means to "set your affection on things above, not on things on the earth" (Colossians 3:2).

Examples of Saving Faith

> And they came to Jericho: and as he went out of Jericho with his disciples and a great number of people, blind Bartimaeus, the son of Timaeus, sat by the highway side begging. And when he heard that it was Jesus of Nazareth, he began to cry out, and say, Jesus, thou Son of David, have mercy on me. And many charged him that he should hold his peace: but he cried the more a great deal, Thou Son of David, have mercy on me. And Jesus stood still,

and commanded him to be called. And they call the blind man, saying unto him, Be of good comfort, rise; he calleth thee. And he, casting away his garment, rose, and came to Jesus. And Jesus answered and said unto him, What wilt thou that I should do unto thee? The blind man said unto him, Lord, that I might receive my sight. And Jesus said unto him, Go thy way; thy faith hath made thee whole. And immediately he received his sight, and followed Jesus in the way. (Mark 10:46–52)

Saving faith begins with recognition of our need. The blind man's need was obvious. But those who are spiritually blind do not see it; therefore, God seeks to awaken in us a sense of need. Faith responds to that dawning recognition.

True faith responds to Christ's call on the conscience. Because of the hardness of our hearts, this can take months or years; many will never respond. Like the blind man, we must rise and seek the Lord. This too is a work of faith.

As God's grace is felt, understood, and experienced, we, like Bartimaeus, cry unto the Lord for a deliverance we cannot gain for ourselves. This is faith at work. Jesus will not refuse to save us, for He has drawn us. He has given us faith and a sense of our need. By faith we can be made whole.

As with the blind man who was healed by faith, so we who are saved by faith make it known that we are healed. We follow Jesus, no longer following "the voice of strangers" (John 10:5) or the "perverse disputings of men of corrupt minds, and destitute of the truth (1 Timothy 6:5).

And a certain woman, which had an issue of blood twelve years, And had suffered many things of many physicians, and had spent all that she had, and was nothing bettered, but rather grew worse, When she had heard of Jesus, came in the press behind, and touched his garment. For she said, If I may touch but his clothes, I shall be whole. And straightway the fountain of her blood was dried up; and she felt in her body that she was healed of that plague.

And Jesus, immediately knowing in himself that virtue had gone out of him, turned him about in the press, and said, Who touched my clothes? And his disciples said unto him, Thou seest the multitude thronging thee, and sayest thou, Who touched me? And he looked round about to see her that had done this thing. But the woman fearing and trembling, knowing what was done in her, came and fell down before him, and told him all the truth. And he said unto her, Daughter, thy faith hath made thee whole; go in peace, and be whole of thy plague. (Mark 5:25–34)

Faith hears, faith acts, faith believes. Then God does for us what we cannot do for ourselves.

In this story of a woman's healing, we again find recognition of need. Because of this woman's great need, she gladly heard the good news of Christ's healing virtue. But the work of faith did not stop here. It was not enough for this woman to be drawn to the Savior by what she had heard. Only when this women understood her helplessness and heard about Jesus' healing virtue, and sought for the Savior, and then touched Him was the power of faith unlocked. These steps of faith are the same for each one who will be saved by grace and live the life of faith.

And when Jesus was entered into Capernaum, there came unto him a centurion, beseeching him, and saying, Lord, my servant lieth at home sick of the palsy, grievously tormented. And Jesus saith unto him, I will come and heal him. The centurion answered and said, Lord, I am not worthy that thou shouldest come under my roof: but speak the word only, and my servant shall be healed. For I am a man under authority, having soldiers under me: and I say to this man, Go, and he goeth; and to another, Come, and he cometh; and to my servant, Do this, and he doeth it. When Jesus heard it, he marvelled, and said to them that followed, Verily I say unto you, I have not found so great faith, no, not in Israel. (Matthew 8:5–10)

In this Scripture we see a request for deliverance and an understanding of human helplessness on the part of the centurion.

The centurion, recognizing his lowly estate in the presence of Christ, declares that he is not worthy to have Christ come with him. Yet in faith he asks Christ to simply speak the words of healing virtue, believing that what He speaks will take place.

The centurion then defines the nature of his faith and explains why he has such confidence. In his own life's experience he sees a parallel to Christ. As a man having authority over other men, he speaks words of instruction, and that which he speaks comes to pass by virtue of his authority. If he says, "Come," the soldier under him comes. If he says, "Go," his men go. If he says, "Do this," his servant does what has been commanded. The centurion recognizes Christ's authority and power to accomplish his request. And so he says, "Speak the word only and my servant shall be healed." Jesus, upon hearing the request of faith that was expressed in recognition of His power and authority, " said unto the centurion, Go thy way; and as thou hast believed, so be it done unto thee. And his servant was healed in the selfsame hour" (Matthew 8:13).

If God's Word says, "Come," by faith we come. If His Word says, "Go," we go. If the Word says, "Do this," great faith does what that word has said.

The Substance of Faith

> Now faith is the substance of things hoped for, the evidence of things not seen. (Hebrews 11:1)

Substance is real and can be experienced; it is confidence. We confidently trust in the "exceeding great and precious promises: [of God's word] that by these ye might be partakers of the divine nature" (2 Peter 1:4). Our confidence is in knowing that "all the promises of God in Him [Christ] are yea, and in Him Amen, unto the glory of God by us" (2 Corinthians 1:20). And what will bring about this most blessed experience? Faith! God's Word contains promises regarding our being conformed to the image of Christ, of obtaining His righteousness and holiness for ourselves, of His coming again, and of the deliverance of the dead from the grave. These things can be experienced, and they will happen. To believe and trust in God's Word is faith with substance.

Here are some examples of faith from the book of Hebrews:

- By faith Abel offered a better sacrifice. (11:4)
- By faith Enoch was translated. (11:5)
- By faith Noah prepared an ark. (11:7)
- By faith Abraham moved. (11:8)
- By faith Abraham offered Isaac. (11:17)
- By faith Moses refused to be Pharaoh's son; he chose instead to suffer with God's people. (11:24–25)
- By faith the Red Sea parted. (11:29)
- By faith the walls of Jericho fell down. (11:30)

Let's take a closer look at some of these examples.

Noah obeyed God's word despite all the evidence that said that word could not possibly be fulfilled. In seeing what could not yet be understood, Noah became a preacher of righteousness. His faith built the ark and preached a coming judgment.

Abel followed God's will, trusting in the Lamb to come typified in his sacrifice. Abel's brother Cain also had a form of worship, but he set his feelings above the plainly revealed commands of God.

Abraham moved from his home and family. He had no evidence except the word of God, but he acted upon the word, for he had a faith of substance. By the word of God and his confidence in God's merciful dealings and His promises, he had faith to believe that Isaac, if slain, would be raised again.

Marching around the walls of Jericho was a ridiculous way to conduct a war. Yet the word of God bid the children of Israel to do so. They had a faith of substance that heard the word of God and followed it. And God did that which to human eyes seemed impossible. For those who refused God's word, there was only disaster and great loss.

We need a faith of substance that brings obedience and trust in what God has said to a blessed reality. The Bible is the word of the living God. Therefore the Bible with all its promises, blessings and warnings is evidence enough that what it says will take place, exactly as God has said. And we see that in the examples of faith recorded in Hebrews 11. Faith in God's Word, the Bible, is faith of substance, and such a life of faith will see the accomplishment both in this life and the next of all that God's word has declared.

What is the result of such a life of faith? "Receiving the end of your faith, even the salvation of your souls" (1 Peter 1:9).

In this world of corruption, chaos, and deception, we, like the apostles of old, must pray "unto the Lord, increase our faith" (Luke 17:5). Jesus said, "If ye have faith as a grain of mustard seed, ye shall say unto this mountain, Remove hence to yonder place; and it shall remove" (Matthew 17:20). Though the mustard seed is very small, it contains the power to produce a large plant. When the mustard seed is sown, it utilizes all that God has provided for its growth: soil, rain, and sun.

If we have faith like this, we will take hold of God's Word and ask for all the help He has promised. Thus our faith will be strengthened. The opposition and hardships we meet in this world of sin and darkness, which seem to be as difficult to conquer as climbing the towering mountains, will be overcome by faith. "Nothing shall be impossible unto you" (Matthew 17:20b). We must be developing this faith now, day by day, to meet our current needs and to withstand the crisis at the end. Then we will be among the remnant having the faith of Jesus, sealed in Christ rather than marked by the beast.

Hear the words of Jesus and let them be words of life to you: "And Jesus answering saith unto them, Have faith in God" (Mark 11:22).

Endnotes

1. James Strong LL.D., S.T.D., *Strong's Exhaustive Concordance* (Grand Rapids, Michigan: Baker Book House, 1987).

2. Noah Webster, *American Dictionary of the English Language* (San Francisco, California: Foundation for American Christian Education, 1967).
3. Ibid.
4. Encarta® World English Dictionary (Microsoft Corporation, 1999). Developed for Microsoft by Bloomsbury Publishing Plc.

Chapter Twenty-two

The Faith of Jesus—
Overcoming Faith

Here is the patience of the saints: here are they that keep the commandments of God, and the faith of Jesus. (Revelation 14:12)

What constitutes the faith of Jesus, the faith that gains the victory over this world today and the beast and his mark in the future? To have the faith of Jesus means the acceptance of Christ as Savior and the surrender of our life to Him as King.

Jesus became our sin-bearer so that He might become our sin-pardoning Savior. He was treated as we deserve to be treated. He died the death that was ours. God made Jesus to "be sin for us, who knew no sin; that we might be made the righteousness of God in Him" (2 Corinthians 5:21). Belief in the ability of Christ to save us from our sins and for eternity constitutes the faith of Jesus.

The source of our faith is the Word of God. And what has Christ said? "To him that overcometh will I grant to sit with Me in My throne, even as I also overcame, and am set down with My Father in His throne" (Revelation 3:21).

What does the Bible reveal to us in regard to overcoming as Christ overcame?

For if, when we were enemies, we were reconciled to God by the death of his Son, much more, being reconciled, we shall be saved by his life. (Romans 5:10)

To have the faith that overcomes, we must give our lives to Christ, believing that in Him we are set free from guilt and condemnation. His resurrection life becomes ours, for "as Christ was raised up from the dead by the glory of the Father, even so we also should walk in newness of life" (Romans 6:4).

Christ died for our sins, then rose again for our justification. His resurrection is the evidence that our salvation is assured in Him. Since we are saved by His life, we have the confidence that He lives to make intercession for us. (See Hebrews 7:25.)

The plan of salvation includes the renovation of our character as we await the resurrection unto life, when this mortal will put on immortality. For even now, by the grace of God, we are being restored to the image of God. "Be renewed in the spirit of your mind; and that ye put on the new man, which after God is created in righteousness and true holiness" (Ephesians 4:23–24). The life of Christ in the heart of man is the result of saving faith.

To be saved by Christ's life means to follow Him. "For even hereunto were ye called: because Christ also suffered for us, leaving us an example, that ye should follow His steps: who did no sin, neither was guile found in His mouth: who, when He was reviled, reviled not again; when He suffered, He threatened not; but committed Himself to Him that judgeth righteously" (1 Peter 2:21–23).

Overcoming through the Word

The creative power that brought the worlds into existence is in the word of God, for "by the word of the Lord were the heavens made; and all the host of them by the breath of His mouth" (Psalm 33:6). This same creative power is in the written Word, the Holy Bible. This Word imparts power and brings new life. For we are "born again, not of corruptible seed, but of incorruptible, by the word of God, which liveth and abideth for ever" (1 Peter 1:23).

And when the tempter came to him, he said, If thou be the Son of God, command that these stones be made bread. But he answered and said, it is written, Man shall not live by bread alone, but by every word that proceedeth out of the mouth of God. (Matthew 4:3–4)

When Christ was weak and hungry from His long fast, Satan appeared to Him as an angel of light, tempting Him to use His divine power to alleviate His hunger. The devil began his attack on Christ the way he often does with man. "If thou be the Son of God" was an expression of doubt, and Christ would have no part of it. However, the devil is more successful in creating doubt in a man, then using men to create doubt in other men's hearts in regard to God's Word.

Satan urged Christ to command the stones to become bread. He went on to misapply the word of God in his dialogue of deception and temptation. But in each temptation Jesus met Satan with the Word of God. Jesus knew the Scriptures and lived by their counsel. This was the means by which He defeated the devil. It is also the means by which each of His followers can obtain victory. Our victory is by grace through faith, in submission and obedience to the Word of God, the word of power and victory.

> Wherewithal [how] shall a young man cleanse his way? by taking heed thereto according to thy word. With my whole heart have I sought thee: O let me not wander from thy commandments. Thy word have I hid in mine heart, that I might not sin against thee. (Psalm 119:9–11)

The psalmist asked a vital question: "How can a young man stay pure?" The answer: "reading your Word and following its rules" (Psalm 119:9 TLB). By faith and surrender we are to conform our lives to the Word.

Both the psalmist and Jesus overcame by the Word of God. Both the Old and New Testament "is given by inspiration of God, and is profitable for doctrine, for reproof, for correction, for instruction in righteousness" (2 Timothy 3:16).

To overcome as Christ overcame, we must surrender as He did. The psalmist, writing by inspiration of the Spirit, said we must seek God with our whole heart. We are to give ourselves to Him without reserve.

We must ask God to keep us so that we will not wander from His word. To *wander* means "to go astray (morally) to commit sin of ignorance or inadvertence, err (ignorantly)."[1]

We must act accordingly with our prayers by avoiding that which would tempt or compromise us.

God's Word is not only to be read but also to be followed and internalized so that our thoughts and actions are guided by the Scriptures. This is what it means to have God's word hidden in our hearts.

The psalmist speaks further about the power of the Scripture in gaining the victory. "Order my steps in Thy word, and let not any iniquity have dominion over me" (Psalm 119:133).

Every seed has the power of germination. The life of a plant is hidden within the apparently lifeless seed. Similarly, there is life in God's Word if it is received into the heart by faith and acted upon by the will and mind of man. Christ says, "The words that I speak unto you, they are spirit, and they are life" (John 6:63). In every command and every promise of the Word of God is life. When we by faith receive the Word, we are receiving the life and character of God.

Every seed brings forth fruit after its own kind and is capable of developing into a plant or tree. In the same way, as we receive into our lives the incorruptible seed of God's Word, it will bring forth a character and a life in the likeness of God. "Of His own will begat He us with the word of truth, that we should be a kind of firstfruits of His creatures" (James 1:18).

We all rejoice when spring arrives, and the seeds for food and flowers are placed in the soil of the warming earth. In time those tiny seeds bring forth fruit to feed the body and beauty to nourish the soul. So in the spiritual realm, seed sowing must take place to beautify the soul with the graces of our Savior and to nourish us unto life eternal. Without the reception on our part of the divine seed—the Word of God—we will remain barren, and the unsightly weeds of worldly conformity and rebellion will spring up. This is why many will worship the beast, for they have received the words and doctrines of man into their hearts and lives rather than the word of the living God.

The Father is the husbandman. Through His seed, the "word of truth," He generates and produces within us a being similar to the parent—an image of Himself. This is the purpose of God's Word. "Sanctify them through Thy truth: Thy word is truth" (John 17:17). God's word will sanctify those who hear and surrender their will to follow it. This is the incorruptible seed of "the word of God, which liveth and abideth for ever" (1 Peter 1:23).

> Wherefore lay apart all filthiness and superfluity of naughtiness, and receive with meekness the engrafted word, which is able to save your souls. (James 1:21)

> So get rid of all uncleanness and the rampant outgrowth of wickedness, and in a humble (gentle, modest) spirit receive and welcome the Word which implanted and rooted [in your hearts] contains the power to save your souls. (James 1:21 AMP)

With meekness, which is humble submission to the divine will, we are to have the Scriptures grafted into our lives so that they become a part of us. God plants the principles and teachings of the Scripture within us, through our willing study and our acceptance of what we study. As we do this, we can experience spiritual growth as real as the seeds planted in springtime that burst forth and bear fruit. God's Word is able to save our souls, to deliver and rescue us from the power and pollution of sin. The Word of God, when received into the soul, will mold our thoughts and transform our character.

Overcoming through the Promises of God

> For all the promises of God in him are yea, and in him Amen, unto the glory of God by us. (2 Corinthians 1:20)

> Whereby are given unto us exceeding great and precious promises: that by these ye might be partakers of the divine

nature, having escaped the corruption that is in the world through lust. (2 Peter 1:4)

Having therefore these promises, dearly beloved, let us cleanse ourselves from all filthiness of the flesh and spirit, perfecting holiness in the fear of God. (2 Corinthians 7:1)

Through faith in these promises, we can be delivered from the delusions of error and the control of sin.

What promises was the apostle referring to in 2 Corinthians? That God would shine the light of the knowledge and character of Jesus into our minds and lives as we receive it by faith. This is the power He used when He spoke light into existence in the book of Genesis. (See 2 Corinthians 4:6.) He has promised us the power of creation if we will believe. We can become new creatures, in which old things have passed away and all things are new. (See 2 Corinthians 5:17).

Christ has been made sin for us so that we could live His life and have His righteousness. (See 2 Corinthians 5:21.) He will be a God and Father to us if we will separate from all idolatry. (See 2 Corinthians 6:16–18.) Truly it has been written, "If God be for us, who can be against us?" (Romans 8:31). Let us not grieve our Savior, as the children of Israel did, with unbelief and hardness of heart, but rather believe, for "all things are possible to him that believeth" (Mark 9:23).

There hath no temptation taken you but such as is common to man: but God is faithful, who will not suffer you to be tempted above that ye are able; but will with the temptation also make a way to escape, that ye may be able to bear it. (1 Corinthians 10:13)

God's Word has promised that no temptation will come to us except what we are able to bear. We do not bear temptation alone by our own efforts, will, and resolve. We are empowered by God's enabling strength. Any adversity, affliction, or trouble that is sent or allowed by God will test or prove one's faith. If we accept our condition as being allowed by God, we can rest in His love and seek His strength to meet the trial.

God has also promised to keep us from the enticement to sin, whether the desires that arise are stirred from within or from outward circumstances. But to meet such temptations we must seek His aid and trust in His promises.

> The Lord knoweth how to deliver the godly out of temptations, and to reserve the unjust unto the day of judgment to be punished. (2 Peter 2:9)

The Lord knows how to deliver us. Such knowledge is not a hidden mystery; it is found in the promises in the holy Bible. We must appropriate this for ourselves and accept God's Word as spoken to us personally.

With every promise there is a condition. That condition is to trust and obey, for apart from a life of trust and faith, the promises of God will have no life-giving power.

> He that spared not his own Son, but delivered him up for us all, how shall he not with him also freely give us all things? (Romans 8:32)

What are the "all things" and "spiritual blessings" God has given us if we have faith in Christ?

> Grace and peace be multiplied unto you [how?] through the knowledge of God, and of Jesus our Lord. According as his divine power hath given unto us all things that pertain to life and godliness, through the knowledge of him that hath called us to glory and virtue. (2 Peter 1:2–3)

But how can these things be? We are sinful and unholy. The answer is in the promise of the Word.

> Now unto him that is able to do exceeding abundantly above all that we ask or think, [how?] according to the

power that worketh in us, Unto him be glory in the church by Christ Jesus throughout all ages, world without end. Amen. (Ephesians 3:20–21)

In Christ Jesus all the promises of God are for us. May we cast away our unbelief and believe that He is able.

Overcoming through Prayer

And this is the confidence that we have in him, that, if we ask any thing according to his will, he heareth us. And if we know that he hears us, whatsoever we ask, we know that we have the petitions that we desired of him. (1 John 5:14–15)

Our confidence can never be in ourselves; it is only in God. Our prayers are answered when we pray according to His will.

It is possible to pray sincerely but wrongly. Therefore we must pray not only based upon feeling and perceived need but according to the will of God as He has made it known in the Bible.

For this is the will of God, even your sanctification, that ye should abstain from fornication. (1 Thessalonians 4:3)

To pray according to the will of God is to ask for that which would bring about our sanctification.

Jesus says, "What things soever ye desire, when ye pray, believe that ye receive them, and ye shall have them" (Mark 11:24). There is a condition to this promise: that we pray according to the will of God.

It is the will of God to cleanse us from sin, to make us His children, and to enable us to live a life consecrated to Him. It is His will that we know Him, love Him, and trust Him. It is God's desire that He be an abiding strength and presence in our lives. It is our privilege to ask for these blessings, to trust God that we will receive them, and to thank God, who "is able to do exceeding abundantly above all that we ask or think, according to the power that worketh in us" (Ephesians 3:20).

We are to open our hearts to God as unto a friend. Prayer is not a formality.

Our prayers cannot be directed to saints or Mary.

Others cannot do our praying for us.

As we come to know God through His Word, and by faith following His word and claiming His promises, we become acquainted with God. Then, through prayer, God becomes our trusted companion and friend. If we would avoid falling into sin, and the many compromises of faith that surround us daily, we must regularly be in contact with our God and Friend. Realizing our own weakness, we should be in constant communication with heaven for light, wisdom, and strength. Victory is assured only through unceasing prayer.

Pray without ceasing. (1 Thessalonians 5:17)

We are to keep our minds uplifted to God, the source of grace, help, and wisdom. Unceasing prayer is the union of our hearts with God so that His Spirit and love works in our lives. In turn, prayer and praise flow back to Him. To pray without ceasing is not praying at a certain time or for a set length of time. It is to have an attitude of prayer that can seek God for help or offer Him praise at all times.

Be careful for nothing, but in every thing by prayer and supplication with thanksgiving let your requests be made known unto God. And the peace of God, which passeth all understanding, shall keep your hearts and minds through Christ Jesus. (Philippians 4:6–7)

The word *careful* means "to be anxious, to be troubled with cares."[2] There are many problems in the world, but we need not be anxious if our trust is in God.

We would not be troubled with care if we prayed for everything, from the smallest decisions of the day to the largest. We are to pray for our needs and for the needs of others, intermixed with thanksgiving for the delights and blessings we receive hour by hour throughout the day. Prayer hedges our minds, our thoughts, and our feelings within the boundaries of God's grace and will. In such a life of prayer we will know the peace and assurance of Christ.

We are to develop a prayer life by praying for everything, recognizing our great need and God's great love. Then our communication with heaven will become as habitual and natural as breathing, for prayer will have become to us the breath of our souls.

> Continue in prayer, and watch in the same with thanksgiving. (Colossians 4:2)

To *continue* means "to be earnest towards, to persevere, be constantly diligent."[3] We are to pray on our knees, and as we go about our daily duties, our hearts always uplifted to God. This was the way Enoch walked with God. Enoch's heart was so knit with God that he was translated to glory without seeing death, for "God took him" (Genesis 5:24).

When we have a diligent prayer life, the trials of this world and the onslaughts of Satan can be overcome as our hearts are fixed upon God.

> Rejoicing in hope; patient in tribulation; continuing instant in prayer. (Romans 12:12)

"Continuing instant in prayer" means to stay so close to God that in every trial and every joy our thoughts turn to God, as naturally as the flower turns toward the sun.

> And he spake a parable unto them to this end, that men ought always to pray, and not to faint. (Luke 18:1)

When Jesus taught His disciples (and us) to always pray, He meant we should never give up, never despair, faint, or lose heart. If this was important for the disciples, it is even more so today. We live in an age of unbelief and compromise. With every wind of doctrine blowing, it is a spiritual necessity that we develop a life of prayer.

Overcoming by Beholding

> But we all, with open face beholding as in a glass the glory [character] of the Lord, are changed into the same image from glory to glory, even as by the Spirit of the Lord. (2 Corinthians 3:18)

> If ye then be risen with Christ, seek those things which are above, where Christ sitteth on the right hand of God. Set your affection on things above, not on things on the earth. For ye are dead, and your life is hid with Christ in God. (Colossians 3:1–3)

Those of us who have been born again and have risen to newness of life have a work to do. We are to continually seek after God, setting our minds upon themes of heavenly origin. This desire to seek and know God is prompted by His Spirit, yet it requires our will and our choice. Our thoughts and our lives are to be taken up with God, His kingdom, and His work. This will be the effect of beholding, seeking, and surrendering.

Colossians 3:3 declares we are dead. This means dead to worldly interests and worldly ambitions that contradict the will and word of God. Such a death is the result of surrendering our way to God's way and placing our interests and our affections on heaven's principles.

The life of fidelity to God that was seen in the life of Christ is to be developed in the lives of all those who accept the everlasting gospel. As we study the Word of God, we see Him revealed in its pages, we hear His voice of instruction, revelation, and mercy. As we learn of God and allow His truth and instruction into our hearts, minds, and lives, we are changed into His image. The Bible is a mirror that reveals the character of God to our hearts. Though "for now we see through a glass, darkly" (1 Corinthians 13:12), what God has revealed in His Word, through nature, and by His Spirit speaking to our conscience allows us to know Him by faith. Placing our attention on God and His kingdom changes our sin-darkened hearts. As we study Jesus' life and the teachings of God's Word, and thereby surrender our hearts, we will be changed from "glory to glory, even as by the Spirit of the Lord."

An earnest study of the Bible accompanied by a life of prayer will show us where we are not living by the principles of God. As the mirror of God's Word reveals to us our defects, we are to seek by earnest prayer and faith to put them away. As we strive, motivated by faith and love, to know and live the standard God requires, the human will becomes molded to the divine will. Though we may be unconscious of the change to a great extent, the transformation of our hearts, minds, and character is being accomplished by God's grace. Beholding day by day the glory of the Lord, we are molded into the pattern of His will.

Those who will worship the beast have also been beholding, and their lives and character have changed as well. This is why they are ready to accept the image of the beast and receive his mark. They have learned to follow their own will and the will of man rather than the will of God. By doing so, they have been changed into the image of the beast. This is the spirit of antichrist, which rejects the will and word of God.

> Looking unto Jesus the author and finisher of our faith; who for the joy that was set before him endured the cross, despising the shame, and is set down at the right hand of the throne of God. For consider him that endured such contradiction of sinners against himself, lest ye be wearied and faint in your minds. Ye have not yet resisted unto blood, striving against sin. (Hebrews 12:2–4)

We are to often look upon, think over, and ponder the character of Christ. Looking upon Jesus and considering Him is not a mystical experience that only a few saints at different times in history have experienced. Looking upon Jesus does not mean adoring the Eucharistic host for hours at a time.

To look upon Jesus and consider Him is to have our hearts opened by the Spirit of grace and to surrender our hearts to Christ. To look upon Christ is to receive His word and surrender our lives to it. To look upon Christ is to prayerfully, even emotionally, consider the meaning of God becoming man and then dying on the cross, not just for the world, but for me.

To look upon Jesus is to turn away from the frivolous and the superficial and the temporary and to allow faith, hope, and love to develop in our hearts. Then we can share that faith, hope, and love with others, even as Jesus did.

To truly be changed by beholding also requires turning away from all that would hinder our quest for righteousness and obscure our view by faith of the glory of God.

Overcoming Through Surrender

It is "God that worketh in you both to will and to do of His good pleasure" (Philippians 2:13). This is the key to victory: the uniting of the human will with the power of divinity.

This surrender is a continual and deepening experience, for surrender today is not adequate for tomorrow. The surrender of the soul to God must go deeper until we come to the point where, like Christ, we can truly say, "Not My will, but Thine, be done" (Luke 22:42), even if we face death from the beast. Like Job, our surrender must be such that we can say, "Though He slay me, yet will I trust in Him" (Job 13:15).

> And whosoever doth not bear his cross, and come after me, cannot be my disciple. So likewise, whosoever he be of you that forsaketh not all that he hath, he cannot be my disciple. (Luke 14:27, 33)

Following the will and word of God often presents crosses that we must lift, for our will is often at odds with the will and way of God. The cross Jesus spoke of as ours is to lay down our will and submit to God's will. A life of prayer and praise and consistent en-

411

durance requires faith and trust to believe, regardless of feelings or circumstances. Self-denial is the lot of all who will enter the narrow way, the way to the city of God. "Whither the forerunner is for us entered, even Jesus" (Hebrews 6:20). Jesus has shown us the way of life. Will you follow Him?

> Submit yourselves therefore to God. Resist the devil, and he will flee from you. Draw nigh to God, and he will draw nigh to you. Cleanse your hands, ye sinners; and purify your hearts, ye double minded. (James 4:7–8)

Submission is not something worked up in the heart of man. Mere religious zeal and fervor cannot bring true submission to God. Though surrender requires our choice, God's Spirit helps us to see our need.

In like manner, resisting the devil is not accomplished by human effort alone. It comes when we submit to God. Then the change worked out in us by His grace enables us to choose the way of God and resist the way of the devil.

God does not tell man, "Come to Me and then I will give consideration to you." We come to God by His drawing, for our sinful hearts do not seek God of their own accord. Naturally, we seek our own will and way.

A clean heart, life, and works that are free from sin and corruption do not come of our doing either. It is the result of faith and surrender. This is how we overcome.

> My son, give [yield] me thine heart, and let thine eyes observe my ways. (Proverbs 23:26)

If you desire to give yourself to God, this desire is the evidence of God's Spirit drawing you. We are all weak in moral power; we have doubts and are controlled by the habits of sin. However, the fact that you are recognizing your weakness is evidence of God's Spirit drawing you. He desires that your needs be met in His grace and strength.

Whether or not we can overcome the beast in the future, and gain victories in Christ now, depends on the exercise of the will. Our will does not save us; salvation is the work of God. However, He has given us a will, the power of choice.

We cannot give God our affections of ourselves. However, as His Spirit draws us, we can choose to serve Him.

Give God your will. Choose to serve and follow Him. Ask for His help. Then God will work in you to will and to do according to His good pleasure. (See Philippians 2:13.) As you make this surrender day by day, you will be brought under the direction of the Spirit of Christ. Then your heart's affections will be centered upon Him, and your life will be in harmony with Him.

God will awaken a desire in you for Him, and as you yield your will to that drawing, God will become more of an abiding presence in your life. As you continue to yield your heart and mind, His love and grace will fill you more fully. "Blessed are they which do hunger and thirst after righteousness: for they shall be filled" (Matthew 5:6).

Overcoming Through Trials

> For whom the Lord loveth he chasteneth, and scourgeth every son whom he receiveth… that we might be partakers of his holiness. Now no chastening for the present seemeth to be joyous, but grievous: nevertheless afterward it yieldeth the peaceable fruit of righteousness unto them which are exercised thereby. (Hebrews 12:6, 10–11)

> For the time being no discipline brings joy, but seems grievous and painful; but afterwards it yields a peaceable fruit of righteousness to those who have been trained by it [a harvest of fruit which consists in righteousness—in conformity to God's will in purpose, thought, and action, resulting in right living and right standing with God]. (Hebrews 12:11 AMP)

Trials are God's means of developing our character. If we truly understood this, we would "glory in tribulations also: knowing that tribulation worketh patience; and patience, experience; and experience, hope" (Romans 5:3–4). In trial and difficulty God wants to strengthen us. In mercy He may be showing us areas of weakness that we may turn into areas of strength.

The trials we pass through are for God's glory. How? He can make known the power of the gospel when we respond to these trials with the meekness and strength of Jesus. The object of the trial of our faith is to prepare us to resist the allurements of evil and to develop in us the faith of Jesus so that we will stand true to Him, with consistent endurance, keeping His commandments, even in the midst of global apostasy.

To bring glory to God in the midst of trial will be the privilege of the saints who are alive just before Christ comes and the mark of the beast is implemented. God will not rapture His children from this world and free them from that trial. Rather, He will strengthen them and enable them to stand as His witnesses to His glory in the midst of trial.

> My brethren, count it all joy when ye fall into divers temptations; knowing this, that the trying of your faith worketh patience. But let patience have her perfect work, that ye may be perfect and entire, wanting nothing. (James 1:2–4)

Conflicts and trials are allowed by God to develop Christian character, so we might partake of the faith of Jesus, standing true to Him in the midst of a perverse and crooked world.

Why is the trying of our faith part of the Christian experience? Trials put our faith to the test. Gaining victory in Christ shows that our faith is true. Such experiences bring courage to our hearts as we learn to patiently persevere in the midst of difficulty.

> Though he were a Son, yet learned he obedience by the things which he suffered. (Hebrews 5:8)

Christ, our perfect example, walked the road of trial as a man subject to temptation. Thus He learned complete submission to His Father. And He bids us, "Follow Me."

> For unto you it is given in the behalf of Christ, not only to believe on him, but also to suffer for his sake. (Philippians 1:29)

> For you have been granted [the privilege] for Christ's sake not only to believe in (adhere to, rely on, and trust in) Him, but also to suffer in His behalf. (Philippians 1:29 AMP)

To truly overcome we must undergo trials and difficulties. Believing is not enough, for many say they believe. To truly believe is to trust and surrender. By relying on Christ, we can pass through difficulties solely because we are the children of God.

In fact, it is our privilege to suffer as children of God. Why a privilege and not a curse? Our Master went through difficulty for us to secure our salvation, and we are to follow Him through the straight gate and the narrow road to heaven. To follow Christ means to go through what He went through, to some degree. "The disciple is not above his master: but every one that is perfect shall be as his master" (Luke 6:40).

The faith of Jesus is the only faith that will take us from this world to the next. And such a faith cannot be obtained from the religions of Babylon or in receiving the beast's mark.

The faith of Jesus cannot be worked up by any human endeavor or secured from any church or religion. It cannot come from anyone but Jesus Himself. The message of Revelation speaks to each person through the everlasting gospel, telling us of "Jesus Christ, who is the faithful witness, and the first begotten of the dead, and the prince of the kings of the earth," of "Him that loved us, and washed us from our sins in His own blood" (Revelation 1:5).

I pray that Jesus and His faith would be yours this day. Amen.

Endnotes

1. James Strong LL.D., S.T.D., *Strong's Exhaustive Concordance* (Grand Rapids, Michigan: Baker Book House, 1987).
2. Greek lexicon based on *Thayer's Lexicon* and *Smith's Bible Dictionary* plus others; keyed to the large Kittel and the *Theological Dictionary of the New Testament*. Online Bible, 1996.
3. *Strong's Exhaustive Concordance*, op cit.